TICKLING
THE
IVORIES
A PIANO JOURNEY

KEITH JACOBSEN

CRANTHORPE
——MILLNER——

First published by Cranthorpe Millner Publishers (2022)

ISBN 978-1-80378-047-4 (Paperback)

www.cranthorpemillner.com

Cranthorpe Millner Publishers

Novels by the same author

No More Sea (2010)
Out of the Depths (2012)
Place of a Skull (2013)
Sisters of Fury (2015)
The Eye of God (2016)
Evil River (2020)
Shadows of Fury (2022)

For David Crystal, fellow scouser, music lover and St Mary's old boy, in gratitude for sixty years of encouragement, inspiration and friendship.

Liverpudlian by origin and once a Catholic, Keith Jacobsen read French and German at St Catherine's College, Oxford, during the heady days of the late 1960s. A former civil servant specialising in international health relations, he divides his time between music and writing. A performer and teacher of piano, he has a special interest in the keyboard music of Bach. He is the author of seven novels, exploring themes of guilt, revenge and the search for redemption, finding a rich seam of inspiration in his Catholic upbringing and the humour of his native city. He also writes poems, short stories and articles on musical subjects.

CONTENTS

PRELUDE

The expression 'tickling the ivories', though well-known, may need some explanation. Piano keys used to be covered in ivory. That is no longer the case, thanks to wildlife conservation laws. If you come across an old piano with yellowing keys the chances are that the key surfaces are of ivory. If you own such a piano and want to send it abroad you need to be careful. Recently an antique piano arriving in New Zealand had its key covers removed by customs officials because of laws against the introduction of ivory products into that country.

As for tickling, the origins of this usage are unclear. Somebody may once have thought that the action of a pianist at the keyboard was suggestive of tickling and the idea took hold. But that impression could hardly be further from the truth. Tickling a piano key with your fingers will produce no sound whatever. It will not even begin to depress the keys. Just watch any professional pianist in action. The energy flowing from the arms down into the keys through wrists, hands and firm finger-joints could hardly be further from a tickle.

Every work of an autobiographical nature has to be selective. This one is explicitly so. It focuses on just one

1

strand in my life: the musical one. I write fiction and was a civil servant for twenty-seven years, but these get only passing mention. So why the emphasis on music? One reason is sheer longevity. Music was ever-present in my very early childhood and is still there now, in my seventies. It has sometimes receded but never gone away. Chance combined with a curiosity and determination which have never released their hold on me have woven the musical threads of my life into a pattern which may form an interesting story in itself. That story may offer encouragement to readers who have fallen under the spell of music in general and the piano in particular and do not want the spell to fade away any time soon if at all.

It may perhaps be a presumptive delusion for me to imagine that younger readers would be able to follow a path anything like my own. Times have changed. Not many five-year-olds these days can expect to set out on a voyage of exploration at the piano which will last their lifetimes. In my early days, and those of my parents and grandparents, a house with a room big enough to contain an upright piano would usually have one, whether or not it was played. Not so now. Rarely is it just a matter of room. I knew a family with a spacious house who told me they did not have enough room for a piano for their children. This was evident nonsense. The available space had become crowded with desks for computers and laptops. Even then they could have found room if they had really wanted to. For some years in my early adolescence our family piano was squeezed into a kitchen at the back of a hairdresser's shop.

No, the real problem is with the nature of the beast. It

does not do what we expect our modern machines to do. It does not download or upload. It does not send or receive messages on social media. You cannot Skype or Zoom on it. If for any reason it stops working altogether it cannot reboot. Maintenance and repair require traditional manual and aural skills of the highest quality, learned over many years and not available cheaply. You cannot solve a piano's problems by calling someone up and getting them to talk you through pressing a few buttons. A piano does not do anything apart from what your fingers, hands and arms tell it to do. Even then it keeps no memory of what you have done for next time. It is not difficult to make a noise from the piano but it is hard work getting anything worthwhile out of it. It is seriously old-fashioned. The basic mechanism of the piano has not fundamentally altered since it was invented in Italy in 1709 by Bartolomeo Cristofori. Materials have been strengthened, some refinements have been introduced and others removed, all in the interests of a bigger, richer sound. But the way it works as explained hereafter has not really changed in three hundred years.

Our current musical environment does not encourage early interest in the piano. That may seem a strange thing to say, given that we are surrounded day and night by musical sounds of all types coming from all directions. But this is a passive rather than active experience. The neural pathways of young brains do not have the chance to develop the connections which build music inside them. That is because the young owners of those brains do not sing hymns or songs at school or church or at home with family, whose older members will be in their own worlds, glued to their computers and laptops. Should music make an appearance in their later years, they will tend to download what they like and let it play as background to other mental activities rather than experience the total immersion of live performance. How and why this cultural degradation in the quality of our national life has been allowed to take hold is a topic outside the scope of this book. Perhaps my story can show that there is another way, if we can only let ourselves find it again. But it will mean an intense struggle to recapture a space which has been lost from our hearts and souls as well as from the schedules of our daily lives.

If I have had the good fortune to have known that space and how to fill it, my story has a dark side which I profoundly hope few will have experienced. I have not found it possible or desirable in this account to separate my musical development from my difficult, sometimes tragic family history. They are too deeply interconnected. Neither I nor any seriously musical person I have met could or would sincerely want to achieve that separation. Music is not and can never be distinct from real life.

Abuse and neglect in all their forms are still there in far too many childhoods today. But often the neglect of our children's deepest cultural, emotional and intellectual needs arises not from deliberate intent but from the impossibility even well-intentioned parents face in finding the time and space to devote to those needs. The division of the day into work and leisure has been elided at the expense of the latter. Short-term contracts, twenty-four hour mobile phone contact, job insecurity in all its forms, all create pressures and anxieties out of proportion to any gains from the move away from the nine to five culture of the past. But there have been positive developments. Gone is the cultural norm

4

whereby parents and children were kept at an emotional distance from each other, where children were only criticised and never praised. Perhaps we sometimes go too far the other way. Undeserved praise can be as damaging in its way as undeserved criticism. But we are surely on the right path to finding a healthier balance.

The main danger with any autobiography is that of wearying the reader with an endless stream of sentences beginning with 'I'. Nobody's life can be that interesting, unless you are Nelson Mandela. The solution I have attempted is on two levels. The first is to weave into my narrative descriptions and anecdotes about the people whose paths I have crossed. The other is to interleave the narrative chapters with interludes of practical advice on piano technique at the most basic levels. Readers who decide to skip the interludes will lose nothing of the narrative. Those interested in exploring them in any detail will need access to a piano, preferably a real one. What I mean by real you will discover in the first of those interludes. What you will not need is knowledge of how to read music. You can learn that from any good manual. If you follow the interludes through and do the exercises therein, you will be able to play a well-known tune, using all your fingers, in time, with the tune in one hand and an independent supporting accompaniment in the other. You will have a much deeper understanding of what the piano is and how it works and how to get real musical value out of it. You may well irritate your friends and family at first. But who knows, they may end up envying you, especially if you decide to make what you have done so far only the beginning of a deeper and wider adventure.

ONE

ANTECEDENTS

We'll miss the Mary Ellens
And me dad'll miss the docks
An Gran'll miss the washhouse
Where she washed me granddad's socks;
Don't want to go to Kirby
Or Skelmersdale or Speke;
Don't want to go from all we know
On Back Buchanan Street.

Liverpool folk song on the 1960s slum clearances

One of the most precious items on my bookshelves is a four volume series, each bound in handsome blue cloth with an embossed gold leaf cover design, entitled *the Music Lover's Portfolio.* The portfolio was originally published in magazine form in two dozen issues and combined into the four hardback volumes about 1920. My copies show all the signs of wear and tear from nearly a hundred years of use, storage and transport. They came into my possession probably about the time of my first marriage in 1974, and have survived numerous moves since. It is a matter of sheer luck that they had already been shifted out of my mother's house when she moved to sheltered accommodation in the early 1990s. Within days of that move the entire contents of the house were cleared out by a local odd job man. I knew nothing of this devastation until after it had happened. Many of my books and other possessions, including sheet music, manuscripts of music I had written myself, and my vinyl record collection built up over many years, were lost. But Aunt Molly's four books had long been safely in my custody.

The contents of the volumes form a potpourri of sentimental songs by composers now faded into obscurity and mostly easy piano pieces of the Romantic school, interspersed with ludicrously difficult transcriptions, including whole movements from Tchaikovsky symphonies. Each volume opens with essays by prominent musicologists of the day. Many of the essays are perceptive and informative, with practical advice on how to sing or play the works in the volume. Some contain curious opinions. Apparently Beethoven's slow movements are starting to sound dated. That was written a hundred years ago, so they should have disappeared for good by now. But the world seems to find them more profound and vital to our emotional lives with each passing year.

Who was Aunt Molly and what did she make of her treasure, which must have cost a lot of money for those days? Her signature is on the fly page of the first volume, inscribed in careful copperplate:

Molly Rogers, 1923.

She was one of nine children, born and raised in Bootle. Bootle, while never administratively part of the City of Liverpool, is in character, history, politics and social, economic and ethnic make-up an integral part of the life of the great port city. It grew up along the banks of the Mersey as the docks and warehouses expanded northwards from the centre and attracted migrant labour from Ireland to take advantage of the growing job opportunities. Bootle natives can claim as much right to regard themselves as Liverpudlians as anyone born or living within the defined city boundary, though no doubt there are some in the latter group who would dispute that. Bootle nonetheless has its own distinct identity and sense of civic and community pride, much of which derives from the now long gone era of prosperity and strong local government in the 1960s.

Despite subsequent economic decline Bootle has retained a strong sense of community. It is proud of the fact that the area resisted the massive post-war housing clearances which tore the life out of so much of inner city Liverpool. From 1960, just as the Beatles were preparing a musical revolution that would resound across the world, one hundred thousand people began to leave their homes in the historic inner city districts including Everton and Scotland Road, the latter famous as the birthplace of Cilla Black and as home to no fewer than forty pubs. Hundreds of streets were bulldozed. Families, relatives, friends and neighbours who had spent their lives together were separated. Most were moved to new overspill developments at Kirby and Skelmersdale. As a result of rapid increases in population not matched by provision of amenities these developments soon developed serious problems of unemployment, crime, poverty and drug abuse. Others of the displaced were moved to nearby new but shoddily built flats in Everton Valley, now since demolished themselves. Much of

Everton Valley is now an open space with no indication of the inner city life which once teemed there. The only visible monument to those times is a plaque on which can be found the words of the poignant *Ballad of Back Buchanan Street*, reproduced at the head of this chapter.

My mother was the youngest in the family, born in 1917. She always claimed there were ten children, but every time I counted the names of my aunts and uncles I could never make the total come to more than nine. There was never any mention of a child being stillborn or dying in infancy. I did for a long time think there were several more aunts than there really were as a consequence of my mother's insistence that I should always address her female friends as 'Aunt...'. I once inadvertently caused a terrible rumpus at home when, after my mother had fallen out with one of those spurious aunts in spectacular fashion, I had suggested that as the woman in question was her sister (there was a strong physical resemblance) my mother might want to mollify her hostility somewhat. My mother told me in no uncertain terms that she would never have had such a dreadful person as a sister. Why then had I always been told to address her as aunt, I most certainly did not have the nerve to ask. My mother would have been only six when Molly acquired her precious books. What was Molly's real name? The children were given elaborate and formal names, such as Benjamin, Alexander (after my grandfather), Fiona, and, in my mother's case, Stephanie. Molly could never have been christened as such. Monica, perhaps.

My grandparents on my mother's side were Liverpool-born of largely Irish descent. They were Catholic and large families were traditional. Their house still stands, solid and respectable, in a well-tended street in Bootle, within sight of the docks and the since dismantled gasworks. Around the corner, a few minutes' walk away, stands the huge fortress-like structure of St Monica's parish church, temple of guilt and strict Sunday observance. My mother and those of my aunts and uncles I got to meet were extravert, in some cases extravagantly so. What a lively and noisy household it must have been before the children began to leave home to seek their fortunes, some in America and Canada. At some point the family, at least those members who did not emigrate, must have decided to renounce their Irish provenance in favour of becoming more English than the English. My mother inherited from hers a knitted map of the world which showed British imperial possessions in red. By the time it came into my mother's hands nearly all those possessions had gone, something she saw not as an inevitable historical development but as a personal bereavement.

My Aunt Stella (christened Estelle, surely?) emigrated to Canada to pursue her career as a piano teacher. On her return she undertook some research into the family history, though I never saw any documented results. The family name in Ireland was Neville, a Norman name in origin. Stella apparently believed the family were descended from the Nevilles whose most famous son was Richard, Earl of Warwick, of 'Kingmaker' fame. By coincidence this warlike gentleman was killed less than a mile from where I am writing this, at the Battle of Barnet in 1471. There was indeed a branch of this family in Ireland over hundreds of years. If Stella had found any evidence of a family connection with the historical Irish Nevilles it might have persuaded my mother that there was nothing to be ashamed of in her Irish provenance. My mother could have argued that she was not of Irish peasant stock but descended from Norman/English nobility transplanted into Ireland to keep the peasants in their place. But to the best of my knowledge none of this narrative ever reached my mother, who remained, as we shall see, viscerally opposed to all things Irish to the end of her days. In any case, there must be many thousands of families all over the world who can, authentically or otherwise, trace their ancestry back to the aforementioned earl. Would even a drop of ancestral blood be found in any of their bodies if there were a means of identifying it?

There was certainly music in my mother's house when she was growing up. The piano which moved with her to our own family home in 1953 and followed us thereafter must already have been at least thirty years old and probably more. I never knew when it had been acquired. But in the days when Molly came into possession of those volumes pianos were a standard furniture item in houses big enough to accommodate them. My grandparents clearly saw themselves as respectable middle class Catholics, unlike those in the nearby teeming inner city streets on whom they could afford to look down, as their ancestors in Ireland, perhaps, had looked down on the local peasants.

My mother told me her father had run a Hansom cab business. (A Hansom cab was a form of light horse-drawn taxi.) The truth as set out in her birth certificate, which I saw only recently, is less impressive. His occupation is listed as 'time keeper'. No doubt Hansom cab businesses would have had need of such a person and he must have earned enough to keep a large family in a reasonably sized house, with a piano included. But by the 1920s Hansom cabs were beginning to disappear and his job would have gone with them. Belts were tightened. My mother wanted dancing lessons but was told they could not be afforded. Her sisters Molly and Stella had had piano lessons but that was in earlier, better times. None of the nine children went on to further education. My mother left school at fourteen and was apprenticed to a hairdresser. My grandfather died in 1935, by which time my mother was eighteen and the older children had dispersed.

What about Molly? What pieces in the volumes did she play and how did they sound? Did she accompany friends or siblings in the songs? I never knew. She died of leukaemia in her forties, long before I was born. Her brothers and sisters spoke of her as an angel. By all accounts she played beautifully. All this may be true. Maybe the anger, crudity, frustration and snobbishness which had to some extent affected all her siblings had indeed passed her by. I like to think so. Of those siblings only Stella, the one who emigrated to Canada, had shared Molly's musical interests. Stella had tried to give my mother piano lessons at home but without success. My mother wanted to dance and have a good time, not to sit through laborious hours at the keys wrestling with notes and scales.

But at least the piano came with her, to the front room of our comfortable suburban house in Crosby, where she moved with her husband, my older brother, Neil, and myself a few years after the war. It was the house her mother had bought after selling the now nearly empty family home in

Bootle. It still nestles in a cul-de-sac on the edge of the Lancashire countryside. About half a mile away stand the walls of the Blundell estate, and, crouching against those walls, the ancient village of Little Crosby, surrounded by farmland. The Blundell family and the village were and remain staunchly Catholic, not Irish but Lancashire. Their ancestors had resisted the Reformation and the persecutions of Tudor times, keeping alive the traditions of the Latin Mass and the sacraments.

The backgrounds of my parents were very different in many ways but shared one striking similarity. They had both been brought up in quite spacious houses suggesting an early degree of comfort later declining into relative poverty. In each case there was an upright piano in the home. My grandparents on my father's side were both Norwegian immigrants. My grandfather's imposing full name was Jacob Jacobsen, my grandmother's before marriage Dagny (meaning 'new day') Gurine Hoysager. My father's birth certificate records his father's occupation as 'master mariner'. I do not know when they first arrived in Liverpool. It was probably shortly before the outbreak of the First World War. They came from a small remote fjord town. The opportunities for a certified merchant seaman offered by a life based in one of the world's largest and busiest ports would have been tempting enough. Or perhaps like many thousands of emigrants from Scandinavia throughout Liverpool's history they originally had their sights set on the New World, Liverpool being the first major port stop on the way. It would have been one of life's many ironies if my father had been born an American, given his lifelong detestation of that country, which he never visited, and all its works. Whatever their intentions at the time they left Norway it was in Liverpool that his parents decided to settle down and raise a family.

Their first home was in Bootle in a working-class area close to the docks, where the streets are incongruously named after Oxbridge colleges and characters from Shakespeare plays. (Balliol College is pronounced 'Bayliol' but Bootle locals pronounce the 'a' of their corresponding road short as in 'rat'.) My grandparents' street is Benedict. The neighbouring one is Beatrice, naturally. Benedict still stands in its entirety, the tiny houses well maintained but by no means gentrified. With its continuation, Bianca (!), descending down towards the docks it forms a double terrace about three quarters of a mile long. The fact that it and its immediate neighbours are still there is a consequence of Bootle's resistance to the policy adopted by neighbouring Liverpool in the 1950s and 60s of wholesale clearances. On a recent visit to the area, I approached Benedict from the Liverpool end via Othello, Macbeth, Celia and Wolsey. For some reason Hamlet has the misfortune of not having a local street named after him. None of the original houses of those streets survives. There is some new housing in them, but as a result of the clearances the original denizens were moved out long ago. Benedict Street is just a few yards over the boundary into Bootle. It appears to have been saved from demolition and the dispersal of its inhabitants solely because of where on a whim a planning bureaucrat once decided to draw a line on a map.

The births of my father's elder sister Ida in 1913 and my father in 1915 were both registered to the address in

Benedict Street, where they spent the early years of their lives. The outbreak of the First World War would have disrupted my grandfather's seagoing opportunities and with them his plans to move his wife and children to a more spacious house in a more salubrious area. I sometimes wonder what my shy, diminutive Norwegian grandmother would have made of her new life in the working-class Bootle of the day with its dirt, pollution and overcrowding. In her small coastal town in Norway she would have been used to space, fresh air and majestic scenery. It is most unlikely that she would have arrived in the country with any knowledge of English. Even if she had, the local accent and dialect would have mystified her. I never heard her speak of those times. I like to think that the natural openness and friendliness of the local community would as it would today have welcomed her and helped her with the care of her two young children.

When after the war my grandfather was at last able to move on, he chose to relocate to the Walton area of Liverpool. It is as a result of one of the many quirks of local government organisation in the region that while the move took him further away from the city centre it brought him into the administrative ambit of the City of Liverpool. It was in this house in Walton that my brother and I spent the first few years of our lives. Thus we can claim the title of full Liverpudlian, or, as Liverpudlians always prefer, 'Scouser', despite our having been born in hospitals just over the border in Bootle. (The traditional explanation of the origin of 'scouse' is that it is a contraction of 'lobscouse', a type of stew Norwegian in origin once popular among sailors. How appropriate in our case, given

15

our descent from a Norwegian mariner!) Though Walton now contains some of the most deprived parts of the city, the street where my grandfather settled had its attractions, including solidly built housing and a large recreation ground just behind the house on the site of a former reservoir. As a child of four I was free to explore the 'rec' as it was locally called on my own, having once wandered off so far that I was escorted home by a concerned policeman. I have no memory of the event. These days there would be no policeman on the beat to find me. But then I would never have been allowed out on my own in the first place.

From a hill at one end of the rec there were views overlooking the massive Hartley's jam factory and workers' village, by far the biggest local employer. Scrambling up and down the sides of the hill and watching for the passage of steam trains on the line running beneath it were favourite pastimes. The hill is now almost completely overgrown, and the railway line no longer there. Much of the factory site is now derelict. The massive dark-red brick factory tower still stands and is visible for miles around. What remains of the industrial site is used for various purposes, including concrete manufacture, wooden boat restoration and car servicing. The workers' village is now a conservation area, an estate of large, comfortable houses. Gone is the excitement to be had from observing the vast noisy complex where the main ingredient of that favourite food of Liverpool children was made, the jam butty, though butter as such was rarely part of the treat.

My grandfather brought relatives from Norway with him to stay in or near the Walton house and was financially generous to them. The immediate post-war boom would have brought him work and relative prosperity. It was at this time that he would have decided to purchase a piano and allow his daughter Ida to have lessons. But the good days did not last. My grandfather died when my father was only six, the result of a botched surgical operation, so the story goes. Whatever wealth he had accumulated by then did not survive him. My grandmother did not work. Probably the relatives who had relied on my grandfather provided the support she needed. They may also have ensured my aunt was able to continue with her piano lessons. Some of the Norwegian relatives were still living in my grandmother's house after the war, where my parents also lived for the first few years of their marriage. There was an acute housing shortage as a result of the intensive bombing of the entire docks area and hinterland during the war.

Fortunately, both houses where my grandparents had lived survived the war without damage. My maternal grandmother's response to the bombing attacks was not to go to a shelter but to sit at home with a cushion on her head, her eyes closed, repeating to herself 'Jesus, Mary and Joseph.' It worked, obviously. Soon after the war, she was left alone in the Bootle house, the children having dispersed. My mother was the last to go, marrying the year after the war ended and going with her new husband to live in the still crowded Walton house. It is one of many mysteries surrounding this part of the story why the newly married couple did not live with my maternal grandmother, where there would have been much more room. Perhaps she disapproved of my mother's marriage to a non-Catholic. Feelings on such matters could run high in those days.

After a few years my maternal grandmother sold the Bootle house and moved into the modern semi-detached in Crosby. My parents, my brother and myself joined her there for her final years, any animosity apparently now forgotten.

Over the post-war years the Norwegian relatives in the Walton house also dispersed. My paternal grandmother lived out her last twenty years alone in a house much too big for her and despite the painful memories it must have held. Fiercely independent and with a lively local social life, she chose not to live with either of her children, not until she moved in with my parents for the last few months of her life after suffering a stroke. She died in Walton Hospital, the same hospital which saw the birth of Paul McCartney. She had long since forgotten how to speak her native language, though she always retained the ability to understand letters from relatives written in Norwegian.

The Walton house still stands, in a street of solid terrace houses backing on to the rec. The absence of housing to the rear meant that many of the houses, including that of my grandparents, had been able to expand to contain far more space than would appear likely from the front. In my early days there we could escape directly from the back of the house onto the open spaces of the rec. Now, a high metal fence with gates at either end, no doubt installed as a security measure, separates those spaces from the back yards of the houses. These days the rec is much more attractive in appearance, with spectacular banks of wildflowers. Corn poppy, blue cornflower, corn marigold and meadow buttercup bring the sights and sounds of the countryside into inner city Walton. But where I and my brother and our friends once roamed freely I saw not a single child playing, not one on a bright and dry autumn afternoon. In this football mad city ball games are no longer allowed on the rec. A small adventure-style playground designed for pre-school children, though quite new, is almost derelict, its moving parts removed so it appears like a modern abstract metal sculpture. This neglect clearly dates from well before the Covid crisis. Cat Stevens once sang, 'Where do the children play?' He was referring to urban jungle environments. But here where I first played there is plenty of space for the children to play. Only it seems that they do not want to use it or are not allowed to.

Where my Aunt Ida lived after her marriage, in the inner city suburb of Old Swan, the terrace houses still stand and have been well maintained, with enough space at the front for miniature gardens. The streets are wide enough for cars, but are packed closely together so that at the back there is room only for those narrow cobbled passages known locally as 'jiggers'. (The word 'jigger' in this context was recorded as long ago as 1902. It was often used to refer to something small or narrow and developed other slang uses, such as a narrow door, a prison cell, even an illegal distillery.) I recall playing in the jigger behind my aunt's house. Once I had to run the full length and out into the street to escape a pursuing dog. Now a child playing there and pursued by a similarly aggressive animal would be trapped. The same high metal fences and gates as now cut off the back of my grandmother's house from the rec enclose the jiggers in my aunt's former neighbourhood and similar ones in the city. Only adult residents and council refuse collectors have keys to the gates. Before the burdens of piano practice, homework and church duties descended on me all too soon I enjoyed far greater freedom to roam and explore than the children of today.

My father was always known as Norman and his death certificate records that as his first name. But he was actually christened Amund, after several Norwegian relatives. Norman was his middle name. Either his family decided to use his more English-sounding middle name as his first name or he decided himself to reverse his names, perhaps as a result of school teasing or bullying. In the latter case he should have stuck to the name by which he was christened and told his teasers what it meant, namely protected by the sword. But 'Norman' also has its resonances of conquest and victory, none of which were at all in character with his passive nature.

My father remained in the Walton house until his mid-twenties, when he left to join the army, returning to the same house after his marriage. He never spoke of his early years. Perhaps he had no memory of his own father, who remains in my mind a shadowy figure, stern and enigmatic in a long-lost faded sepia photograph. I do not know if my grandfather loved music or if he enjoyed listening to his daughter's early efforts at the piano. It may have been he who bought the collection of 78s which passed into my father's possession, only to be lost in the later clearout. Those records were all of famous opera singers of the early twentieth century. Did my grandfather sing, as my father was later to do? Did the relatives also sing, perhaps one of them playing the piano on which the young Ida was learning? Perhaps it was for a few short years a real musical household. I like to think so. Though I never knew my grandmother to show any special musical interest, she would surely have enjoyed listening to musical evenings in the home.

When Ida married, the family piano moved with her to their house in Old Swan. She kept up her strong musical interests all her life, despite what must have been literally painful memories. Her teacher had been very severe and would correct mistakes by rapping her knuckles with a ruler, a practice not unusual in those days. Sadly, those punishments created in Ida a chronic nervousness when playing, such that her hands shook badly. I observed this for myself. Though by then well into middle age she had never been able to overcome the legacy of those lessons, though there could be no doubt as to her love of music and her natural ability. With more sensitive teaching I am sure she would have become a wonderful pianist.

Ida also had a strong interest in languages. As well as German, she studied Norwegian in later life, perhaps drawing on her childhood memories of the language when it was still spoken around her. She kept in close contact with relatives in Norway, from whom she learned that one of them had spent some years compiling a family tree. Ida asked them to send her a copy, which she brought round to our house to show us and to leave with us so we could peruse it at leisure. It was a substantial document, the conclusion of which was that the Norwegian side of the family were descended from the first Viking ever to rule over the whole of Norway. (Yes, here we go again with those warrior ancestors!) I think his name was Olaf. It certainly should have been, as that is the name of no fewer than five kings of Norway. The name is of course much more familiar these days as that of the benevolent, wisecracking snowman in Disney's animated film of 2013, *Frozen*. I shudder to think what our Olaf had to do to obtain power over all of Norway, certainly nothing benevolent. On examining the family tree more closely – it is an annoying habit of mine to examine things closely – I realised that the thread back to Olaf was not straight but led there through a series of zigzags back and forth between the male and female lines. In any case the population of Norway is very small and I am in no doubt that there is hardly a family there who could not with a little time and effort compile a tree leading to exactly the same destination.

While Ida was clearly enthusiastic about her discovery, my father was distinctly unimpressed, as would be expected. As for my mother, she was tight-lipped. She always looked down on Ida for having married a policeman, even though Ida was that comparative rarity in those days, a professionally qualified woman. She had a diploma in librarianship. She would have resented Ida having a daughter. Now, to add insult to injury, Ida had come round to our house bearing evidence of royal lineage on the Norwegian side which my mother, still no doubt ignorant of the possible Neville connection on her side, must have found galling in the extreme.

Of all those of my relatives who as children had access to the pianos of my grandparents, only three – Molly, Stella and Ida – had lessons and of course all three were girls. Not a suitable pastime for boys in those days, so it seems. And of those three, it was Stella and Ida who researched family history. I saw no sign that either of them was driven by vanity or grandiosity in their search for the past. Certainly Ida showed no inclination I could detect to go over to

Norway and claim the throne by ancestral right. I believe their interest was another aspect of the curiosity and imagination they had already displayed in music and in other fields; Stella in art, Ida in language and history. Ida had had the good fortune to work as a librarian before her marriage, as I did myself for some months between school and college. Like me she would have found the library an Aladdin's cave of treasure to explore, especially during those magical quiet periods when there is time to look along the shelves and take down a volume or two. Typically for these days of wanton cultural destruction the beautiful Carnegie library where she worked at the end of her parents' street has now closed. The building is to be refurbished and used by the NHS as 'Life Rooms', described as a 'centre for learning, recovery, health and wellbeing'. All very worthy aims, no doubt. But wasn't the original library all of that all along? Would Molly have displayed the same wide-ranging curiosity as Stella and Ida during her short adult life? She certainly loved books. The evidence for that is on my own shelves. Given that curiosity and appetite for intellectual exploration, the appeal of family history, the need to look beyond the immediate time and present to ask the perennial question: where do we come from, does not surprise me in the least.

What were those family pianos like? The piano left to my mother was the one I learned on throughout my childhood. It was strong and robust, built to last, hard to the touch. Too sensitive an application of the hands and fingers would be met with a stubborn silence. Ida's piano was similar. But they served their purpose, which was to bring the joy of live music into those homes.

But what exactly is a piano? The first interlude examines a question which in those days nobody would have even thought to ask.

INTERLUDE I

WHAT IS A PIANO?

Piano, n. A parlor utensil for subduing the impenitent visitor. It is operated by depressing the keys of the machine and the spirits of the audience.

Ambrose Bierce, *The Devil's Dictionary* (1911)

The question does not arise with other instruments. A double-bass is a double-bass. There are different types of clarinet, horn and saxophone but there can be no question as to the general category to which each type belongs. But there are instruments sometimes called pianos which are actually not pianos. An electronic keyboard, sometimes very misleadingly called an electric or electronic piano, is not a piano. Neither is a so-called digital piano, though the best ones do a pretty good job of pretending to be one. You may sometimes hear or read that a piano is a percussion instrument, that is, one like a drum which works by being hit. Do not believe it. A piano, a real piano, is a string instrument, like a harp or a violin. Have a look at the strings inside a piano. You can see them by lifting the lid of a so-called 'grand' piano or taking off the front of an upright (more about 'grands' and 'uprights' below). They may remind you of a harp. But a violin? Could that small, sweetly singing instrument you tuck under your chin and carry about with you as easily as a laptop possibly have anything in common with the nine-foot long behemoth of wood and metal we call the concert grand?

The answer is most definitely yes. In each case sound is produced as the vibration of strings is picked up and amplified. With the violin it is the wooden casing beneath the strings which provides the amplification. Piano string vibrations are caught and amplified by a sheet of wood known as the soundboard. What produces the vibration in the first place? A violinist draws a bow made of a stick and horsehair across the strings, the hair being the part of the bow which actually touches the strings. The pianist uses keys to work a mechanism which throws a hammer at the strings. A violin has only four strings. To find the different notes the violinist uses the fingers of the non-bowing hand to shorten or lengthen the portion of the string which is made to vibrate. The pianist's job is easier when it comes to finding particular notes. Each key on the piano represents a different note. As the pianist presses a key a hammer inside the piano is thrown at a string or group of strings which sound the desired note. Piano strings are made of steel stretched to a high degree of tension. High and medium pitch notes have three strings each, lower ones two, the very lowest ones only one. But these lower strings are much thicker than the higher ones. It is because so many strings are needed, well over two hundred, that a piano is so much larger than a violin. That is one reason. The other is that the key mechanism enables a wide range of notes to be reached by one player, from a deeply growling bass to a high twitter like the song of a tiny bird. It also means that many notes can sound at once. A device worked by a pedal enables many more notes to sound simultaneously than those which can be reached by the ten fingers. The epithet 'one-man band' is sometimes applied to the piano and with some justification.

So what about these pianos that are not pianos? Electronic keyboards are what they say on the tin, no more, no less. They can be great fun, able to produce a range of pre-determined sounds and background effects. The layout of the keys corresponds to that used in the design of the piano. This can be useful for learning, but only for learning that layout. You can no more learn to play the piano from such a keyboard than you can learn to swim by studying a book of diagrams. Digital pianos are likewise sophisticated electronic instruments capable of reproducing a wide range of musical effects, including piano. In recent years the quality of piano-like sound obtainable from such instruments and the closeness of the 'feel' required to obtain that sound to that of a real piano have improved a great deal. A good digital piano can be very useful, if for example you need to practise silently to avoid disturbing family or neighbours or upsetting the cat. But it is no substitute for the real thing. Nothing can take the place of the experience of creating through your own body the beauty of sound from the vibration and resonance of piano strings through the medium of a good 'real' piano.

Broadly speaking, pianos are divided into two categories: 'grand' and 'upright'. We may sometimes think of the grand as the equivalent of a luxury end car as opposed to the family saloon of the upright. But this would be a mistake. The shape of the grand, like a table with an indented curve on the right hand side away from the keyboard, is the shape in which the piano traditionally evolved from its early development in the eighteenth century and was itself derived from that of the piano's predecessors, such as the harpsichord. The piano, originally called fortepiano meaning loud and soft, was developed by its early pioneers to do what the harpsichord cannot, which is to play loud or soft according to the touch of the player. The popularity of the piano combined with its tendency to take up a lot of space as it grew in size and power led to searches for compromise designs for domestic use. The upright was an ingenious answer to the need to save space, by turning the strings upright instead of laying them out flat. But it remains a compromise. A real piano, yes, but limited in its scope for expressive power and dynamic range.

As a piano teacher I found a surprisingly widespread reluctance on the part of prospective pupils or more usually their parents to secure regular use of a good piano. These are typical responses I met when I was approached about lessons and I asked about access:

(a) We will 'see how it goes and maybe get one later'. (This is a guarantee that it will not 'go' at all.)

(b) We've got him/her a decrepit old piano on E-bay and we'll get them a decent one later if they show promise. (So how are they to show musical promise on an instrument that cannot produce a musical sound?)

(c)   We've no room for a piano but we did get them an electronic keyboard. That'll do, won't it? (No, it won't!)

If you are serious about taking up the piano or encouraging your children to do so you will need access to a good quality instrument, for practice and for the pleasure of playing what you have learned for yourself or for family and friends. A good piano resonates well in a reasonable size room, which means a soundboard in good condition. It has even key mechanisms which are not too hard or soft, and pedals that work and are silent to operate. It is in tune and is kept regularly so. An adjustable stool is also needed. Too much to ask? I don't think so. You don't start to learn to swim in discarded dishwater and graduate to a good pool later. The same with the piano.

Yes, a piano can be expensive. But so are family cars, trips to Disneyland and season tickets to a premier league football club. Nobody ever said it would be cheap. But good quality pianos have advantages those purchases do not have. They last for decades if well maintained. And they keep their value far better than your car. Pianos can be resold if interest has waned, without too much financial loss. They can also be hired, if the cost of purchase is prohibitive.

In a later interlude I will address another question which is rarely asked and often taken for granted: how does a piano actually work and what is involved in getting from it a musical sound as opposed to the sound generated by your dog, cat or toddler confronted with what might well seem to be a fascinating and noisy new toy?

TWO

ME LIVERPOOL HOME

In me Liverpool home
We speak with an accent exceedingly rare
Meet under a statue exceedingly bare
If you want a cathedral we've got one to spare
In me Liverpool home.
(Peter McGovern)

So there I was, five years old, in a house with a comfortable living room containing a serviceable upright piano. A good start. But it is not enough to put a child in the same room as a piano and expect wonderful results, or indeed any musical interest at all. A trigger is needed. Most often this comes from parents or siblings. If a mother or father or older brother or sister plays it will be natural for a younger child in the family to try to imitate them and to respond to encouragement as to how to go about it. The great jazz pianist Erroll Garner learned from watching his sister receiving lessons. He absorbed it all through his ears and from there to his hands and never learned to read musical notation. Most often, musicians are the offspring of musicians, not because they carry some sort of musical gene but because they grow up in a musical environment where to play an instrument seems as natural as breathing. Daniel Barenboim grew up believing everybody played the piano, as their only visitors were those who were already pianists or who came to his parents for lessons.

So, were my parents musical? Not in the sense that either of them played an instrument. My mother had resisted the piano lessons offered by her sister, Stella, and to my knowledge my father had no interest in learning the piano as his sister had done. But musical they were, to a point. My mother loved the musicals of Rodgers and Hammerstein and the standards from the Great American Songbook. She was fond of tenor Kenneth Mckellar and his recordings of Scottish folksongs. While Beethoven terrified her, she could take readily to the melodies of Schubert and Mozart. Certainly her ear was better than that of her sister, Fiona. Fiona once asked me in later years as we watched an orchestral performance on television what piece the orchestra were playing at that moment. But at that moment they were still tuning up.

My father was a much more complex case. Before I come on to him, some more background is needed.

Liverpool was and remains an intensely musical city, and not just because of the Beatles. It boasts a first class concert hall – the Liverpool Philharmonic Hall, henceforth just 'the Phil' as Liverpudlians always call it – and a world class symphony orchestra. But more importantly perhaps, there is a strong tradition of amateur music making in all fields, pop, folk, jazz and classical. Liverpool is at least half Irish, most of those Catholic. Catholic children sing from an early age at school and in church. Singing is a fundamental part of what it is to be Irish, and the Liverpool tradition of song and love of music infects the whole population. The most musical football ground in the country is Anfield, home to Liverpool Football Club. Their adopted anthem is *You'll Never Walk Alone* from the Rodgers and Hammerstein musical *Carousel*, made popular in a 1960s top ten version by Liverpool pop singer, Gerry Marsden. When the team is doing well or just needs encouragement the supporters sing it with astonishing fervour and tonal and rhythmic accuracy. During the Beatles heyday, imitation pop groups could be found in every school and youth club, anywhere where someone could be found who could afford a guitar and drums. The snobbish divide I have since found elsewhere between classical and other forms of music was simply not there. Fritz Spiegel, the principal flautist in the Liverpool Philharmonic Orchestra, arranged Beatles songs for string quartet. The same orchestra put on so-called industrial concerts at the Phil, with reduced price tickets for factory and office workers in the city. Those concerts were so popular that each was given on three successive nights. The growth in mass-produced record players and radiograms in the late 1950s and 60s along with the arrival of cheap label long playing records were taken up enthusiastically in working class and middle class households alike. There was a thriving culture of mutual lending of records between families and friends, a process which introduced me to a wealth of music at a young and impressionable age.

My father was not immune to the musical influences surrounding him, which of course included his sister's exploration of the piano repertoire at home. As a young man he had sung in the chorus of one of those amateur opera companies. He admired singers with deep voices such as Chaliapin. Though as racist as any white middle-class man of his generation he made an exception for the glorious voice of Paul Robeson. He was knowledgeable about classical music up to Tchaikovsky and Rachmaninov, both of whose music he loved. Anything later was deemed too modern. He had a stock of old 78s which he might have bought for himself in his younger days or inherited from his father. In the late 1950s he bought one of those enormous radiograms which were by then fashionable and showed some interest in my own growing gramophone record collection, bought with my carefully saved pocket money. But never once do I recall him buying a record for himself. From 1960 onwards, by which time I was twelve and attending grammar school, my Aunt Ida, aware of my intense musical interest, took me and her daughter to the annual series of Saturday concerts at the Phil. Never once did he think of joining us. Never once did he stir out of the house to see an opera by a visiting professional company. Certainly never a ballet. His contempt for male ballet dancers knew no bounds. The only times he took me to an opera were to performances put on by his former amateur company when people he knew would be in the cast. He treated the music of the Beatles and other pop groups of the era with contempt, the long hairstyles a barrier closing off their melodies to his ears. The one exception he was ready to praise was the American group, the Beach Boys, and then only when I pointed out that sometimes they sang in five part counterpoint.

So I never heard him sing. Well, yes, actually, just the

once. By then I was in my late teens, waiting to go up to university. There was a party at home which had turned into a musical evening, with me at the piano to accompany anyone who fancied a sing. It was the sort of occasion which by then was a decades old anachronism but which would have been staple fare in middle class households before the arrival of radio and television. At one point I had the score to *South Pacific* on the stand, knowing it was one of my mother's favourites. I started to play *Some Enchanted Evening*, expecting to continue as a piano solo. I was suddenly aware that he was standing behind me. He began to sing. Somehow I held myself together and concentrated on the accompaniment. All those years his fine baritone voice had lain disused. It was still in good condition. I had never heard it before and I never heard it again.

My father was a man of his time. He kept all his emotions in firm check. For him to express himself in music or even to show the emotional effects it had on him was anathema. He was the polar opposite of my mother, whose emotionalism drove her every word and action and led in later years to successive breakdowns. I could never imagine how they had come to marry. As will be explored in more depth later, my mother's attitude to the opposite sex was complex. She expressed a taste for gallant charmers, preferably with wealth attached. But the presence of men often evinced a mixture of fear and distaste. My father was the polar opposite of those expressed tastes. He could be stubborn and self-righteous. He despised social snobbery. While always courteous in company he could be merciless about anyone he thought intellectually or morally inferior.

He was never gallant or charming. He never sought wealth. He taught disadvantaged children in a local secondary modern school, a sink school for those who had failed or never attempted the notorious eleven-plus exam. His salary was meagre for many years but he had no extravagant tastes, liking only a weekly pint of beer in the company of two younger men he had met during the war.

I will never know what caused the ice to break that one evening when he chose to sing, but it quickly re-formed. He must have always feared what might happen if just once he allowed free rein to his emotions through music. When it did happen that night all his fears would have come flooding back. He did not dare take the same chance again. That was perhaps the only moment, certainly the only one I saw, when a spirit touched both my parents and revealed a closeness which might have been. Instead, the story of their marriage was one of a growing chasm, such that he withdrew from any close involvement in the early years of Neil and myself while my mother steeped herself ever more deeply in anger and self-pity, finding an outlet in acts and words of cruelty towards her husband and children. My father also lived in anger, but his was mostly hidden away and simmering inside him. In particular he was angry that his wife despised his lack of material ambition. It is small wonder that I needed another reality in which to take refuge. It was there at hand in the form of the piano sitting in our front room, dormant, waiting to be reawakened. But it was clear no adult's touch would reawaken it.

There are two other mysteries in my parents' life, other than the fact that they married in the first place. The first was why she did not leave him. The second was why he did not leave her. As for the first, my mother was raised a Catholic and the doctrine of till death us do part was central to her beliefs. But I am sure there was more to it than that. Though the girls in her family outnumbered the boys by five to four, the boys, to judge from those of my uncles I met, were very much the prominent gender as was the usual case in those days. Her brother Ben, sixteen years older, was a domineering bully. On the few occasions he visited our home my mother was visibly terrified of him. When their brothers left home to seek their fortunes my mother and her sisters had the chance, if not of freedom as we understand it these days then at least of a life where their contribution was valued for its own sake and not for how it could enhance the lives of their menfolk. My mother, after her early training in hairdressing, worked in armaments during the war, like many women. But after the war she found herself once again in an environment dominated by men, or rather a husband and two small boys. She must have feared that the overbearing male ambience of her childhood would return. Her reaction to that fear was to become a bully herself. Leaving my father would have deprived her of the chance for surrogate revenge.

My mother was never any sort of feminist in the economic or social sense. She believed women were the superior gender, but men had a role to play in providing the means for social and economic success. She did not believe that women should drive cars or go out to work. Yet she worked throughout her marriage until retirement, resenting every minute of it. Much of that work was in hairdressing, the occupation to which she had been apprenticed as a teenager. She always gave every impression of detesting it.

How it had come about in the first place that she had been channelled into that occupation I have no idea. There was no family history of interest. I can only assume that in economically straitened times it was one of the few opportunities which presented itself and her parents had pressured her into it. She had dreamed of a life of wealth and leisure supported by a successful husband, preferably a charmer, and including perhaps the feminine companionship of a daughter or two. Instead she spent many of her days in a job she found demeaning, forced to please her customers and be polite to them. Many of those customers she would have been brought up to believe were her natural inferiors. There was nothing glamorous about hairdressing in those days, before the arrival of the likes of Vidal Sassoon and his innovations in cutting and styling. (Ironically, Sassoon was, just like my mother, apprenticed at the urging of his own mother to a hairdresser at the age of fourteen, though he had known much greater poverty than my mother ever did.) As for her marriage, it could not have been more different from her dreams.

She particularly envied her elder sister Fiona, intensely to the point of visceral hatred. Fiona had married a charming man and led a comfortable life in affluent Formby once he had retired from his postings in India as an employee of the British and American Tobacco Company. My mother ludicrously exaggerated their wealth. They were frugal and had few expenses, having had the chance to save enough while in India to buy a comfortable detached house on their return. The many beautiful ornaments in their home had been bought in India for a song. Fiona for her part had cause to envy my mother for having children.

Life in the tropics had caused her to miscarry more than once. My mother had no sympathy for her on that score.

My father faced classes of difficult teenagers every day at work with all the fortitude he and his companions had shown against Rommel in North Africa. But at home he let himself be bullied by his own wife. Though he rarely talked about the war, I suspect he suffered from survivor guilt, a syndrome much better understood now than then. He returned intact when many of his fellows suffered life-changing physical injuries or did not return at all. He felt in need of punishment so accepted in silence whatever she handed out to him, also rarely interfering when she bullied his own children. I spent the first few years of my life in fear of her and barely aware of his existence. So maybe they were well suited after all. The successful, wealthy, charming husband of her dreams would never have tolerated a bullying wife. And he would never have known what to do with a wife who respected his values, who set more store by his work in giving life chances to deprived children than by material goods. When I consider the life stories of my parents as they came down to me, inevitably with gaps I can never now fill, I feel anger that they put so much pressure on Neil and myself to fill the lacunae in their lives, but also sadness that they found so little fulfilment, either within themselves or with each other.

The immediate pre- and post-war social and economic landscapes were certainly grim. But after the war there were opportunities a-plenty for those with ambition and initiative. My father had attended a local grammar school, where his favourite subjects were languages and literature. In those respects and up to that point his life and mine were very similar. He then spent a year at Liverpool University before deciding to leave to obtain clerical work. Financial pressures would have played a role in that decision. The era of the Great Depression had arrived. But after the war he could have taken up any of the opportunities available to ex-servicemen to take a degree, perhaps in the humanities in which he had excelled at school. He maintained a lifelong memory of the French and English literature he had studied and had a good working knowledge of spoken French. His favourite French novel was Hugo's monumental masterpiece, *Les Misérables*, which he had read in the original. He had also read the most difficult novel in the English language, Joyce's *Finnegans Wake*. (I have yet to rise to that challenge though *Ulysses* is one of my favourite novels.) I once heard him recite from memory a few lines from Chaucer in the 'original' pronunciation as he had been taught it. He knew a lot of Shakespeare and could discuss at length the roles of real and assumed madness in *King Lear* and *Hamlet*. He was familiar with all the set texts I studied for A-level English.

But all that, like his musical interests, was part of his past, recalled only occasionally. He never re-read those favourite works or went to see any of Shakespeare's plays in live performance. The reading matter he brought into the house for himself consisted mainly of the hyper-masculine adventure stories of H Rider Haggard, John Buchan, Alistair MacLean and Hammond Innes. His intellectual curiosity and hunger to explore great writing had faded away, leaving only memories. As with literature so with music: at some time in his early life, probably long before I was born, he had decided to turn off the taps that feed the soul. Nobody knew why. Did he even know himself? Did he think it was the price he had to pay to become a 'real' man in a man's world?

Whatever the reasons, it was the dreary certainties of basic mathematics and technical drawing he chose as the subjects he would teach, useful subjects but hardly the stuff of passionate involvement. He must have realised at the time that that decision, like any major life choice, would involve a trade-off. Teaching subjects for which he had no natural love in the grim environment of a secondary modern school would have cost him both inherent job satisfaction and earning opportunities. What did he get in return? In the early days of his teaching career he would at least have had the satisfaction of knowing that he was helping deprived children gain skills valuable in the rebuilding of the country after the war. But that motivation would also fade in time. Disillusion with almost every aspect of British society would take hold and he would no longer think the country worth rebuilding. He favoured capital punishment for killers and birching, as still practised then in the Isle of Man, for delinquents. He came to loathe both his job and school, though at no point did he consider a change of either. Things might have been different if his wife had encouraged him to continue to believe in the value of his work and helped him at difficult times. Instead she never lost a chance to remind him of the poor material rewards and lack of promotion opportunities and how her own life was blighted as a result.

My mother had no formal education beyond the age of fourteen. But she had a natural intelligence and curiosity and also a vivid imagination, the latter sadly often misused to the cost of others including myself, and plenty of energy. There were opportunities at what was then called night school, and later, the Open University. For the first few years of her marriage there were always free baby-sitters ready to hand. Both of my parents when young had friends who, often with far less natural ability, went on to achieve considerable professional success, that very success weakening and eventually ending those friendships. My mother, once she had accepted that a life of kept luxury was not to be her lot and that she would always need to work, could have found ways to discipline her natural intelligence and find work which would bring some fulfilment. Instead both my parents chose relative failure and victim status, for which they blamed fate, bad luck, politicians, and yes, marriage and parenthood and the shortcomings of their partner and offspring.

It would be wrong to suggest that my mother was incapable of affection. She had a niece, Pauline, ten years my elder. Pauline had had a difficult start in life, having been born out of wedlock and not knowing her father. My mother showered affection on her, often telling her that she saw her as a daughter. My father helped her to find and form a bond with her own father. But by the time Neil and I appeared Pauline had moved to the Midlands with her mother. She and my mother could not be as close as before though they were in regular contact. The separation left a gap in my mother's emotional life which her own children could not begin to fill. We had auditioned but were just not right for the part.

My father had no more natural interest in fatherhood than most men of his generation. From comments he made later to Neil and myself it seemed that he saw our arrival as somehow sealing him into his punishment, ensuring there could be no escape. Later he was able to see Neil, who played team sports and joined the school army cadets, in his own masculine image, even compensating for his own lack of ambition when Neil achieved material success in adult life. Neil showed no interest in the piano, and at school would spend orchestra lessons with a cello idling between his knees while he studied the Latin verbs he had placed on the music stand. But he had a good ear and could sing well.

I, on the other hand, was my mother's project from the start, as she tried to fashion me into something which could reflect well on her. My father was suspicious at first of my musical development, perhaps fearing it could bring to the surface that musical side in himself he had worked so hard to suppress. It has to be remembered that playing the piano in those days was not generally considered an activity suitable for boys, even though most professional pianists were and probably still are men. My mother often told me that she had wanted me to be a girl. It was out of the question for them to have tried for more children in the hope of having a daughter. That could have led to the nightmare for her of an even larger all-male family. But encouragement of my musical interest was perhaps a way to introduce at least an element of femaleness into one of her existing offspring. It would also mean that through me she could compensate for her own failure to respond to the piano lessons her sister, Stella, had given her. But as we shall see, if she had indeed hoped to tame her childhood demons in that way she could not have foreseen the adult demons which would be unleashed in their place.

INTERLUDE II

ONE NOTE

Upholding the lid he (who?) gazed in the coffin (coffin?) at the oblique triple (piano!) wires. He pressed (the same who pressed indulgently her hand), soft pedalling a triple of keys to see the thicknesses of felt advancing, to hear the muffled hammerfall in action.

James Joyce *Ulysses*

You thought one note was a note-taking app for your smart phone? Read on and think again. This interlude will take you on a voyage of discovery using just one note played with one finger.

So, how exactly does the piano work? In particular, why is it so easy to make a sound at the piano but so hard to make that sound musical? If you are curious about this and have access to a piano in good condition, try the following steps.

Adjust the stool so you can lay your hands flat on the keys with your forearms level. Sit far enough away so that your arms are not cramped but not so far that your elbows and upper arms are uncomfortably strained. Choose any key to start with. There is no qualitative difference between black and white keys. The black keys are raised above and placed between the white ones to enable the hands to reach as many notes as possible with minimum lateral movement. For now, choose a white key, preferably one immediately in front of you. You should be seated about the middle of the keyboard. Usually this is where the maker's name is to be found and this is a useful indicator of where to sit.

Press your chosen key down very slowly. Nothing will happen. This is where the piano differs from its electronic cousins, or its more distant cousin, the pipe organ. To make a sound at the piano you need to generate enough energy to throw a hammer against the strings which correspond to your note. In a grand piano the hammers, covered with felt, are thrown up from a bed below the strings. In an upright they are thrown away from you towards the strings. To make a musical sound on the piano, even just one sound, does not require great physical effort but it does call for care and concentration. All pianos differ in their actions, but generally a movement equivalent to the weight of a couple of ounces is enough to overcome the resistance of the key and trigger the hammer-throwing mechanism. What happens as a result of this movement depends on the speed with which the key descends to the point where it will go no further, that is, the key bed. The faster the speed of key descent, the louder the sound.

Now choose a finger with which to play your first note. I suggest the index finger of your right hand. Crook it into a curve, keeping the two joints of the finger firm. The first joint in an adult finger is slightly less than an inch from the tip. The second joint is around the middle of the finger.

This is the joint that enables the finger to curve down and under and so to grasp small objects. From a few centimetres above your chosen key press down with your firm, curved finger to the bed of the key. Do not force the touch, but also do not let the finger joints collapse or the energy needed to make the sound will be lost. Keep the finger down in the key bed, but there is no need to press. You need no more effort than is required to hold the key in place. Listen to the sound you have made. Feel and hear the resonance of the instrument. It is not only the strings which are resonating, but the whole instrument in sympathy, an effect which no electronic substitute can provide.

As you listen you will notice that the sound starts to fade as soon as you have made it. This is called evanescence. It is at once the piano's great beauty and its biggest disadvantage. You cannot prolong the sounding note or make it louder. The vibration of the strings slowly weakens and eventually ceases altogether. The string and wind player and the singer all have the advantage here, especially the string player, who can prolong a note indefinitely by repeated bowing. But evanescence has its own special beauty. Listen for it as your sound fades away. It is an exquisite effect which the great composers for the piano such as Chopin and Liszt knew how to exploit to the full in their writing for the instrument. You have only played one note so far. But already you are tuning in to a pianistic effect which has caught the imagination of composers, pianists and audiences down the years.

Now play your note again but this time take your finger off the key after a few seconds. What happens? The sound abruptly stops. Look again inside your piano. Apart from those for the very highest notes, you will see that each group of strings is covered by a damper. The dampers literally damp the sound. If you are playing a drum and you want the sound to stop you put your hand on the skin of the drum. That is damping. When you press down a piano key, as well as a hammer being thrown at the strings the damper holding those strings is simultaneously released to allow the strings to vibrate. Release the key and the damper moves back into place and stops the sound. The high notes do not need dampers as their vibration time is very short and the sound fades to nothing almost at once.

So, with your one finger on one note you can do a lot already, though there are limits. You can decide how loud or soft your note is going to be. You can experiment with different speeds of key descent and listen to the results. Try to hear in your head the sound you want to produce before you try it at the piano, and then listen carefully to judge how closely your actual sound matches what you heard. This is the three-stage key to all musical piano playing at all levels and standards, from a grade 1 exam piece to a recital by a pianist who is a household name: hearing, playing, listening. What else can you do? You can decide whether and if so when you are going to end your note before it ends naturally. What you cannot do is vary the quality or nature of the sound for any given speed of key descent or affect its dynamic level once it has started to sound.

THREE

FROM POPPA PICCOLINO TO BACH

So if my parents did not show me how to get music out of a piano, and my musical aunts were not around, then who did?

The answer, so I was later told though I have no memory of her, was a lodger who stayed in our house while playing with a visiting orchestra. I would have been about five or six at the time. My maternal grandmother had been living with us during the years of her final illness. She died in 1953 and I doubt if there would have been time or room for a lodger before then. Our visitor was given the use of our piano for her own purposes, but was prepared to spend time helping me to pick out tunes. From that I acquired the habit of playing songs I heard on the radio. One of these was *Poppa Piccolino*, recorded by Diana Decker in 1953. This song in its English version was about a concertina-playing vagabond and the monkey who collected his takings. It was hugely popular around the world and reached second place in the UK charts. The song, though very much of its time, proved to have unlikely staying power. Petula Clark recorded a version as late as 1998.

My way with this song, surely just with one finger, was clearly enough for my mother to decide I should go for piano lessons. I have always believed that the start of any sort of worthwhile career, amateur or professional, on the piano requires one or preferably more than one stroke of good fortune. For me the first two strokes were the presence of the piano in our home and that chance encounter with our musical lodger. The third was Miss Penhall.

Miss Penhall was our local piano teacher. She lived no more than a hundred yards away. I was seven when I was sent to her for weekly lessons. She was probably about sixty at the time but to me she seemed infinitely old. She could have been of the school to which my Aunt Ida's teacher had belonged, in which case my playing career would have ended very quickly. At the first application of the ruler I would have burst into tears and run home, never to return or to touch any piano ever again, whatever punishments my mother would have decided to inflict on me. But while Miss Penhall was firm in her belief in the discipline of basic techniques such as scales and arpeggios she was kindness and patience itself, even though it must have been clear to her how much I hated that first lesson. It seemed to have nothing to do with what I enjoyed getting up to at the piano at home. But gradually she coaxed me into an appreciation of how much more rewarding it was to make careful and systematic progress, to tame and control my wayward fingers and master the mysteries of the printed score with recitation of the formulae: 'Every Good Boy Deserves Favour' and 'All Cows Eat Grass'. The moment to which I always looked forward with almost unbearable excitement was at the end of a lesson in which I was due to finish one piece and start a new one. 'Time now for a new piece,' she would say, going over to her cupboard, her treasure chest of sheet music. The words 'new piece' were magic to my ear. Whatever the new piece was, she played it through to me, always just the once. After that, it was up to me.

I know even now, nearly sixty-five years on, that she played beautifully. A musical future of any kind depends on the sounds that enter the brain while the neurons have yet to form solid pathways. This is why the biography of any pianist of note will nearly always state that they started lessons about the age of six or seven or eight. That is the optimal age for learning to translate musical sounds into pathways in the brain that lead directly through the arms and fingers into the keys of the piano. That aural legacy remains deeply embedded in the brain for life, often remaining there after other functions have started to ebb away through dementia. Miss Penhall gave me the sound for each piece. It was then up to me to learn to recapture it, with her help.

The only piece I worked on with her which she did not choose herself was, bizarrely, Tchaikovsky's Fifth Symphony; well, just the first page. I have referred above to the inclusion in Aunt Molly's *Music Lover's Portfolio* of several 'ludicrously difficult' transcriptions of movements from Tchaikovsky symphonies. The first movement of the fifth was among these. During my early practice sessions when I felt like a break from the music she had set me I would browse the volumes of the *Portfolio*. I had learned notation well enough by then to have a go at the opening of the fifth, which, though of course I did not know this at the time, consists of a slow haunting clarinet solo accompanied by lower strings. I sensed that Tchaikovsky was not a favourite of Miss Penhall so I intended to keep this indulgence to myself. However on hearing me struggle through that first page my mother promptly telephoned Miss Penhall to inform her that I would bring the piece with me to the next lesson. I was furious. Nevertheless I took it along as instructed and for just one lesson she worked patiently with me on it. I knew she realised that in terms of my progress at the piano it was a pointless exercise. I would never get beyond that first page. But the experience was enough to ensure that a deep love of Tchaikovsky's music would always stay with me. The Fifth Symphony was one of the first records I bought. How dark, how Russian, how soulful, that opening clarinet solo!

Miss Penhall had worked professionally as a singer in her younger days. One day she told me the following story, which has stayed with me ever since. I even incorporated it into one of my novels.

She had been due to sing an aria by Handel, probably at the Phil. I must have already played it for her in the piano solo version I knew from *the Music Lover's Portfolio*. In those days it was known simply as 'Handel's Largo'. I was later to learn that its proper title is *Ombra ma Fu,* literally, 'Never was a Shade'. It is the opening aria from Handel's opera, *Xerxes.* I knew about Handel, of course. He composed *Messiah.* Every Christmas at the Phil there would be several sold-out performances. We all knew we had to stand for the Hallelujah Chorus. Years later I played the piano in a school Speech Day performance of this same chorus in the same hall. Apart from the hundred plus performers and the piano the massive organ took part in full throttle. It was surely the loudest and least historically informed performance of all time. So I knew about Handel and I knew he wrote sacred music. Certainly not Italian operas. But in those days a performance of a Handel opera was almost unheard of.

As I recall her story as she told it to me, Miss Penhall was due to sing the Aria with the orchestra conducted by that renowned maestro, Sir Adrian Boult. At the rehearsal the orchestra started to play the introduction. Right away she knew there was something wrong. It was too high. They were playing in the key of G, actually the key in which I had learned the piano version. She knew it in the key of F, Handel's original key. But the orchestra had all the parts there on the stands, all in the wrong key. No time to get new parts before the performance. Sir Adrian understood the problem right away. He turned to the orchestra. 'Gentlemen,' (it would have been all gentlemen in those days, unless there was a harpist on the platform) 'the key of F, please.' They played it there and then, transposing the music at sight. Just for her.

Any music critic will tell you that not all pianists, even the greatest, play every composer in their repertoire equally well. It is not usually a matter of technique. I sometimes find myself saying of a particular pianist that while I love, for example, 'their' Bach I am not moved or convinced by 'their' Beethoven. There are some composers who seem to live inside certain pianists. Their interpretations of those composers give the impression of coming from within their heart and soul direct into the heart and soul of the listener.

But the same pianists with other composers may struggle to convey their meaning, however accomplished the performance.

I believe that when a particular composer enters a pianist's soul this happens at an early age. A teacher may give a young pupil a piece to which he or she takes readily. It may be pure chance, or it may be that a perceptive teacher has understood the pupil's temperament and tastes. It is important that the piece is heard performed by a sympathetic interpreter, either the teacher in person or through a performance, be it live, on radio or via a recording. What takes root in the pupil is not just that one piece, it is the essence of that composer's artistic and emotional character. For the most part the pupil will in later life take just as readily to other pieces by that composer. Three such composers were introduced to me by three different teachers.

With Miss Penhall it was Johann Sebastian Bach. Now Bach's writing for keyboard, though always immensely rewarding, can be complex and resistant to early appreciation. Often it does not yield its secrets until after long study. But that is not the case with many of the movements from his cantatas and other religious works. They appeal directly to the soul of the listener. The great pianist Myra Hess, who lived from 1890 to 1965 and was renowned for her wartime recitals in London's National Gallery, understood this when in 1920 she first heard the chorale from Bach's Cantata 147. Bach had taken an existing hymn (chorale melody) and woven an orchestral accompaniment around it. The accompaniment not only has its own extraordinary melodic quality, it surrounds the simple chorale melody with a musical halo and transforms it into a deeply spiritual statement. Hess was so moved that on returning home she played the movement repeatedly from her own full score. It was only a few years later, after sometimes including it in her programmes as an encore, that she was persuaded to write the arrangement down and publish it. The usual English title is *Jesu, Joy of Man's Desiring,* taken from a poem by Robert Bridges to which the chorale melody can be sung. The piece has ever since been a firm favourite and many pianists apart from Hess have played and recorded it.

Miss Penhall gave me the piece to learn in a simplified version of Hess's arrangement. Soon afterwards, she asked me to perform at a concert of her pupils. I had only been studying with her for a couple of years. Though I loved to play the Bach I was sure that it would be too difficult to play at the concert. My preference was to play a piano solo version of a traditional Irish song Miss Penhall had also given me about that time, *The Rose of Tralee.* I did not know then about my mother's pathological aversion to all things Irish, be they animal, vegetable, mineral or musical. Even if I had, I could never have understood because it is still a mystery to me now. It is particularly curious because she was at least three quarters Irish herself. She always denied to me that she and her family had any Irish connections, even when Aunt Stella on one of her visits to us in Liverpool announced she was taking the Dublin ferry to visit 'her Irish relatives'. According to enquiries I made recently of surviving relatives in England, my mother when young had herself visited those relatives in Ireland. So why would she deny to her own family ever having been there?

And if there were no Irish connection, as she claimed, whence the large Catholic family? I can only conclude that there had been some sort of almighty row with the Irish branch of the family, which not only led my mother to repudiate her Irish relatives but the entire Irish nation and its whole cultural and spiritual heritage.

She was particularly horrified to meet Mary, my first girlfriend. I say first. There had been Jennifer, a neighbour's daughter, but we were only nine at the time. Mary and I met while I was working in a library between school and university. Mary was as Irish as they come, with long black hair and green eyes. If I had deliberately wanted to shock my mother I could not have made a better choice. The relationship did not last. But it must have been the stuff of my mother's worst nightmare, that after all she had done to distance herself from her own Irish origins a son of hers might marry into an Irish family. It would be years before I understood her hostility to Mary, who was Catholic, polite, well-spoken and doing well at school. But what was there to understand? My son is my possession and I hate you for threatening to take him away from me. Always plenty of that about, in life and literature. But mostly I hate you because you are Irish. There had to be more to it than that. I hate you because you are proudly Irish, while I am ashamed of my own Irishness. That would be nearer the mark, though still beyond any reasonable understanding.

So, for reasons which could never but be obscure to any nine-year-old especially as they remain obscure to me over sixty years later, *The Rose of Tralee* had to go. By then my father had begun to notice what I was playing and declared that he liked the Bach arrangement. He would have let me decide for myself what to play at the pupils' concert. My mother's way was slightly different. While I was practising *The Rose* one day she simply tore it off the stand and put the Bach in its place.

I do not know where the concert took place, probably in some draughty church hall. I had to stand in front of the audience of doting parents and introduce it before playing it. Someone had made a recording of the concert and I later had to go through the embarrassing experience of listening to it. It was not the playing which embarrassed me but the timid, squeaky voice which introduced it. However, my father told me that my playing had gone down well. He had heard someone near him say after I had finished, 'By Jove, that was good.'

That was surely the trigger, though my father would never have intended it as such. I now knew I had reached out to at least one person who was not a parent, teacher or acquaintance, someone I had never met and would not know from Adam. Playing was no longer just about me and those who knew me. That was the moment the idea and the meaning of performance took root.

So there I was, with a serviceable if not great piano in a comfortable home, a kind and sympathetic teacher, one parent had who begun to take notice and another who would on no account let me duck practice to play outside. I had a firm grounding in basic techniques, been introduced to some of the most beautiful music ever written, and gained early performance experience. What could go wrong? The answer, as is so often the case, is life.

But more of that later. Time for another diversion, for

those of you wanting to engage further with your own piano. You have learned a lot from just one note. Time for an important step forward. What does someone ask you when there is a piano about and they know you play? They ask you to play something or maybe just to 'play a tune.' So let's do that now.

INTERLUDE III

LET'S PLAY A TUNE

HORTENSIO:
Madam, before you touch the instrument,
To learn the order of my fingering,
I must begin with rudiments of art,
To teach you gamut [scale] in a briefer sort...
BIANCA:
Why, I am past my gamut long ago.
HORTENSIO:
Yet read the gamut of Hortensio.
BIANCA (*reads.*)
Gamut I am, the ground of all accord:
A re, to plead Hortensio's passion;
B mi, Bianca, take him for thy lord;
C fa. Ut, that loves with all affection;
D sol, re, one clef, two notes have I;
E la, mi, show pity or I die.
Call you this gamut? Tut, I like it not.

Shakespeare: *The Taming of the Shrew*

You now know how a sound is produced from within the instrument and how your contact makes that sound possible.

You know from playing just a single note how to play loudly and softly and everything in-between. You know how to start and finish a note, or just to listen as it fades naturally. Now you can use what you have learned to play your first real tune, and to play it in a way which anybody would recognise as musical. Your tune will be genuinely tuneful.

First of all, revisit what you read in Interlude II about the three-stage key to all musical piano playing. Remember those three all-important words: hearing, playing, listening.

Why is hearing top of the list? The prerequisite for playing any instrument in a controlled, musical way is to have before you start to play what is sometimes called an aural image. An easier way to put this is to say that you must first hear it in your head. Before you say that you cannot do that, think of a tune you know very well. It could be a nursery rhyme you learned as a very young child. Or a hymn you sang in church along with the rest of the congregation. Or maybe even something you chant with fellow supporters at a football match. Recall it and go over it in your head. If you can sing a bit and there is nobody around for you to worry about hearing you, then go ahead and sing it. On your own, you may feel that you are not as in tune as you would be as part of larger forces. That's perfectly normal. The important thing is that you have the tune in your head. You know how it goes. You would recognise it if someone else sang or played it.

Why is singing so important when it comes to playing an instrument? The human voice is the first and most important musical instrument. It is through singing that we learn to internalise the tunes and rhythms which make up most of the music we will meet in our daily lives. And the earlier singing is part of our lives the better. Parents who sing to their babies and toddlers are not necessarily creating a new generation of Mozarts but they are laying the foundations for a life in which music plays an important part, either as listeners or performers or both. And performers are first and foremost expert listeners. While there are some rare conditions which make it impossible for some young children to respond to music, they are indeed rare. For the vast majority the ability to respond is innate. Very young toddlers can often be heard singing in the bath or as they wake. At that age they are more likely to sing confidently and with rhythm and in tune than in later life, unless they are taught in time to overcome the self-consciousness which comes all too soon as part and parcel of growing up. Very young children learn music as naturally as they learn to speak.

When self-consciousness has made itself felt and made solo singing in the presence of another human being impossible, social singing can come to the rescue. Opportunities for this should be embraced eagerly, for the musical as well as social advantages. The innate musicality to which I have referred is never wholly lost. Sometimes it can rise to amazing heights, in situations of great social cohesion and elevated emotion. You may not be a football fan, but you will understand my point better if you can get hold of a video of a football match at Anfield, the home ground of Liverpool Football Club. Listen out for the singing of the song which has become the club's anthem, *You'll Never Walk Alone*. When the crowd are at their best – usually after a goal by the home side – the level of musicality they can achieve in this song is astonishing. Tuning and timing are perfect. As is expression. The world's greatest choral conductors could not achieve as much. And it all happens spontaneously. To say that the Liverpool crowd, mostly working class youngsters, do it justice is an understatement. But I would bet that only a tiny fraction of them has had any formal musical training. They have learned from listening and joining in.

Sometimes social singing can achieve extraordinary degrees of precision and complexity. I heard this for myself more than once in a village in North Wales where my father, brother and I would stay as a base for exploring the mountains. The local men – male choral singing is a Welsh tradition – were slate miners. In their pub on a Saturday night they would show off their vocal skills. Their abilities were of a standard that would have put some professional groups to shame. Again, this was not the result of formal training but from a tradition where singing was a major part of home and school life.

When it comes to learning to play an instrument the process is nothing like as natural. There are complex motor skills involved, some requiring elements of physical strength and dexterity just to make a sound, elements which will not be available until the child is much older. For example, would-be trombonists will not produce a sound until they learn to flutter their lips. Trumpeters make their sound through pursed lips. A flautist's lips must be strong enough to channel a narrow column of air across a small aperture. A different sort of strength is required for the oboe, where air needs to be forced between two reeds compressed by the lips. The larger stringed instruments require strength and agility in the bowing arms and the fingers which press down on the strings. Progress at this stage of transition from the aural and vocal to the instrumental can be slow and may well fail altogether. The physical obstacles may simply become too much. Or in focussing on them the player forgets the initial purpose of the exercise, to make music as opposed to just a sound. As we have seen, making that initial sound on the piano is much easier than with many other instruments. Failure to progress with the piano usually comes at a later stage, when the two hands are called upon to play different notes at the same time and in a coordinated way. Even when quite a high level of two-handed skill has been achieved progress may falter when the focus is too much on the mechanical process of identifying notes from printed score and playing the 'right' ones in the right order, with inadequate attention to the quality of the sound or the musical effectiveness of the result.

Playing has to be musical to be rewarding. To play any instrument musically there is a universal requirement, which is a sense of how the player understands the music and how they want it to sound. In other words, they need the prior aural image that comes from careful listening and, preferably, from the natural internalisation of musical elements from early singing experience. The stronger and more deeply rooted that aural image and sensitivity, the greater the chance that the inevitable challenges particular to their chosen instrument can be overcome. It is essential to start slowly and simply.

So at last we are ready to play our first tune. Before you try it out on your piano, you need to recall it and remember how it goes and, especially, how you want it to sound. I have chosen a particular tune for what follows, one I am sure you will know. But you can apply the same principles to a simple tune of your own choice.

As I cannot be with you in your room to show you which notes to play, we need a coded system we all understand. There are many such codes in music. The simplest is that which identifies notes by letters of the alphabet. Different instruments have different what could be called focus notes, or notes which form the basic reference points from which all other notes can be found. For a string player they are the 'open' strings, that is, the strings which sound a note without any alteration by the player of the length of string which vibrates. For the piano the main focus note is called Middle C.

Where is it? Take up your position at the piano, around the middle of the keyboard. If the name of the manufacturer is displayed, sit opposite that. Look at the keys. You will see that the black notes are grouped in twos and threes. Find the nearest group of two and locate the white note immediately to the left of the group. This will be Middle C. Play it as you learned to do above. If you can, sing it. Now play the white notes to its right, going up to the next group of two black notes, and listen carefully. Again, sing them if you can. You will notice that the pitch of the notes changes. Each note sounds at a higher pitch than the one to its left. Now go back to Middle C and play the white notes going to the left. You will hear that they get lower in pitch.

Our tune will use the notes from Middle C upwards, that is, to the right. Play these notes again, this time calling out their names (or, even better, singing them) according to the letters of the alphabet. Only seven letters are used, so after G you go back to A. So the sequence is C, D, E, F, G, A, B. This sequence of notes in order of ascent or descent is called a scale. (It is easier to remember the sequence this way than through the elaborate code urged by Hortensio on Bianca in the extract from *the Taming of the Shrew* quoted at the head of this interlude. But then Hortensio has an ulterior motive, doomed to fail, to seduce Bianca while teaching her the scale. His scale is a six-note mediaeval scale beginning on G.) Now play the white note immediately to the right of the B. This is also C. Because it sounds with twice the vibrations of Middle C the ear perceives it to be the same note. Use both hands now and play both Cs together. You will hear that they are essentially the same, though at different pitches.

You should by now be reassured. All those dozens of different keys on the keyboard do not mean dozens of different notes. Not really. There are only seven different notes, leaving out the black notes for now. They just appear at many different pitches. They can always be recognised from their position relative to the groups of two and three black notes. So finding your way around the keys is easier than you thought.

There is no logical reason why our focus note is labelled C rather than A. The reasons are lost in musical antiquity. Well, not lost exactly. But it has to do with the scales used in Ancient Greece and how they came to be notated in the early Middle Ages. A fascinating subject for musicologists with a historical bent, no doubt!

Our tune is French in origin and dates from the 18th century. If you are an adult, do not feel insulted because I am suggesting you play what you may know as a nursery rhyme. It was originally a pastoral love song with poignant and distinctly adult lyrics. Children's lyrics were adapted to the melody later. Its French title is *Ah! Vous Dirai-je, Maman* ('Ah! shall I tell you, Mother, [what is the cause of my torment?]'). English lyrics include *Twinkle, Twinkle, Little Star* and – to a rather more complicated version of the tune – *Baa, Baa, Black Sheep*. The tune has an impeccable pedigree in the classical repertoire. The simpler version we are going to play was used by Mozart in a set of brilliant variations for solo piano. In an alternative but still recognisable form it provides the main theme of the slow movement of Haydn's Symphony 94, the *Surprise*.

The tune starts on Middle C. Use your right hand only, and move to your right from Middle C. Play it with one finger, in the manner explained above. Proceed as follows:

C C G G A A G – F F E E D D C

Niceties of timing will be dealt with later. For the time being, pause on the third G and take a breath, literally if you are singing along, as I would strongly recommend. This is the first phrase. Songs traditionally open with two phrases in the form of a question and answer. What you have just played is the question. In the original French lyrics the words to what you have just played do actually pose a question. The answer follows and is identical. So play the whole thing again.

Now follows what singers often describe as the middle eight. This is about what are called bars and will be explained later. Again there are two identical phrases, as follows:

G G F F E E D

Pause on the D and repeat the phrase. Now the opening returns, so play what you started with, again making the repeat.

Now, let us go back to the three stages which are the key to musical playing. We have dealt extensively with hearing. You have just played your first complete tune. So where does the third one, listening, come in? Play the tune again, and this time listen intently as you play. It can be surprisingly hard to listen to yourself while playing, because you are naturally focussed on what your hands and fingers are doing. But the ability to listen to yourself as you play is essential if you are to make progress. It takes concentration and practice. Also, honesty. Did your playing correspond to what you heard in your head before you started? Did it measure up to your aural image of the tune? Honest answers to these questions mean that you will never be satisfied just with sounding the right notes in the right order. As you repeat the process of listening while playing you should find that the tune as you play it and your idea of how you want it to go are coming closer together, though at this stage a gap is likely to remain.

Later you will learn how to close that gap through techniques of timing, touch and tone. You will learn to use all your fingers, not just the one you have used up to now. You will also learn to play with two hands, at first with both playing the same notes, then with a left hand independent of the right. You will be well on the way.

To what? You need to be realistic. Few beginners will become professional concert pianists or concert standard amateurs, certainly not if they only start later in life. But if you have got this far, then an ambition to be able to play even simple pieces musically and sympathetically is well within reach, provided you proceed methodically and patiently.

FOUR

WINDS OF CHANGE

There is always one moment in childhood when
the door opens and lets the future in...

Graham Greene, *The Power and the Glory*

My intense early involvement with the piano, as well as
with a toy theatre I had made myself and for which I had
written some long-lost and thankfully brief plays, was a
refuge not only from my mother's sometimes violent moods
and my father's distance but also from my primary school,
Saints Peter and Paul. Neil and I had no choice but to go
there as it was the only local Catholic primary school.

It is worth recalling some background for those who
have no personal or family memories of those times or have
not studied the history of education in this country in the
twentieth century. To a large extent your social and
economic destiny from 1944 up to the mid-1970s rested on
success or failure in a single examination, the notorious
eleven-plus. This exam still exists in parts of the country
with selective state secondary schools, but varies in format
from place to place and is much more flexible than in the
past. It was originally intended to 'stream' pupils at age

eleven according to their aptitudes for either academic or technical secondary education. But because of the national neglect and underfunding of technical education it became in effect a fiercely competitive 'pass or fail' moment (with no option for a re-sit), determining admission either to a high quality grammar school or a poor quality so-called secondary modern. The latter was the type of school in which my father taught. The primary school which Neil and I attended had a very poor record of eleven-plus passes. It was essentially a waiting-room for entry to the local Catholic secondary modern school, St Bede's. I do not know if St Bede's deserved its sinister reputation. But the very name was enough to send a shudder down the spines of my parents and their friends and relatives and thus by osmosis down the spines of Neil and myself. It was not open to our mother to consider a better primary school for us as she was committed to sending us to Catholic schools. Our father had no part to play in such decisions.

Saints Peter and Paul was run by a couple of severe and exotically-dressed nuns, one of whom was called Sister Serafina. We naturally nicknamed her Sister Semolina. Academically the school had a poor reputation and thoroughly deserved it. Though it was not all bad. Among the lay staff there were some compassionate and caring teachers. One of them was Miss Walsh, so loved by her pupils that on their discovering she lived very close to the school an adoring group would greet the poor woman every morning outside her home and escort her into work. But there were not enough of the well-intentioned ones to spare me from an ordeal, which as far as I can remember lasted a full year. I was not one to make friends in my early years there and would usually spend playtime cowering in a corner of the playground. I had good reason to cower. Several larger boys would take time from their games to come up to me and punch me several times in the stomach. I imagine there were supervising teachers but they took no action. I told my parents about the bullying. I was even able to give them names. But they also did nothing. They seemed to think it was just part of life and I would need to accept it. Neil also heard me tell what was happening. He decided he would do something about it. His playground was for older children, separate from ours but linked to it by a path. One day at playtime he brought some of his classmates along the path to see for themselves what was happening. As they were older and bigger they were soon able to deal with the bullies, who never bothered me again. What my teachers and parents had done nothing to stop was ended by my ten-year-old brother and his mates.

One day at the age of nine I was sent along to a huge house in 'posh' Blundellsands. I had no idea what it was about, other than that I had to sit an exam. I learned later that the house was the preparatory school, known usually as just 'the prep', for St Mary's College, the local Catholic grammar school. I was later surprised, as were my parents, to learn that I had gained admittance and would be leaving Saints Peter and Paul from the following academic year. I say surprised because I do not recall having shown any academic potential at all. I was just an irritatingly shy, introverted, pale-complexioned child with an obsessive interest in music and reading.

From the start I could sense that this school was different. The first and most obvious difference was that it was single sex. That also applied to the teachers, apart from a severe lady each for dance and elocution. The purpose of the elocution classes was to remove any traces we might betray of the distinctive Liverpool or scouse accent. It worked only in part, as most of us learned to speak in two accents. For some it was scouse at home and posh at school, though only in class and not in the playground. Talking posh in the playground could get you if not a beating then at least derision from fellow pupils for 'talking like a fruit.' In my case, posh was required at home as well as in class. This was before the Liverpool accent would lose its anchor in the working class and become world famous and infinitely desirable through the medium of the Beatles and their irreverent interviews on radio and television. But a word of warning: the Liverpool accent cannot be taken up convincingly by anyone who has not been steeped in it in childhood. A Liverpudlian can always spot when even the most skilful actors who try it are not genuine scousers.

The second difference in the new school was the presence of strange creatures with male voices but wearing black ankle-length dresses with a black belt around the midriff. This was my first encounter with the Christian Brothers. The Brothers are not anointed priests but take similar vows of poverty, chastity (which in practice means celibacy) and obedience. These alien beings seemed to be in charge. They enforced strict discipline with the use of a leather strap on the hand. But the main difference was work. Hard work in class and at home and with one aim in view. There was no time or inclination for bullying, any sign of which would have been promptly stamped on. We all had to focus on the job in hand. The prep achieved passes in the eleven-plus for nearly all its pupils. It was expected.

Not that it was all work and no play. Apart from dance and elocution, there was music. A teacher called Slade, whom we will meet again at what we called the big school, that is, St Mary's College, came each week for hymns and to teach the rudiments of playing the recorder. I played in a recorder group at annual speech days in a local hall, where we would also put on a short play. I did not get a part but was allowed to stand in the wings, pretending to be the assistant stage manager. Strangely, while music would feature very strongly at the big school, drama would be totally neglected.

I had started in the lower of the two streams but was promoted to the upper stream for my second and third years. We were so well drilled that the eleven-plus exam came and went without stress. I gained a place in the upper stream at the big school after winning my first form prize. From just about scraping into the lower stream in my first year at the prep I had progressed by my third year to fourth place in the upper stream.

What about Neil, who had stayed on at Saints Peter and Paul after rescuing me from the playground bullies and who was apparently destined for the horrors of St Bede's? I do not know if he ever tried for entrance to the prep. I do know that our parents held increasingly gloomy conversations about the hell which would await him if he failed the eleven-plus. I also know that Neil overheard some of these conversations and resolved that he would put his head in the gas oven if he failed. He passed, a rare distinction for that school, well enough to get into the second highest of the four streams at the big school.

The year of my ninth birthday was memorable for another life-changing event; a traumatic one which at different times and in different ways would leave its scars on all of us. It was, in the words of Graham Greene, the moment when the door opened and let the future in. It was to be a future of insecurity and anxiety, tearing at the already fragile heart of the family. No longer and not for several years would we live in a space we could call home, for on every working day our living area would be invaded by outsiders. Once the invaders had gone for the evening we would still feel cramped and crowded. What had happened? Had we lost our home to unemployment and overwhelming debt? Not at all. It was simply that my mother had tired of my father's modest salary and the supplement she earned from part-time hairdressing. She had decided to go into business on her own account. She announced the decision dramatically with the words, adapted from the film *Gone with the Wind,* 'I'm never going to be poor again.' Note the personal pronoun. She was not doing it for us.

The immediate impetus for her decision was a wretchedly uncomfortable caravan holiday my mother and I took in North Wales with one of her friends and her three children. My father and Neil had wisely managed to be elsewhere. The main problem with the holiday was the weather, hardly unexpected in that part of the world. We were not in fact poor. We had a comfortable house on the edge of the countryside with no mortgage attached. My father had a secure job with a regular if not large salary.

True, we had no car and did not go on foreign holidays. But this was 1957. Rationing had ended only three years before. Few enjoyed the luxuries she craved. Many would have envied what we had.

Nevertheless, she sold the house she had inherited from her mother and with the proceeds bought a hairdressing business in nearby Waterloo. We rented the premises, which apart from the very small shop comprised a living room, kitchen, two bedrooms and a bathroom, all small and cramped. The bathroom could only be reached through the bedroom which I shared with Neil, so a screen had been put in place to allow passage. Although the premises were old even then and the brickwork surrounding the tiny backyard already crumbling the building still stands to this day. Poodles were later groomed where my mother had groomed the hair of the local ladies. Now the much refurbished shop sells ice cream and milkshakes.

It was not only our domestic situation which changed. The flat arable landscape near our first family home and the neighbouring Blundell estate and village of Little Crosby had not altered in centuries and remain unchanged to this day. The surroundings of our new home were very different. Change was all around us. The shop was only a few yards from a popular beach fringing the Mersey Estuary. A short walk onto the sands and we faced wider, more distant and more turbulent vistas than any we had known in Crosby. Across the water to the West lay the Wirral Peninsula and, lining the far horizon on a clear day though more often veiled in mist, the Welsh Hills, home of ancient legend and language. It may be that that sight evoked in my father a nostalgia for the youthful time he had spent exploring those same hills and the mountains of Snowdonia which lay beyond, cycling there on a tandem with a childhood friend. Or perhaps he had already started to return there with Neil before our move. In any case, I persuaded him when I was a few years older to take me with them on those excursions to the tops of mountains whose names breathed their own Celtic music, such as Tryfan and Carnedd Llewellyn. My mother was horrified. A strenuous outdoor pastime with an ever-present element of danger was never remotely part of her plan for me. But high on those ridges I could see something in my father's face I never saw at home: peace of mind.

To the North of Waterloo Beach lay Liverpool Bay and the Irish Sea. Ships of all sizes ploughed the channel marked by wave-tossed bell-sounding buoys, heading along the Welsh coast to Llandudno or over to the Isle of Man or Dublin, or in the case of the vast ocean-going liners further out and onto the Atlantic. The western and northerly winds scoured the coast with blown sand. Sometimes the water was lashed into fury by the winds, sometimes it was no more than a sullen swell. But it was never at peace. Always it threatened. To the South lay Liverpool, port and city, built by wave on wave of migrant ships, from China, the West Indies, and, bearing my ancestors, Ireland and Norway. At the end of the long beach the lighthouse beckoned. Beyond it, huge cranes and warehouses unloaded and stored cargo bound for destinations across the country. Change would come there as well, when the massive container base arrived downriver. The old docks fell into disuse. The former dockers, once the elite of the skilled port labour force, would wait in vain by the locked gates for the return of their proud past. The huge docks in the city centre by the Pier Head just beyond the so-called 'Three Graces' – the Royal Liver, Cunard and Port of Liverpool buildings, a trio of giants which tell so much of the history of the port – are now theme parks to attract tourists. Older, smaller docks to the south now sport trendy waterfront developments.

The area immediately by the hair salon, as we would pretentiously call it these days but not then, was thriving and diverse. An elderly Dutch lady opposite kept two adjacent shops, one selling sweets from huge jars which she sold by the quarter pound in little paper bags. Her shop next door was opened seasonally to sell cheap plastic buckets, spades and beach balls for the day visitors to the beach. Just up the road from her was an alluring Swiss cake shop. There was a Chinese laundry and a Chinese restaurant. Next door to us was a fishmonger, who provided delicious Manx kippers and displayed a notice promising to supply anglers 'in strictest confidence.' But above all, at least as far as I was concerned, only about a hundred yards away, was a record shop amply stocked with budget price long-playing classical records. Wow!

Some of our furniture had been sold because of the more restricted space. Fortunately, the piano came with us. The only room which could be found for it was in the kitchen. It was not just a kitchen. During the day it served as a meeting and tea room for the shop staff, whose number increased steadily over the years. It always smelt of peroxide, a pungent odour which leaked into our food and tea and no doubt into the insides of the piano itself. The peroxide was used to bleach hair, though judging by its concentration in the confined downstairs atmosphere it could well have served its other main purpose, as an ingredient of rocket propellant. There was time for piano practice only after the shop had closed and before my parents had settled in by the radio next door. I was lucky if I could get in half an hour's practice before I had to leave my parents in peace and go upstairs to do my homework. I was puzzled that after those years in which my mother had insisted on my daily practice she had so changed our domestic circumstances as to make practice very difficult.

Some years later the radio took second place to a television which they had belatedly acquired, my mother having for years denounced the invention as sinful and resisted its introduction into the house. My father had already been paying for his mother to rent a television. Neil and I made long weekly journeys after school to our grandmother's house to watch the original *Quatermass* series. This terrifying programme, all the more scary for being in black and white, was scheduled in the very early evening just in time for children to catch it on getting home from school and then to have nightmares when they went to bed. These days it would only be put on after 11.00 p.m. When our own television arrived I was only allowed to watch it sparingly. But what I did see left lasting memories, in particular, the first ever televised series of Shakespeare's history plays, *The Age of Kings,* and a never to be surpassed *Maigret* series starring Rupert Davies. Thus was born in me a lifelong love of Shakespeare and the novels of Georges Simenon. Television also provided my introduction to opera, with broadcasts in Russian of Tchaikovsky's *Eugene Onegin* and *the Queen of Spades*. The former remains one of my favourite operas, heartfelt and intimate, a moving story of real people rather than a vehicle for stars. My mother in the meantime found emotional refuge in another sort of opera, becoming an early devotee of *Coronation Street*.

The new accommodation was too far for me to continue to go to Miss Penhall, who by then was coming close to retirement. My father enquired about the availability of a popular and respected local teacher, Edgar Brown. He had no vacancies but strongly recommended one of his own former pupils, James Firth, always known as Jimmy. Jimmy was in his early thirties and already well established locally as a teacher. He had been a pupil at the same school as Neil and myself.

Jimmy lived in an upstairs flat in which, as far as I can recall, the only furniture was his piano. He was a superb pianist. He performed regularly in local festivals. The huge technical challenges of Chopin studies he met with fluency and ease. His lifestyle was somewhat chaotic and often it was he who would be late for my lesson, running up the road and waving frantically as I waited outside. But I adored him. My father was less sure about him. I now understand why, from this distance in time. His manner was very open and rather camp, which only endeared him to me all the more. Such a refreshing change from the stern and studied masculinity of my father and his drinking companions.

Jimmy started me off with a Debussy piece, his quirky G major Arabesque, which I never began to master. Then something magical happened. He introduced me to the second composer to enter my soul. Schubert. He gave me one of his impromptus to learn. The name impromptu, which in Schubert's time was often attached by publishers to single-movement piano pieces to enhance their appeal, suggests something slight which you might improvise on the spur of the moment. Schubert's eight impromptus could hardly be more different. They are all substantial and technically challenging works. The one which Jimmy gave me was the second of his second set, a hymn-like tune with a brilliant arpeggio middle section. The piece has its technical difficulties but such was the overwhelming beauty of the music that they simply melted away. My fingers found immediate solutions to them without my being aware of how they were doing it. I never had to think what the piece meant or how to interpret it. I just played it.

I was not with Jimmy for long. My mother, who to the best of my knowledge had never met him, told me that my lessons with him had stopped because he had 'gone to London to become a concert pianist.' For many years afterwards, failing to see his face on television or his name on programmes of concerts at the Phil, I had visions of poor Jimmy practising at night in a tiny garret while fruitlessly touring agents and promoters during the day, eventually succumbing to a life of destitution on the streets. But what my mother had told me was yet another of her inventions. As far as I can tell from my recent research, Jimmy never had ambitions to earn his living on the concert platform, being well established as a teacher in schools and private practice. He had already studied in London, at the Royal College of Music. He might have gone down to London again to further his studies or elsewhere to develop his teaching experience. He would return in due course to his roots in Crosby, where he would regularly play in local festivals until well into his eighties. Whatever the reason for the cessation of my lessons with him, I was devastated and cried for a long time.

I next went to a musical couple, both professionals. Emily Mair was a singer and her husband, Wilfred Simenauer, the leading cellist in the Liverpool Philharmonic Orchestra. I managed very recently to get hold of a copy of Wilfred's autobiography, *Slaving Over a Hot Cello*[1]. Before that it had never occurred to me that he was anything but English born and bred. I now know that he was Jewish, given the name Wolfgang at birth, born in a part of Germany now Polish, who fled the Nazis with his parents at the age of nine. His developmental years were spent in New Zealand before he came to London to study at the Royal College of Music. My main memory of him has nothing to do with my piano lessons. In 1962 I saw him give a very fine performance of the Elgar Cello Concerto at the Phil. The conductor was Colin Davis. It seems from Wilfred's autobiography that he had what he called 'demons' about playing from memory and was very nervous that night that he would forget his way during the performance. All I can say is that he did not forget and there were so signs of nerves that I could detect.

The lives of Wilfred and Emily were as chaotic as one would expect from two busy professionals with separate careers. I never knew which of them would give me my lesson or how long it would last. I liked them both but I recall very little of the actual lessons. I have the impression that after my rather improvisatory, hit-and-miss time with Jimmy they took me back to basics, probably no bad thing.

It must have been about this time that I started to learn more about the use of the sustaining pedal, though I had surely used it instinctively in the Schubert impromptu. Only much later on did I learn to use it with proper control and focus.

But the truth was that I was beginning to lose interest. I was twelve by then or nearly, attending a grammar school obsessed with homework. Finding time and motivation for practice in our cramped and often occupied kitchen was getting harder. I missed Jimmy's fire and inspiration. It was a dangerous time. I do not recall exactly how my lessons with the couple came to an end. Their professional commitments and my own increasingly crowded schedule, which at my mother's insistence now included serving on the altar at the local church, no doubt combined to create a mutual decision to call it a day. They would have ended soon in any case as Wilfred and Emily were planning to move to New Zealand. They left England for good a couple of years later. It could so easily have been the end of my piano story.

FIVE

EDUCATION, SENTIMENTAL AND PRACTICAL

Two factors combined to ensure it was not the end. The first was my father's promise to make further enquiries of Edgar Brown, the teacher who had steered me to have lessons with Jimmy. The second came later, in the form of the musical environment of my secondary school, St Mary's College.

Edgar had by then retired from private teaching but his son Gerald was now a piano teacher and had vacancies. I was invited to their house to audition for Gerald. Edgar was also there. I took along the piece which I had continued to play for my own pleasure and consolation in those difficult times, the Schubert impromptu. I put the music on the stand and started to play before the assembled audience of my father and the two Browns. After a short while Edgar stood up and approached the piano. He told me I should carry on playing but that he wanted to follow the score more closely. Without warning he removed it from the stand. He knew already what I did not know myself. That I knew the piece by heart. I finished playing. Edgar then announced that he would take me himself.

Edgar, like all my teachers so far apart from Jimmy, was more than a pianist. He had studied organ with Caleb Jarvis, official organist at St George's Hall in Liverpool. He still taught singing at a local grammar school. I had lessons with him until I was sixteen. He was kind and patient and he certainly needed to be. My ever-increasing commitments at school and church meant that 'practice' was often a quick run-through before each lesson of the piece he had given me the week before. Later, as a teacher myself, I could very readily spot such last-minute preparation, as of course could he. I became an adept sight-reader. We worked much too rapidly through a very wide repertoire. I was not putting down the technical or interpretative roots I should have been at that age. That was not his fault. He knew that it was essential to maintain my interest despite the many other pressures and distractions. He ensured that I never got bogged down in music which was not amenable to me. He soon realised when something did not grip my interest and moved on.

But there was one composer for whom I always managed to find some extra time. He was the third composer to enter my soul. Chopin. Mazurkas, waltzes and nocturnes. But especially the mazurkas, for which I have retained a deep love to this day. I had already been exposed to the mazurkas through a recording I had borrowed from a friend as part of that free exchange of records I have mentioned earlier. This was a 1959 recording of ten mazurkas and the B Minor Sonata played by the late Chinese pianist, Fou Ts'ong. We often read and hear that to play the mazurkas with proper understanding you have to be

Polish. But Fou's way with the mazurkas was acclaimed around the world. He had won a special prize for his interpretation of them at the international Chopin competition in 1955. To those who say to me I should be Polish to play the mazurkas I respond that I first learned to appreciate them from a Chinaman.

Other great interpreters of the mazurkas who are not Polish include the Argentinian pianist, Martha Argerich, and the Italian, Arturo Benedetti Michelangeli, both of whom I have heard in live performance of this music. Both have well-deserved legendary status among the greatest pianists of their times. Michelangeli died in 1995 but Argerich, who had some lessons with Michelangeli, is still with us and still full of her distinctive fiery virtuosity and musicianship. Like Fou T'song she won a special prize for her playing of the mazurkas at the international Chopin competition, ten years after Fou T'song won the same prize. Though she has long since ceased to give solo recitals I was fortunate to hear her play one of the three Opus 59 mazurkas, special favourites of hers, as an encore after a concerto performance at the Royal Festival Hall. She spun such a web of magic sound that I did not want to spoil the effect by hearing anything else, at least not that evening. I left the hall before the second half.

I have been lucky enough to see Michelangeli perform live, though only on the one occasion, at London's Barbican Hall, some time in the late 1980s. Luck certainly came into it because he had a reputation for cancelling more concerts than he actually played. When I rang the hall to book my ticket the lady at the box office asked me for my telephone number. When I asked why, she told me it was so she could ring to tell me 'when he cancelled.' The expected call never happened. I made my way to the hall, expecting to see the cancellation notice displayed outside and wondering whether I would then go straight home or find something else to do in the concrete desert which surrounds the Barbican at night. But there was no indication of a cancellation. Expectation was rising as the audience gathered. Would the maestro actually appear? He did, playing a programme including the F Minor Fantasy of Chopin and the second book of Debussy's Preludes. The performances were of a chiselled perfection which I found somewhat cold. Then he came back onto the platform for the encore, Chopin's Mazurka in B Minor, Opus 33 Number 4. This was a different experience altogether. Some of the mazurkas are short and light-weight, but others are among his profoundest inspirations and this mazurka is one of them. It opens with a melody full of nostalgia and longing, which then alternates with startlingly contrasting episodes, some harshly dissonant, others songlike and dreamy, still others full of joyous rhythm and dance. Before the final return of the main theme is a passage in a single line which could have been written for the cello, by no means the only such passage in Chopin's solo piano output (he had a profound love of that instrument.) In my view, none of his longer works covers so many differing emotions with so many contrasts of light and shade, all distilled within a piece lasting only a few minutes. Michelangeli had a way of drawing out the line so that the audience held its breath. The performance was utterly mesmerising, once heard never to be forgotten.

Edgar also gave me many pieces by Grieg to work on,

perhaps having picked up a hint from my father about our Norwegian ancestry. Grieg is without doubt a superb and underrated writer for the piano as a solo instrument. Though I believe his finest work is to be found in his songs, which rarely get a hearing in the English-speaking world, probably because of the language factor. My favourite Grieg piano pieces remain his own transcriptions of two songs, *Heart Wounds* and *The Last Spring*. As well as the piano versions, he thought enough of them to make superlative arrangements for string orchestra under the collective title *Elegiac Melodies*. From the start I loved his piano music for the yearning harmonies derived from Norwegian folksong and the sprightly rhythms of the festive pieces with their open fifths suggestive of the Hardanger fiddle.

But did I feel my playing of his music to be more 'authentic' because of my part Norwegian blood? If that were the case, how could I explain my affinity with the mazurkas of Chopin and my later love of the quintessentially French Debussy and the culturally much more remote Moravian, Janacek? In any case, I have only visited Norway twice and then only briefly. I have no knowledge of the language. I am sure Grieg would have been horrified at any suggestion that the Norwegian folk elements he wove into his music to put his own original stamp on it would have somehow sealed it off from the wider musical world. Composers who flavoured their work with their own national seasonings, as many did from the latter part of the nineteenth century onwards, were surely no different from their predecessors in seeing music as a universal language. The reason Grieg's piano music tends to be neglected by virtuosi is not because of its national character but precisely because it tends to lack any obvious virtuosic element, calling rather for sensitivity of touch and phrasing. One notable exception to this neglect is the great Soviet artist and peerless virtuoso, Emil Gilels, who recorded and performed many of Grieg's pieces in his later years.

Lack of equivalent nationality should never in my view inhibit anyone from exploring whatever music appeals to them, any more than anyone with the same nationality as a particular composer should feel entitled to claim privileged access to their musical secrets on that ground alone. The great British guitarist and lutenist Julian Bream was once asked if he had Spanish blood as he played Spanish guitar music with such passion and intensity. I was born in Battersea, he replied, between the park and the dogs' home. To Segovia goes the credit for establishing the classical guitar in the concert repertoire. But his Spanish blood did not make him a greater interpreter of Spanish music than either the London-born Bream or the Australian John Williams. And what of composers? Are they not allowed to take into their own artistic imaginations the experiences of other countries and cultures? What of the 'Scottish music' of German-Jewish Mendelssohn or Salford-born Peter Maxwell Davies, or the vivid evocations of Spain achieved by Ravel and Debussy? Are they to be condemned in retrospect for cultural 'appropriation?' Deep waters indeed, and time to move on.

Edgar always wrote down his comments about my playing after each lesson, using a blank notebook 'borrowed' from his own school. He would then leave the book with me to study the comments in preparation for the following week. It was a practice I was to remember and adopt myself in my own teaching. At the beginning of each lesson he would ask me for what he always called 'the book of words.' He would then listen carefully, pen in hand, though mostly he wrote only after the lesson was over and at great speed with very few corrections. His comments were models of clarity and relevance. By some miracle the notebook covering the period March 1963 to July 1964 has survived and is in my hands. It is a sobering and moving experience to read through his comments. They were the essence of the man, perceptive, generous, understanding, warm. Through them I get a clear picture of the sort of pupil I was, not darkly through the glass of my own memory but through the insights of a teacher of great wisdom and experience. He always spotted when I was sight-reading work which should have been prepared. Often I was too loud, sometimes even aggressive, and used excessive sustaining pedal. He commended my gift for memory but warned me of the need for a controlling intellect. He well understood the pressures on my time and made allowances. I believe he also understood that for me at that time playing the piano was as much about emotional release as anything else.

A composer who is of the utmost importance to every serious pianist is of course Beethoven. He was not one of those who entered my soul, softly as in a morning sunrise. Rather he overwhelmed and overpowered me. The trigger again took the form of records lent to me by a friend, of Beethoven sonatas played by Joseph Cooper. The sonatas were five of those well known enough to have acquired names: *Moonlight, Pathétique, Appassionata, Pastorale* and *Waldstein.* Cooper was well known in later years as the genial host of a TV musical quiz show, which rather overshadowed his very real pianistic accomplishments. Certainly he was a fine Beethoven pianist. I will never forget the first time I listened to his recording of the *Moonlight.* I had first come across part of the score in the *Music Lover's Portfolio*, but only the first two movements are there. There is no suggestion of what might follow. When I first heard the uprushing arpeggios of the finale I was swept away as in a whirlwind. How were such sounds possible? How could any one individual create such a maelstrom of sound and passion? I had barely had time to recover before the opening chord of the *Pathétique* came crashing in. It is scarcely an exaggeration to say that a whole new world had opened up to me.

I continued to work on my own on the first two movements of the *Moonlight* from the Portfolio, feeling quite rightly that I would not be able to tackle the finale for some years yet. I bought the score of the *Pathétique* and tried to storm the citadel of the first movement. Success was limited but there was always the heavenly Adagio to follow. I did not work on any Beethoven with Edgar, though towards the end of our time together he did ask me if I would be interested in the *Appassionata.* (How well he understood me!) I needed no further encouragement. I bought the score and studied it intensely over the following years, but always on my own. If ever there was a piece which could act as a safety-valve for teenage angst this was it.

The friend who had lent me the Cooper records was also

responsible for my first visit to a live Beethoven performance at the Phil. He was David Crystal, quite a few years older than me and already in the sixth form of our school. David later became world-famous as a professor of linguistics and author of many books on the subject. My mother and his had met and become friends through the local church. Through his mother I was introduced to David and was thoroughly taken by his charm, confidence, lively intellect, curiosity and energy. What he saw in me, a shy, awkward introvert so many years his junior, I will never know. But we met frequently to share our mutual interest in music. His was deep and wide-ranging. He was an accomplished player of clarinet and saxophone, the latter his instrument of choice in a group which played in Crosby and Liverpool clubs, including the tiny, cramped Cavern where the Beatles and Cilla Black among many others forged the famous Liverpool sound. When I later embarked on composition it was David I asked to look through my manuscripts, to which he readily agreed, making helpful suggestions. After he had gone up to university we corresponded for several years and I visited him in London. He was an expert in the lost art of witty and entertaining letter-writing. We lost touch once my own university days began but resumed contact as recently as 2009, when his autobiography[2] was published.

I would have been about ten or eleven when David offered to take me to the Phil to see the renowned pianist Clifford Curzon play Beethoven's *Emperor* Concerto. I remember not only the glorious sounds of Curzon's playing but the look of sublime joy on his face as he brought Beethoven's music to life. I always took whatever opportunity offered to see Curzon again, as I did to see another British pianist who represented, sadly for far too short a time, the very pinnacle of pianistic achievement, John Ogdon. Ogdon died at the age of only fifty, after suffering years of severe mental illness. I was able to attend one of his last recitals in London. When he came onto the platform the huge, shambling, white-haired figure was barely recognisable from the titan I had first seen in Liverpool, sporting a little goatee beard which gave him an almost diabolic aura. The pianistic genius was still there, but subdued, even in Beethoven's massive *Hammerklavier* sonata. After the scheduled programme he played a string of encores from remote corners of his vast repertoire, chatting with the audience and obviously making up his mind on the spot as to which pieces to play. It was as if we were at a musical house party rather than in a concert hall. I like to think he enjoyed the informality which he had himself created. Certainly the audience did.

David also introduced me to the BBC Proms on one of my visits to London. The two concerts we attended together on successive nights featured favourite Tchaikovsky concertos, the violin concerto played by Henryk Szeryng and the first piano concerto played by yet another distinguished British pianist, Peter Katin. The unique atmosphere of the proms and its lively young audience has been a special love of mine ever since.

The grammar school I attended from the age of twelve, St Mary's College, was run by the Irish Christian Brothers, already familiar to me from my prep school. Though intensely focussed on examination success St Mary's was also very active in sport and music. Singing and orchestra were compulsory for all pupils for the first three years. After that it depended on whether you had secured a place in one or more of the choirs and orchestras. Performances by these were given at the annual Speech Day which took place at the Phil. I sang soprano in my first two years. The highlight for me on my second Speech Day was the thrilling experience of being in the choir to sing Wagner's *Hail Gift of Song* from *Tannhauser*. I knew then that Wagner was another world waiting to be discovered, though that would not happen until I was well into adulthood.

Orchestra lessons gave me a chance to learn another instrument apart from the piano. I dearly hoped it would be the oboe, an instrument I had always loved from the time I had first heard it. Our first orchestra lesson was a curious experience. We were still in our form rooms when the two instrumental teachers arrived. Eugene Genin taught strings in several Liverpool schools and was a noted orchestral player of violin and viola and a private teacher. He was short and rather rotund, with ferocious energy. He loved to drive huge classic cars, in which he was barely visible behind the steering wheel. He continued to teach in local schools until he was eighty. William Flood was small and self-effacing. As well as teaching wind and percussion he played trumpet in several Liverpool orchestras. While it was Genin who as conductor stood in the limelight at Speech Day performances it was Flood who did all the arranging of the orchestral parts, incorporating discreet little solos for the more accomplished players. At that first lesson Genin took the lead, asking us to stand and choosing the tallest boys to play double bass. In the meantime I was sending out unseen vibrations to Flood to choose me for his wind class. I was successful. I already knew I liked him. It was not too difficult after that to persuade him to allocate the oboe to me. It was much harder actually to get a sound out of the instrument but eventually I succeeded.

Our singing teacher was Frederick Slade, like Flood an accomplished arranger. He was often difficult and tetchy, impatient with any pupil who could not respond to his direction. In private he could be congenial and had many good stories to tell. I sensed that he was a frustrated man. His love of music ran very deep but emerged only occasionally. He often did not seem to like even the music he had arranged himself. It was clear he had wanted to be a concert pianist but had somehow found himself channelled into a teaching post in which he was inevitably faced with pupils who were hard to motivate. Genin and Flood had less of a problem with motivation because playing instruments, or even just playing around with them, was fun. They did not seem to mind if their efforts produced a shocking cacophony, at least at the early stages.

There was always a school pianist to serve the choirs and orchestras. At the time I started in the school there were senior boys well qualified to take on that role. When they left I found myself called on to replace them. My mother had spoken to the headmaster. Several boys in my year auditioned for Slade and I was chosen. This meant I had to leave Flood's wind class to join the string class as support pianist. I was moved when Flood told me he was sorry to lose me. I also became the accompanist in our form class for singing. Slade coached me intensively in the special art of accompaniment. It is indeed an art and takes a lifetime to learn. What I learned at school only scraped the surface but stood me in good stead in later life. My sight-reading abilities were also tested and developed. Often in choir or class I would have a score placed in front of me and was expected to play it right away and in a way that helped rather than hindered the singers.

A particularly memorable moment in singing class came when Slade chose Schubert's great song about an elusive but ultimately deceived fish, *The Trout*. The accompaniment depicting the darting to and fro of the fish under the water is notoriously tricky. I practised it carefully. On the day the class were due to sing it I had to work on it before leaving for school, knowing that my fingers would otherwise be too stiff. Another world had opened up for me, that of the great German lieder and the rewards to be had in partnering singers with those wonderful piano parts.

I had in fact already had a glimpse of that world within the covers of Aunt Molly's *Music Lover's Portfolio,* in the form of perhaps Schubert's greatest song, *Erlkoenig* (the Earl King), set to a poem by Goethe and written when the composer was only eighteen. Apart from a complete transcription of his 'Unfinished' Symphony, this is curiously the only music by Schubert to feature in the entire series of volumes. Curious because the editors could have chosen any number from the treasure of wonderful Schubert songs whose technical demands fall comfortably within the ability range of the good amateur at whom the volumes were aimed. *Erlkoenig* is strictly for professionals and only a select few of those. The introduction contains advice for the singer considering tackling the song but none at all to help the pianist with one of the most difficult accompaniments ever written. Nevertheless I explored the music as best I could and the song has never lost its fascination for me. I do not recall when or by whom I first heard a performance. Perhaps that by Dietrich Fischer-Dieskau accompanied by Gerald Moore will always reign supreme.

Repertoire for the Speech Day concerts was not generally on such an inspirational level. It would be chosen not by the specialist music teachers themselves but by the Christian Brothers, whose tastes were not always so elevated. They had a special passion for the music of Sullivan, from the operettas in which he collaborated with W S Gilbert. It featured on the programme year after year. Sullivan was more in vogue then than he is now. There can be no doubt that he was a consummate craftsman with a superb melodic gift and a genius for pastiche which on occasions he could lift to the level of its models. A couple of my school friends caught the bug, as did I for a while. We collected recordings of many of the operettas and played them to each other in our homes.

Playing with the school orchestra was time-consuming but fun. I had to attend all the weekly sectional rehearsals of the string players as well as the later rehearsals as the whole ensemble took shape. Normally there would be one piece for the orchestra alone and another to provide the climax to the Speech Day concert, when the orchestra and senior choir would combine. It was fascinating to experience from the inside how an orchestral sound is built up from all the individual sections. The school orchestra would never have put the Berlin Philharmonic to shame. Very few of the players could afford their own instruments on which to practise at home. The school instruments, while serviceable, were not of high quality. For most of the players, the only time they could get their hands on their instruments was in class or at rehearsals. In the circumstances it is astonishing that the orchestra sounded as well as it did.

I found accompanying the choirs far less satisfying. With a solo singer you know who to follow. But often a choir and conductor are not on the same page (musically speaking) in the early stages and it is hard to know which to follow. One Speech Day I was accompanying the senior choir in a performance of a choral version of a Strauss waltz. At the end I was so caught up in the flow of the music that I failed to observe a pause the conductor wanted before the final chord, so that the ending was ragged. I learned a valuable lesson from this: if you go wrong with a solo singer you only have one person from whom to ask forgiveness; with a large choir it is much more problematic.

Perhaps the most valuable lesson I learned from so much ensemble playing was the importance of a crucial musical quality which pianists who learn and play only on their own often neglect. Playing in time. It sounds so obvious. Those who play instruments or sing with others from the outset take it for granted. Everybody has to play or sing in time, either a time set by the conductor or one they have agreed among themselves.

That is my cue for another interlude, to reflect on what time actually is in music and how to make it part of your music-making, whether or not you are fortunate enough to play with others.

INTERLUDE IV

TIME

Play strictly in time! The playing of many a virtuoso resembles the walk of a drunkard. Do not take those sorts of performances as your models.
Robert Schumann[3]

The importance of time

What mainly distinguishes music from the other arts is that it moves through time in a regular way. This is certainly true of most classical and popular music, so we will take it to be a general truth. Consider how you first learned to make music, perhaps at school or in church. Your teacher might have made the class clap to the time of the music, after first indicating at what speed to clap. The main though by no means the only function of the conductor of a choir or orchestra is to indicate and maintain timing, so everybody can start together and stay that way to the end. Where there is no conductor, for example where players and singers come together in small groups, usually one is designated as the leader and will mark the timing through gestures such as a nod of the head.

Pulse, beat and rhythm

You will find various words used to describe time as it applies to music. They do not all mean the same. Apart from time itself, the most common such words are rhythm, speed, tempo, beat, and pulse. The main distinction which needs to be made clear is between rhythm and pulse. Beat can be used to mean much the same as pulse. In what follows I will use 'pulse' to refer to the intended pace of a piece of music or a section of it, and 'beat' to refer to the individual components of that pulse.

A good start is to get hold of a recording of that very popular orchestral piece by Ravel, his *Bolero*. I am taking this as an example because it has a particularly notable rhythm marked by the side drum which is repeated constantly and impresses itself on the mind of the listener. This rhythm goes as follows ('*tickety*' represents three light hits on the drum in the time of one heavier '*tom*'):

Tom tickety tom tickety tom tom, Tom tickety tom tickety tickety tickety

The pulse underlies this rhythm and is the same throughout. It can be represented just by the '*toms*', with one '*tom*' for each '*tickety*':

Tom tom tom tom tom tom, etc.

Now here is an important distinction. Compare several versions of the *Bolero* and you will find they do not all take the same time to perform. Some are quicker than others. That is, the underlying pulse is quicker. This is the choice of the conductor. But what is the same in all versions is that rhythm or rhythmic pattern on the drum, because that was

97

the decision of the composer. Composers may give an indication of how fast they want a piece to go. They may even suggest a precise setting for a metronome, a mechanical device for the audible marking of a wide range of speeds. But these are only indications. The precise speed or tempo, or pulse is one of the things which the conductor has the sole right to determine, taking account of the composer's guidelines and the conductor's own insights into the character of the piece. Sometimes, confusingly, the word rhythm is used to mean something more akin to a sense of pulse, such as in Gershwin's *I got Rhythm*. For our purposes we will use rhythm in the more restricted sense I have chosen here.

Your own experience of music and what I have just said here should be enough to make it clear that a sense of timing is paramount in any music making. If you sing or play you need not only to do so in time with the underlying pulse but also to fit the rhythmic patterns precisely into that pulse. If you are singing in a choir or playing in an orchestra you will take this sense of timing for granted. You will follow the conductor's baton and find timing support from your fellow singers and players. Most singers sing in choirs, but non-singers also have occasion to perform with others. Those who sing solo will nearly always have someone to accompany them with whom they will have worked on timing together. Most instrumentalists play in orchestras or in smaller groups. Timing only usually becomes a problem when someone is playing on their own.

That, sadly, is the experience of many, perhaps most pianists. The instrument does not require the support of others. Sometimes its function is to support others, and where this happens a developing pianist has a golden opportunity to develop a sense of timing. If he or she is accompanying a singer the latter will indicate how fast or slow the song is to go. As the song unfolds the pianist will be careful to follow the singer in maintaining the pulse and in matching any slight variations the singer chooses to adopt.

But unfortunately, many pianists only ever play on their own. Why unfortunately, given the wonderfully rich solo piano repertoire? It is not only that they miss the enjoyment of shared music making. They risk failing to develop the deeply refined sense of time which comes from that sharing. Music played without that sense, however brilliantly and quickly the fingers move across the keys, will lack an essential vitality. At worst, it will become incoherent. I always urge developing pianists to seek out opportunities to play with or in support of others. Those opportunities are there. Singers are always in need of sympathetic accompanists. Chamber groups need pianists for a large segment of their repertoire. Duets (four hands at one piano) are a wonderful way to develop a sense of time. Imagine the chaos when one or other duettist insists on playing in a different time from that of their partner. It happens.

Of course you need to have developed to a certain level to take advantage of those opportunities. But you will be far better prepared for them and will derive far greater pleasure from your own solitary playing if you have worked to develop a secure sense of timing from the outset. It can be very hard indeed to catch up later if you neglect this aspect of your playing in the early stages.

Pulse, beats and sub-beats

So let us return to the tune we have already played, *Twinkle, Twinkle, Little Star*. In this tune the rhythm and the pulse are closely allied so the former should pose no difficulties if you can achieve a secure sense of the latter. The first thing is to decide how fast or slow you want it to go. It is surprisingly common to find even quite advanced pianists who have given this no thought at all when they start to play a piece. Easier sections then tend to be played quite fast while the pulse slows down for trickier ones. But the pulse should be decided on musical grounds alone, not on what your fingers can do at your stage of development and/or according to the challenges of particular passages. And, except where the composer has indicated otherwise, the same pulse should be maintained throughout. You will probably agree that this tune will not go at a cracking pace. Imagine you are teaching it to a class of very young children. The first six notes correspond exactly to the pulse. So hear it in your head as you learned in the previous interlude and clap the pulse to your class. It is not yet time for you to play or for them to sing but we are getting close.

Now it is time to introduce an important refinement. The pulse of a piece of music may move as regularly through time as your metronome, but it does not proceed in the same mechanical way. There are divisions and sub-divisions. Musical scores use what are called bars to indicate the divisions. The pulse of most classical and popular music is divided into units (bars) of two, three or four beats each. Our tune has two beats to each bar. So, using the slash sign to indicate the divisions, the opening goes like this:

C C / G G / A A / G / F F / E E / D D / C /

You will see that the third G and the third C have a bar to themselves. Each of these two notes lasts two beats. All the others last one beat. In the last interlude I suggested you just pause on these two longer notes. Now you are counting the exact pulse you can be precise as to how much longer they will be, that is, twice the length of the others. Look again at my representation above of the rhythm of the *Bolero*. You may have been wondering what the comma was for. This is to indicate the division of the rhythmic pattern into two bars.

Now that we have made acquaintance with the concept of bars I can explain what I meant by 'the middle eight' when describing the structure of our tune. We started out with an opening which was then repeated. That opening came back at the end. In between was a section which left us somewhat in the air, requiring the repeat of the opening to provide resolution. Eight refers simply to the number of bars in this middle section.

So why the division of the pulse into bars? Return to the *Bolero* and listen to the opening on the side-drum, before the famous tune enters. Even before you ever heard the tune the first time I am willing to bet you found that rhythmic opening arresting. On its own, even without the tune, it is musical. That is because there are many layers to the pulse and it is our musical personalities which respond to that complexity. This applies to our simple tune as much as to Ravel's huge score. As well as clapping to every beat of our tune you can clap just to the first beat of each bar, a slower underlying pulse. Or you can clap twice or more to each beat. All these different pulses co-exist and our ears recognise them to varied degrees of consciousness.

Clapping very quickly to indicate multiple subdivisions of beats can be exhausting, even painful! There are ways to count out loud which make this easier. If you have a metronome, set it to 60, which is one beat per second. If you do not have a metronome, you can use the second hand of your watch. Count in groups of four, which is the most common grouping in classical and popular music. Now subdivide into half-beats, as follows:

One-and/two-and/three-and/ four-and/ etc

Now three sub-beats per beat:

One-and-a/two-and-a/three-and-a/four-and-a etc

Now quarter beats:

One-and-on-to/two-and-on-to/three-and-on-to/four-and-on-to etc

Because the basic pulse remains steady at 60, it follows that the sub-divisions of the beats get faster the more of them there are. It is easy to understand that in principle. What is not so easy is to master counting them in practice. All the sub-divisions must be placed exactly evenly within the main beat, or they will fall behind or get ahead of the pulse. With experience you will be able to count or sense far more subdivisions within a beat than you could physically be able to clap or count out loud.

When you are playing or listening to a piece of music with a steady pulse, all these subdivisions of beats, and ever smaller ones to the point where they exceed our ability to sense them, co-exist within the music, whether or not notes are actually being played to match them. The famous opening of Beethoven's fifth symphony consists of four notes, three short and one long. Listen to a recording and feel the pulse of those opening three notes continuing through the long note and into the silence beyond. The continuation of that opening three-note pulse is implicit. A few bars later Beethoven makes it explicit and sustains it throughout nearly the whole movement. Even in those few bars where it is not explicit all listeners will be aware at a more or less conscious level of the pulse driving the music on from underneath. Only the crashing chords at the end of the movement can stop it. This is as good an example as any of how timing can generate musical excitement and meaning. If you compare several recordings of this symphony you may be surprised to find that the most exciting are not the fastest but those with the greatest precision and vitality in timing.

Stresses and accents

The way musicians generate that excitement and meaning does not just come from keeping a steady pulse. It depends to a large extent on how they stress certain beats more than others. These stresses are sometimes also called accents, though often that means something stronger than just a stress. A beat at the beginning of a bar will receive a stronger stress than the one just after. Now clap our tune again (two beats to the bar) and take careful note of how you are doing it. You are probably clapping more strongly on the first of each pair of beats than on the second. The tune and the words all guide you to do this. The notes are in pairs, inviting a difference in stress. So do the words, in the English nursery rhyme version. *Twin-kle* has a naturally heavier stress on the first syllable.

Listen again very carefully to the highly skilled drummer at the beginning of *Bolero*. The opening beat will bear a heavier stress than the much lighter intermediate ones (the '*ticketies*'). The other '*toms*' in the bar will be slightly lighter than the opening. All these distinctions will be slight but perceptible. When you recall that our drummer has to maintain this precision and subtlety throughout the twenty minutes duration of the piece your respect for orchestral percussion players will be much enhanced! (By the way, the version to which Torvill and Dean danced their way on ice to perfect scores in those winter Olympics is heavily cut.)

Before we get to our tune again, try this exercise. This time I want you to play just one note, six times. Say, Middle C. We can represent it thus:

C C C C C C

There are different ways in which this could be divided into bars. Three bars of two beats, or two bars of three, or one bar of six (ignoring more exotic divisions for present purposes). Choose one. How can you communicate to a listener what you have chosen? The only way to tell is by where you place your stresses. Stress the first, third and fifth for a two beat pulse, the first and fourth for a three beat pulse.

<u>C</u> C <u>C</u> C <u>C</u> C
<u>C</u> C C <u>C</u> C C

Now back to our tune. You have decided on the speed. Do not play right away but spend some time thinking about that speed and how it translates into a series of beats, two to the bar. Feel the stress on the first beat of each bar. Now clap the pulse and keep it steady. The next stage is tricky. It is to count out loud with each clap, following the pattern of beats to the bar, that is:

<u>1</u> 2/<u>1</u> 2/ etc

Again feel the stress on the first of the pair.

Now have a go at playing. Obviously you cannot clap and play at the same time, but try to count out loud as you play. It may not work the first few times, because you will forget to count as you focus on moving the fingers to their notes. It is well worth persisting, because this technique will help you to play in time when you come to tackle more complex pieces. You could enlist a friend or family member to help, by getting them to clap as you play. But remember to tell them to clap in accordance with the pulse, not to follow your playing! Your job is to follow the pulse. If a few 'wrong' notes result, that is not important. You can correct this later. A 'right' note played at the wrong time is as much a wrong note, or arguably more of one, than one where a note is played in time but is not the intended one. The latter inaccuracy is much more easily corrected than the former.

Now try this. If you can do the following and keep in time you are well on the way to becoming that sadly rather rare specimen: a pianist who can play in time on his or her own. While you play the tune, call out 1 2, as above, and use your free hand to tap the pulse on the lid of the piano. This may sound straightforward, but it is pianistic multi-tasking of a high order!

A word of warning here about stresses and accents. It is very easy to overdo these on the piano. Your tune is a song, after all. A singer cannot and would not want to 'hit' a note the way a drummer can, or indeed the way a pianist can. A singer's perception of the opening stress in each bar will be slight and subtle. Try to match that on the piano. Remember what you learned in the first interlude about how to change the dynamic of a note by altering the speed of key descent. Though of course you only get one shot at it. You can do nothing about it once the key is struck and the hammer is thrown. There are many gradations. A piano sound is not just loud or soft. It is best just to try to feel the stress at the beginning of each bar rather than to make a consciously heavy accent.

Slow practice

If you are already a fairly advanced pianist, you may be at the stage where a complex piece has to be analysed and taken apart first, then practised slowly, before you can decide on the speed you want. In that case, build as much steady timing and rhythmic control as you can into the early stages of preparation and make sure that slow practice already incorporates a constant pulse. That way you will find it much easier to move towards your target speed as the piece becomes more familiar.

Rubato

This is a very complex subject and can only be touched on briefly here. Advanced pianists will in due course need to get to grips with the concept when they come to tackle the music of the Romantic period, especially that of Chopin. First of all, do not be misled by the literal translation of the

Italian words, *tempo rubato* – 'robbed' time. Rubato is not about stealing time from the pulse in order to pay it back later, though there are always theoreticians who will have it so. In his magnificent book, *Piano*, in the Yehudi Menuhin Music Guides series, Louis Kentner[4] describes rubato as 'freedom, taken spontaneously, in the interest of intense expression' (Kentner, 1976, p. 155). He further observes that this flexible modification of time 'must remain this side of what could be expressed in terms of musical notation' (ibid., p. 154).

For the present it is worth bearing in mind that the term has two distinct musical meanings. For the pianist, as explained by Kentner in the quotations above, it refers to a natural flexibility in timing which helps to add meaning and vitality to the music you perform. It most emphatically does NOT refer to that careless and unmusical sloppiness which comes from failure to cultivate a proper sense of time or to make a proper study of the timing requirements of the piece being played. The best way to get a sense of the flexibility to which I refer is to listen to a good singer. There will be places in the music where the singer has to take a breath, and this may be a slight or deep breath depending on the length and volume of what follows. The breath has to be taken in such a way as not to disturb the natural shaping of the music or the meaning of the words. Indeed, it should enhance those aspects. A good accompanist needs to be aware of those breathing points and allow the singer the time and space to negotiate them. The singer may also wish to underline the meaning at certain points, musical as well as verbal meaning, by slight slowing down or speeding up of the pulse. Again, the accompanist needs to be alert to these. This sort of tasteful flexibility should be cultivated in solo piano playing to a greater or lesser extent depending on the genre and period of the piece and the stylistic features peculiar to the composer, discreetly and subtly in earlier music, more openly in music of the Romantic era.

The other meaning of rubato is flexibility about or within a steady pulse. I mention it here only for completeness. This sort of rubato is not called for in solo piano music in my experience, though there is an ongoing and unresolved debate as to whether it is intended in some of Chopin's music. Again, good singers show the way. In this case, there is no variation in the pulse itself. The singer may sometimes be ahead of the pulse, sometimes behind it, but always consciously and with a musical purpose. Frank Sinatra was perhaps the supreme exponent of this skill in popular music.

SIX

ONCE A CATHOLIC

A great deal of music, especially choral music, is described as religious, and much of it has a ceremonial purpose. Many music lovers describe their love and experience of music in religious terms, whether or not the music itself has a specifically religious context. So how important is religion to music and vice versa? My early musical upbringing could not but bring me face to face with these deep and complex questions.

My mother's experience of religion was as difficult and tortured as any of the many demons with which she wrestled throughout her life. She had been brought up a Catholic and was expected to make a Catholic marriage. A mixed marriage, that is, one to someone of any other faith or none, was allowed her so long as she made a pledge that her children would be brought up in the Catholic faith. My father agreed, though he was as firm an atheist as you could possibly hope to meet.

Up to my mid-teens she was a regular church-goer and taker of the sacraments. As far as I could tell she was the only one of those nine children who continued into adulthood to observe the religious practices in which they had been brought up. She persuaded me when I was about ten to serve on the altar at our local parish church in Waterloo. At last she had found a use for a boy which would have been denied a girl. Girls were not allowed to serve on the altar. Her thoughts, I later discovered, went further than that. In the Catholic Church only men can be ordained as priests, a rule which still applies, as does that of priestly celibacy. Nothing would make her happier, she told me, than if I decided I had a vocation to be a priest. What she did not go on to say, and did not need to, was that that would mean no girlfriends and no wives and no more boys in the family, at least through me. If I could not be the daughter she had always wanted I could be the next best thing. The priesthood was an acceptable form of maleness. At the time I became an altar boy she gave every indication of loving the Church and its ceremonies. Also of loving the priests. She would have seen them as safe, blessed, asexual men. Rumours of clerical abuse did not circulate in those days. If they had she would have dismissed them as malicious lies. Priests were special beings, ordained by God, free of worldly temptation. God would never have allowed such behaviour.

Some years later when her moods and behaviour entered their darkest phases she gave up going to church, though she expected me to continue to attend Mass. I did so until well into my second year at university, though because of the pressures of schoolwork I had stopped serving on the altar while still at school. Was she angry with God for not giving her the lifestyle she wanted and had always considered her due? Was she conscious of sins she could not bring herself to confess? Without Confession there could be no Communion, the sacramental heart of the Mass. Though I could only confess my own sins, not hers, I sensed that she saw me as her representative until such time as she could return, which she did many years later. By that time the Church had introduced less burdensome forms of Confession. She would no longer need to go into the confessional box and spell out her sins to the priest in order to obtain the absolution needed for Communion. To my mind there was a very strong whiff of hypocrisy about her return. She would have done better to have said sorry to the victims of her callousness, those who were still alive.

I knew there was one sin which haunted her as long as her memory lasted. One of her brothers, Jim, had in his youth become violent as a result of a head injury incurred in a motorcycle accident. He had been detained in Broadmoor for most of his adult life. He was later discharged, no longer any sort of danger. He had long since lost contact with his own family. He tried to get in touch with my mother but she refused to have anything to do with him. I had not even been aware of his existence until then. Whenever he rang our house she would become hysterical. That word is overused but there is none more suitable to describe her reactions. One day when he rang, Neil went to the phone and told Jim he would kill him if he came near us. I have no idea when or in what circumstances Jim died, which was to happen soon after. Many years later, she attempted to justify to me the way she had behaved towards him. I did not want to listen. After all, thanks to her I had never met him, never known he had even existed. Clearly her rejection of a plea for help from her own brother, that lonely wreck of a man whose life had been destroyed by an accident, had continued to gnaw at her. Another way in which she tried to come to terms with what she had done was to make contact with Jim's surviving son, John, and to lavish concern and affection on him. John died while still quite young. My mother's grief was out of all proportion to the little time she had known him and the limited contact she had with him. Perhaps she felt God had rejected the means she had chosen to atone, so leaving her once again face to face with the original sin against John's father.

But even without her treatment of her brother, there were enough sins I witnessed for myself, including those of which I was myself the victim, to keep her parish priests busy many a Saturday evening. She could never say sorry to those she hurt. But could she say sorry to God, through the prescribed form of the sacrament? It seemed not. I have never been able to reconcile any claim to be a sincere Catholic with the sort of materialism, snobbery, racism, callousness and envy my mother displayed throughout her adult life, not to mention her readiness to lie whenever she felt it would suit her, regardless of the consequences to others. What use is any form of religious observance in a life empty of spiritual values? There was much more honesty in my father's rejection of religion, which in no way precluded him from believing that all should strive to live by a moral code.

Whatever anybody's reasons for embracing the Catholic faith, whether it be family or national tradition or genuine belief in a universal Church as the gateway to a spiritual life, there can be no doubt that for the prepubescent and the elderly the observances can be wonderful. I loved the ceremony, the Latin prayers, the many warm friendships I made, and of course the music. I have always love hymns, whatever their denomination. Catholic hymns were an important part of school life, including the glories of plainchant, of which Slade had a profound and rare knowledge. Plainchant lies at the heart of much later music and it is rewarding to develop an acquaintance with it. It is both pre-harmonic and pre-contrapuntal, and may date back to the earliest days of Christianity, long before music came to be written down. It comprises single line melodies in fluid rhythms following enhanced speech patterns. The best known plainchant is probably the *Dies Irae*, setting a sequence of Latin verse forming part of the Requiem Mass. The melody was taken up with powerful effect by later composers such as Berlioz, Liszt and Rachmaninov.

My first trip abroad was a school pilgrimage to Lourdes in the foothills of the Pyrenees, the site of miraculous visions of the Virgin Mary to Saint Bernadette. I was twelve at the time. These days, parents might with justification balk at the idea of sending their sons at that age on a week-long visit abroad in the care of the Christian Brothers, against whom there have in recent years been many substantiated accusations of sexual abuse, mostly in residential settings. Certainly some of the Brothers who taught at our school had wandering hands but I was never aware of any more serious problems. The majority with whom I and my schoolmates came into contact, as well as being excellent teachers, were kindly and well-meaning. Many memories of the pilgrimage remain, not just of the extraordinary beauty of the setting but of the experience of singing, along with literally thousands of others, the so-called Lourdes Hymn (*Ave, Ave, Ave Maria*) in the torchlight processions, a breathtaking river of light, the queue of pilgrims so long that the singers at the back could be heard several bars behind those nearby. There was of course much distasteful commercialisation within the town itself. And there will always be controversy concerning claims of 'miracle' cures. But there could be no doubt that as a whole it was a truly uplifting experience.

One of the friends I met at our local church was Gerard, a devout Catholic who attended Mass every day and more than once on Sunday. He was a bachelor who would surely have become a priest or lay brother, but for the fact that he suffered from a mild form of cerebral palsy. Speech was sometimes difficult for him, as holding sacred objects at Mass would have been. My mother took a dislike to him, despite his piety and good nature, solely as a result of his disability as far as I could tell. My father had no time for him either, as he was not exactly his idea of a 'real man.' Gerard was warm-hearted and generous. He arranged frequent outings for the altar boys, including annual retreats to a monastery run by the genial Passionist Fathers near Ilkley in Yorkshire; a serene, remote location high on the side of the valley.

Gerard was a fervent music lover. He introduced me to the pioneering countertenor, Alfred Deller, and not just in musical terms. Gerard kept up a regular correspondence with Deller and took me to meet him after one of his concerts at the Phil. Gerard's favourite composer was Berlioz. He never made any attempt to pronounce the French titles of his works other than with straight English pronunciation. He genuinely failed to understand why his friends were amused when he described Berlioz' *Grande Messe* as a grand mess.

I was once invited to deputise for the organist at our local church at High Mass and Benediction. I had never played the organ before. Someone showed me how to operate the mechanisms. The sense of power was extraordinary. I only had to press a key with no effort for a rich vibrating sound to fill the whole space. When it came to the final hymn I did not have the score, though I knew how the accompaniment went. What I did not know was what key would be most suitable for the congregation. I chose one which was far too high. For all but one of the congregation, that is. The exception was a lady in the front row. She soared effortlessly up to the high Gs. When had she last had a chance to shine like that? She did not thank me afterwards, perhaps because the rest of the congregation were glaring at her for showing them up. No doubt they were glaring at me too, though from the safety of the organ loft I could not see them. I had enjoyed the experience but decided that the organ was not for me. The double keyboard had been confusing enough and many organs have up to four. I had not even touched the foot pedals. It was too late for me to contemplate mastering such complex controls, much as I loved the sound.

For those who have reached puberty and are not yet into their dotage Catholicism is always likely to prove problematic. Unless you can ignore much of its teaching, it means to be in a constant state of impurity in its many forms or the producer of an intolerably large family like my maternal grandmother's. I clung on as long as I could, but by the second term of my second year at university the faith had abandoned me. My Catholic upbringing undoubtedly widened and deepened my musical education. But did it make me a better musician? Hymns aside, the strict Catholicism to which I was subjected as a child was obsessed with sin, punishment and repentance, hardly the sort of spiritual nourishment which enhances the making or understanding of music. Throwing off the shackles of dogma and punitive morality was an essential step in life for me. But a strong sense of spirituality and a deep belief in the values taught by Christ have always remained. They have, I am convinced, helped me to love and understand all music that has an undoubted spiritual dimension, whether or not it was created, as in the case of much of Bach's output, for specific religious purposes or indeed whether the composer was himself or herself a believer. Bach was a devout and strict Lutheran but that in itself did not make him a great composer, any more than Beethoven's sublime late works owe their spirituality to his rejection of formal religion. Whether or not my religious background and inheritance have made me a better musician I cannot say. Such routes as I have taken and the milestones I have reached could have come my way in any case. I am however convinced that an awareness of the spiritual dimension of human life, however you define that dimension, has greatly enriched my understanding of music and its contribution to what makes us human.

SEVEN

INVITATIONS, VISITS AND MAGIC MUSHROOMS

Although it had been my mother's decision to take over the hairdressing shop she made it clear from the outset that she hated it as much as we did. While now her own boss she was still bound to a customer service she had always seen as degrading in a line of work she had never chosen for herself. She had acquired enough aptitude to meet her customers' requirements but never any sense of enjoyment or satisfaction. As always, she took it out on her immediate family. Over the years her moods became increasingly extreme, from outbursts of anger at one end of the spectrum to long periods of morose silence at the other, all unprovoked. Worst of all, she was impossible to predict. A day when she seemed reasonably content and we dared to relax just a little could turn in a second into an electric storm of unbearable tension. It was impossible to reason with her or try to pacify her. My father remained passive as always. I decided it was best to keep out of her way as much as I could. If I deemed it too perilous to stay indoors I could go to the church or to visit friends or for long walks on the beach.

It was about this time that I became acutely aware of the danger of the spoken word, of even using my voice at all. My mother could react explosively to anything I said, whatever my meaning or intention, or, when not taking issue with the words as such, to the way she heard them. I recall trying to read out loud to her something which I thought might interest her, only for her to insist she read it for herself as my voice was 'not very charming to her.' Ever since I have had an acute self-consciousness about my speaking voice, which created problems in my civil service career I had to work very hard to overcome. Little wonder that the piano provided a safer means of expression. Note for note and for any given speed of key descent, the sound of a piano does not depend on the player having a 'charming' touch but is entirely the result of the way the instrument has been built and maintained. This element of distance was vital to protect me from any identification of my own physical qualities with the instrument I was playing. It explained why I continued with the piano rather than other instruments which at different times in my life have appealed to me, such as the oboe or the Spanish guitar. As for singing, that was out of the question. As a boy soprano I had always enjoyed singing. But after my voice broke I had no idea, and still do not, whether my natural adult voice is tenor, baritone or bass.

It is hard to recall those times behind the shop with any affection, but there were lighter moments. Behind the kitchen and outhouse was a small backyard giving onto a narrow lane. To avoid going through the shop Neil and I would use this back entrance when we got home from school. The yard was paved but there was a narrow strip of soil about a foot wide and eight feet long. Nothing was growing there when we moved in. Neil had discovered a sudden interest in horticulture and expressed a wish to grow mushrooms. Nobody told him mushrooms were best grown in dark and compost. One summer he obtained some spawn from somewhere and planted them in the strip of soil. Every day on his return from school he would examine the soil to see if anything was emerging. Nothing happened of course, but he continued to watch. We decided his optimism should be rewarded. We bought a pack of grown mushrooms from the greengrocer's and planted them in the soil. We then waited for him to return from school. His eyes lit up as soon as he opened the gate and saw the miraculous mushrooms. Then he realised we were watching. Slowly, the penny dropped. He took the joke in good part. The strip did in time and under his care yield some tiny flowers.

During school holidays the piano was not available to me during the day for as long as the shop was still open. I found another musical refuge, that of composition, which I could pursue in the relative quiet of the bedroom where I did my homework. After a couple of years I had to my credit three large-scale works, a concerto each for oboe, violin and piano. I think there was also a string quartet, but it was never completed. I say 'credit' but there was little by way of originality in the works. David Crystal showed one of the scores to a friend of his, the Welsh composer William Matthias. Matthias was a prolific composer of choral and orchestral works, later to become professor of music at the University of Bangor where David was by then a lecturer. I recall that at the time of my visit Matthias was working on the score of what was to be his Opus 27, a concerto for orchestra. A civil and charming man, Matthias recommended that I should study ways of writing in a more contemporary vein, suggesting a study of the piano music of Bartok, a composer who was clearly a strong influence on him. Though later I would come to know and love Bartok's music, at the time I had little or no feel for so-called contemporary music. When eventually I did, I no longer had the appetite to write anything but the occasional small-scale piece, which I did in a style that remained stubbornly un-contemporary.

After the 1964 Speech Day and my problems with the choir, Slade obviously decided that it would be safer next time to let me loose on my own with a solo. I was still playing with the orchestra but other pupils were coming forward who could take on accompanying the choirs. The solo piece chosen for me was Weber's *Invitation to the Dance*. It was not a piece I would have chosen myself. I found it musically rather trite and it bristled with technical challenges. It would be a long time before I would learn to recognise Weber's true worth, notably through his operatic masterpiece, *Der Freischutz*, and also through some of his works for clarinet and piano. It was clear that Slade also had his reservations about the choice. But the decision had been made, not by him but by those of the Christian Brothers who ruled on such matters as Speech Day repertoire. While I was prepared to tackle the piece it was soon clear that there was a serious problem. My hit and miss, try it out and move on approach with Edgar would not work. This time I would need to practise the piece hard and long, every day during the summer holidays. But such practice was simply not possible at the back of the shop where the room housing the piano was always noisily occupied during the day. I needed time, peace, solitude and for preference a better piano.

Salvation came in the form of a neighbour who was one of my mother's customers. She had a good grand piano in a large house on the sea front, just fifty yards away. The house was usually empty during the day. I was given a key and allowed to come and go as I pleased. I do not recall ever meeting my good Samaritan. But without her I would never have been able to give the work the time and effort it needed, though I have to admit that sometimes I took a break to watch the cricket test match on her television. On my return to school after the summer break Slade coached me on the finer points of my performance. He was pleased with the progress I had made on my own. I was also grateful to him for suggesting that some musically unnecessary and difficult flourishes could safely be omitted, another useful lesson for the future: the score is sacrosanct except where it is not. I had agreed with him and Edgar that it would only confuse matters if I took the piece to Edgar as well, so for a while I had two teachers for entirely separate repertoire.

That autumn brought another momentous change in our family circumstances. For some time the shop had been losing money. It had never made much, helping at most to finance the purchase of a Morris Minor car, a model which would later become a sought-after classic. Ironically, given that it was an uncomfortable holiday that had first driven my mother to take on the business, the shop had never provided the means for holidays as we now understand the term, though there were a few occasions to get away. I recall a week in Scotland when I was fourteen, during which my mother conspicuously and methodically wrote down every single item of expenditure, however trivial, in a notebook she had brought for the purpose. By way of a holiday within a holiday, this time from my mother's ostentatious penny-counting, my father and I made the ascent of Ben Nevis in glorious weather. One summer we hired a cottage for a couple of weeks as a base for climbing in Snowdonia. We also had a few days at Port Erin on the Isle of Man. None of these could be described as a family holiday any more than the original wet week in Wales had been. My father did not join us in the Isle of Man, Neil did not join us in Scotland and our mother did not join us in Snowdonia. These breaks were like games of musical chairs in which whoever managed to stay at home claimed the prize.

The area around the shop had been in decline for some time. Pollution was ruining the beach and those looking for seaside holidays or days out moved further up the estuary, towards Ainsdale and Southport. My mother, eager to shed some of the physical burden of dressing hair after so many years, insisted on increasing the number of staff as the number of customers declined. The shop was in any event tiny and could not have accommodated more custom. There may also by then have been competition from more progressive and adventurous stylists responding to changes in tastes. My mother's practice was still rooted in the comb back and lacquer days. Customers came in for a shampoo and set or a permanent wave and that was that. For drying they sat under a huge noisy helmet of the sort used in science-fiction films for brain swaps. The books no longer balanced and no capital had been accumulated. Much of the revenue went to pay rent for the premises and the landlady was a ruthless businesswoman. My mother still seemed to expect something to turn up but it was clear my father did not.

What has happened to the area since? Curious to find out, I went back there very recently. The shop itself is now an ice cream parlour. A hotel close to the beach which was closed and derelict only a few years ago is now a lively bar and kitchen. The fishmongers is now an outlet for burgers and pizza. The shops of the Dutch lady and the Swiss confectioner have been replaced by a huge Turkish and Mediterranean bar and grill. Where the record shop once stood there is a Chicago … yes, you've guessed it, bar and grill. That's right, bars and grills all around the approaches to the beach. But the beach itself is no longer there. In its place is the Crosby Coastal Park, the sand nearest to the shoreline having been grassed over. There is a large marina and a small lake for wildfowl. Sheltering the park is a sea wall and a row of sand dunes. The dunes have accumulated over the decades since our time there, created by the natural forces of wind and erosion and by the shifting of tons of sand to clear the spaces for the container base and marina. Beyond the dunes and the sea wall the views of the estuary and the Welsh hills are still there, but they reward only those intrepid visitors with time and energy enough to get across the park and the dunes. The day visitors are back and the area has revived to some extent. But the revival is only skin deep. A few yards further inland from the cluster of fast food outlets, the signs of urban decay are everywhere. The nearby stretch of road leading north towards prosperous, or 'dead posh' as locals would call it, Blundellsands had once been well provided with little newsagents, grocers and sweet shops. But all are gone, the life drained from them by inconveniently located supermarkets. Shop fronts are boarded up. There are no hairdressers in sight, even though having their hair done regularly is a way of life for Liverpool ladies. With the exception of one Indian restaurant, no restaurants serving a local clientele, no shops selling books or CDs or DVDs or even mobile phones. My mother would have had few customers if she had taken up her business now, unless she was prepared to sell ice cream or fast food. Time with the help of human intervention has continued to work its changes and not all have been to the good. In the end, wind and sand will change the area more than people ever will, as the marks of high tide continue to recede. Unless, of course, the melting of Arctic ice brings the waters of the estuary close into shore again. None of us will live to see those changes. But they may be witnessed by the one hundred cast-iron life-size statues placed in the sands further up the coast by sculptor Antony Gormley.

While the shop's finances had declined those of my father had improved. Teachers had secured some worthwhile basic pay awards on top of which he received payments for extra responsibilities. He negotiated a mortgage on a largish house in Crosby – after the cramped accommodation behind the shop almost anything would have seemed large – into which we moved in December 1964. My mother continued to work in the shop until the business could be sold. It was clear by then that the physical and emotional demands of the business were becoming too much for her. She was to have one last venture into the trade soon after, which turned out to be something of an adventure. She secured a one-off job as a hairdresser on an ocean liner called the Empress of Canada and took the opportunity to visit her sister Stella, long established in that country.

The move to the new home was a mixture of blessing and curse. Finances were extremely tight and that put a continuing strain on the mental and eventually physical health of both my parents. The beloved Morris Minor had to go. The mortgage took a large chunk out of my father's salary, as he had only a few years to pay it off. If he had taken it out earlier in life it would have been paid off by then or been reduced to an insignificant amount. When my mother eventually got rid of the burden of the shop and returned from Canada she still had to work to supplement the household income. There were by then all sorts of clerical jobs brought in to save a city where traditional industries were dying. She could do undemanding work without the responsibility of running her own business. Successively, she worked in a couple of city centre department stores, then for a pools company, the Giro bank, and the Inland Revenue. But economies still had to be made and that included my lessons with Edgar Brown.

If we thought the move would lessen the intensity and frequency of my mother's moods we were doomed to be disappointed. I could see that my father was proud that relatively late in life he had been able to secure a spacious house in a pleasant area. I was delighted that at last there was real space for the piano and radiogram downstairs away from the television, and another room upstairs I could use as a study. But from the day we moved in the expression on her face told us that she was determined not to join the party. It was a good enough house for anybody by any standards. But obviously it was not the palace she had dreamed of. She ordered redecorations and room alterations, but of course nothing satisfied her. It was just as important in the new home to keep out of her way, only this time there was more refuge space available. The worst of the crises arising from her mental states still lay ahead and most of them were to happen in that house.

In the meantime, in the run up to the 1965 Speech Day concert, I could practise the Weber piece at home for as long as I wanted or needed. When the day came my slot was between the performances of the senior choir and the orchestra. The audience was by far the largest I have ever played for, over one thousand seven hundred. It is true that none of them had come specifically to hear me. Most of them were parents there to see their child perform and maybe receive a prize for their schoolwork. So they had no choice but to sit through my rendition of the Weber. I knew the piece well by then and could let it run on auto-pilot. I enjoyed the atmosphere and the quality of the superb Steinway piano. I was surprised to find that the applause was enthusiastic and went on for longer than I expected. There was a party at home afterwards, and I was called on to play the piece again. I have to my relief never touched it since. On the day and for some time afterwards I received compliments from teachers and other parents and was told they had enjoyed the performance. My mother, however, made a point of telling me she had not enjoyed it. Clearly she had feared I would fail, which would reflect badly on her.

As a final flourish before the financial curtain came down, my mother joined David Crystal's mother on a short holiday in Austria. She did not have enough spending money and borrowed from a fellow traveller on the same tour. On her return she instructed my father to send this man he had never met or heard of a cheque for the sum she had borrowed. He obeyed, of course. She decided that I should also visit that country as it would help with my spoken German (I was studying German for A-level). The only way this could practicably be done was by means of an exchange system run by the Anglo-Austrian Society. I would spend a month there at the expense of the parents of my exchange student, while we would host him the following year.

So off I went in the summer of 1965 to a remote part of rural Styria, close to the border with Yugoslavia. The name of my counterpart was Franz. His father was a station master on a line that saw about four trains a day. He dressed up proudly in his uniform for each arrival. The family accommodation, over one of the stations, was primitive, with no running water. Both parents were delightful people, but Franz was a Nazi who hated the British and never lost a chance to make his feelings clear. His strongest regret must have been that he was born too late to join the Hitler Youth. So while the visit had its tensions, as would his return visit to us the following year, it did prove to be very rewarding in a musical sense. Franz and I were supposed to have been matched for mutual interest, but that did not extend either to fascism, which had no appeal for me, or to music, in which he had no interest whatsoever. But during a spell of sickness as a result of exposure to the sort of sun which never reaches Liverpool I had the chance to listen on the radio to a live concert from the Salzburg Festival. The music was by a composer of whom I had barely heard, the fourth symphony of Anton Bruckner. It is rare, I am sure, for any sixteen-year-old to fall under the spell of this composer, who usually requires the attention span of much greater maturity. But I was in the ideal place, among the massive mountains and valleys which had inspired those majestic musical paragraphs. On my return I was able to get hold of Otto Klemperer's famous recording of the symphony. Bruckner was still not fashionable in these islands. It would be some years before I would get to hear his much greater later symphonies. But the fourth has always remained a personal favourite.

On the same visit to Austria I was taken to Salzburg, where the festival was still in full swing. I managed to get one of the last remaining tickets for a concert in the main Festspielhaus, where Daniel Barenboim played Mozart's C Minor piano concerto. Although only twenty-two he was already a veteran of the concert platform. His Royal Festival Hall debut was in 1954! He remains to this day one of the most eloquent, energetic and passionate of musicians. I still take every opportunity to see him perform and was able to attend his cycle of the complete Beethoven piano sonatas at the Royal Festival Hall in 2008.

Back home I knew I could now develop on my own. I had been exposed to a huge range of wonderful music. Thanks to my private teachers and my school I had the equipment to make a reasonable fist of most of it, at least to my own satisfaction. I had a glorious sense of freedom and of boundless possibilities. What I did not fully realise then was that I still had many technical and interpretative deficiencies and nobody to help me with them. But in those heady days nothing like that mattered. Those chickens would come home to roost much later.

After we had been in the new home for about a year Aunt Stella accepted an invitation from my mother to come and stay with us in return for hosting her visit to Canada. I was seventeen by then. I had never met her before. She had moved to Canada while still young and made a good career for herself as a piano teacher. I had often been told by my mother that Stella was the musical one in the family and that I took after her in that respect. She made no mention of Molly, or of Aunt Ida on my father's side. Stella for her part had heard about my musical progress from my mother and was anxious to hear me.

It is no surprise that my mother would never have thought of Ida in connection with my musical aptitudes, though Ida was a much better pianist than Stella. Ida was *persona non grata* with my parents. My father had always disapproved of her decision to give up a promising career as a librarian to marry a policeman. Her husband, Ivor, was a kind, gentle, lovely giant of a man whom my father totally despised. I loved Ida and Ivor and often went to visit them and their daughter, Christine, for music and chat. Ida, Christine and I would also meet at the Saturday concerts Ida arranged for me to attend at the Phil. Ida died while still only in her fifties. My father declared himself devastated. But he had always avoided contact with her and on the occasions when he did see her in my presence he was visibly cold and distant. One of the many ironies in this story is that the policeman brother-in-law my father so despised, who with his family remained in their inner city terrace because of the warmth and kindness of the neighbours, in time achieved far greater material success than my father. Ivor, whom my father once cruelly described (though not in his presence) as 'six foot six of solid bone', was able to retire early with a good pension, then secure a job as a collator in his local police station. Long before my parents he and Ida would be able to afford foreign holidays, though they had never sought money or social advancement. Ivor's reaction to the early death of the wife he loved deeply had none of my father's self-pity. Ivor lived into his eighties, quiet, serene, pipe-smoking to the end, saying he did not miss Ida because he always felt she was still there with him. For sheer humanity and strength of character he would have had much to teach my parents, had they been ready and willing to learn from him.

My father was also cold and distant with his own mother, who had the kindest and sweetest nature you could possibly imagine. A very strange man indeed, my father! My mother does not emerge from these pages with much credit, so I should give her credit for taking care of my paternal grandmother during her time with us after her first stroke. She was affectionate to her and cried at her funeral. My father on the other hand showed no grief whatsoever, regarding the occasion as a tiresome nuisance to be got over as soon as possible.

To return to the visit of my Aunt Stella. Her first comment when I played to her was that I had 'a good touch.' When I heard her play, on that selfsame piano on which she herself had learned in her youth, I could not bring myself to say the same. After all the time and effort my mother had put into raising my expectations, it is very likely that I was unable to hide my disappointment. Not many seventeen-year-olds are natural diplomats. Her touch could barely be called such. She attacked the keys with something very like spite. Her sound was harsh and brittle. While she was staying with us she heard me play on a number of occasions. I sensed a growing resentment on her part. I played in the same way and at the same times as I would have done if she had not been there. I was not trying to annoy her but it was clear that I was beginning to have that effect.

I was puzzled as to how she could have had a successful teaching career. Probably she was able to encourage her pupils to achieve musical results she could not achieve herself. She would not have been the first teacher of whom that was true. Certainly she was not tone deaf or insensitive to musicality. She was able to recognise that there was a difference between my playing and hers. Somehow in her early days of learning, a dichotomy had grown up between on the one hand her understanding of musicality and the way a pianist can achieve it and on the other how to realise it through her own mental and physical mechanisms. Again, she would not have been the first. Once, in an unguarded moment, she said of her piano teaching in Canada that it was 'a racket.' I knew what she meant, that she had been able to charge higher fees than in this country. But in relation to her own playing she spoke more truthfully than she realised.

Later, Stella decided to return to England for good. Her surviving sisters were not happy about the prospect. There was no doubt that Stella could be a difficult, abrasive person. They persuaded her that she would be happiest well away from Liverpool, perhaps somewhere 'down South' by the seaside. After all, she would be able to afford it with all that money earned in prosperous Canada. In Liverpool in those days, when travel was still prohibitively expensive, the phrase 'down South' represented a sort of yearning for a life of ease and comfort not possible in the harsh realities of a northern city blighted by unemployment and scarred by de-industrialisation. My aunt was persuaded. She moved to a small village on the Devon coast.

Neil and I by then were living and working in London. We could reach her quite easily in the cramped, noisy, draughty little sports car he had bought to impress the girls (it sometimes worked, until the moment they got into the car). We were invited to visit. She had brought over from Canada her baby grand piano. I grabbed the first chance I could to play it. I chose Schubert's Impromptu in B flat, a quite lengthy set of variations on a theme which was obviously a favourite of his. He also used it in his incidental music to the play *Rosamunde* and in one of his string quartets. After I had played the theme and one variation, she grumbled, 'You're not going to play all the variations, are you?' I was and I did. She did not on that occasion play the piano herself. But she did produce her violin and asked me to accompany her. The pain her scratching produced in my ears was exquisite. Neil was seated opposite us. Whenever I caught the expression on his face I had the devil's own job to keep my concentration.

Stella had married a quiet, studious Dutchman with whom she had nothing remotely in common. He moved to Devon with her. A few years later she was left a widow. Her own health began to fail. Before she died my Aunt Fiona persuaded her that she should leave her piano to me in her will. She reluctantly agreed to do so. My first marriage had broken up and I was living in a flat which could not accommodate a grand piano. I went down to Devon to arrange for the piano to be collected and put into storage. It was a sorry sight. She had kept cage birds for company and obviously let them loose in the house. There were bird droppings and feathers inside the piano. The condition of both the casing and the interior were very poor. She had badly neglected what was surely her most precious possession. I wondered when she had last even touched it. When I remarried we brought the piano out of storage and into our home. But it was obviously no longer serviceable, either as furniture or as an instrument on which I would want to play or teach. We disposed of it.

Stella's story is a sad one. There is no doubt she suffered greatly from loneliness and regretted the alienation from her siblings, however much she was herself responsible for it. Inside, she must have felt that despite her success as a teacher she was musically unfulfilled. Yet she had artistic gifts. She was an accomplished painter, a skill for which I had no aptitude whatever. Could she have had a more satisfactory life if she had devoted her time and effort to visual art? Had her efforts at the piano been the subject of bullying and criticism from her parents and brothers, those same brothers who had later described Molly as 'an angel' who played beautifully? Was Stella jealous of

Molly? I knew she was capable of jealousy. Fiona did tell me once that Stella had been teased by her brothers for her artistic efforts. My mother never talked about these things. All are dead now and I will never know the whole story.

Ironically, it was Stella rather than any of her siblings who had the most success in life in material terms. Certainly not the boys. The eldest, Ben, a huge, overweening figure who modelled his voice and manner on Churchill, his way perhaps of banishing all traces of his family's Irish origins, was successful enough at first with his own marine insurance business to send his four children to public school. But in time his business failed, as my mother's was to do. Other siblings had tragic lives and/or premature deaths. Only Fiona lived a relatively contented later life as a pillar of Formby society. There can be no one cause for the misfortunes. Difficult economic times, excess ambition, poor judgement, sheer bad luck – all played their part. Stella's eventual fate was as dark as any of them. But though she may have ended her days in loneliness she alone of the siblings had formed an ambition for an independent career which she pursued with determination and ultimate success. Though I respected her for that more than she could ever have known we could never have been friends. Our musical interests were a barrier rather than a gateway to friendship. And like my mother she was of a judgemental temperament and my divorce put me beyond the pale.

Of the few aunts and uncles on my mother's side I actually met, Fiona was the only one with whom I experienced any mutual affection. Though she had adopted something of an air of superiority to go with her role as spouse of a British manager in post-imperial India and later assumed a suitably dignified persona as a leading light in Formby society, I always sensed that these were carefully studied roles. Beneath them lay a genuine warmth and openness. I have already described how intensely my mother envied her. But my mother always urged me to take time out to visit Fiona on my visits to the family home, though she would have stuck pins in her eyes rather than accompany me. Fiona had no children of her own, my mother always reminded me, so I needed to keep in with her so I might inherit some of her money. I did pay those visits, for which I always had a standing invitation, not because I had the slightest interest in 'her money' but because I enjoyed her company and that of her husband, a passionate lover of cricket. The truth was that Fiona had no money of her own. If she had survived her husband, she would of course have inherited and been free to dispose of what remained. But she predeceased him so the issue never arose. What I found revolting was my mother's idea that I would cultivate Fiona solely for material gain. My mother could not understand that I simply did not share her materialistic greed. Nor did she begin to appreciate that though Fiona's manner could sometimes grate she was a good-hearted person whom my mother was wrong to hate and envy as she did. Unlike my mother and Stella, Fiona never took a judgemental attitude to my divorce. Of all the siblings she was the only one whose funeral I attended. My cousin Fergus gave a speech after the service, which summed her up to perfection. The worst she was ever able to say about anyone, whatever wrong they had done, he told the guests, was that they were 'a so-and-so.'

A brief diversion here about Fergus, the one of my many

cousins to whom I found myself closest, personally and professionally. Fergus overflowed with a charm and personality few could resist. His life should have been easy but it was anything but. Pressed by his bullying father to have a safe and respectable career, he tried to qualify as an accountant but repeatedly failed the examinations. The second major blow in his life was when he was diagnosed with a debilitating and incurable condition, ankylosing spondilitis, a type of arthritis which over time causes the small bones of the spine to fuse. This second blow would have been enough to crush most people. But for Fergus it opened up his true vocation in life, as the first director of NASS, the National Ankylosing Spondilitis Society. He ran NASS for nearly thirty years, his enthusiasm and inspiration undimmed until his final fatal illness in 2006. I had first met him when I was twelve, when he escorted me energetically round London on my first visit there. In later life my responsibilities as head of the Department of Health branch concerned with physical disability brought me into frequent professional contact with him. The respect and affection with which he was held in the disability world and beyond was plain to see. His life was an object lesson in how to overcome adversity and use it to benefit others.

In October 1966, just before my eighteenth birthday, I went up to Oxford to be interviewed for a place to read modern languages at St Catherine's College. The day the letter arrived telling me I had been successful was a strange experience, even for that house. My mother opened the letter herself and showed it to me. I was delighted, of course. Then my parents indulged in a bizarre competition, during which I was totally ignored, as to whom they would tell about it and in what order. My mother was particularly insistent that my father should tell his headmaster as soon as possible, as if somehow that would make up for the various humiliations my father was supposed to have suffered at his hand. As always, any achievement on my part had value only to the extent that it could be used to impress others, even people such as the aforesaid headmaster who had never met me nor would ever want to.

The following April I and those of my fellow sixth-formers who had also secured university places by then were allowed to leave school. I found a job which I loved, in the public library at Bootle. It was not my first holiday job. That had been the previous year, in a fishing tackle wholesalers, counting fishhooks! I had just gained three grade As in my A-levels so felt slightly overqualified. But it was relaxing and pleasant work.

The Bootle Central Library building stood proudly alongside the Town Hall amidst crowded working-class streets which had sprung up behind the docks during the area's period of rapid growth. One such street, though I was not aware of it at the time and my father never mentioned it, was the one where my Norwegian grandfather had settled before the First World War and where my father and aunt had spent the first years of their lives. It was an area of deprivation, certainly, but also one of aspiration. Several school friends of mine lived around there, one of whom had secured a scholarship to Cambridge. And one day, a very pretty Irish girl with long black hair who lived just around the corner and whose father was a warehouseman came into the library, looking for something in reference. Luckily I was able to find it for her. She was doing A-levels at the convent school just opposite the school I had just left. For our first date, I took her to the Phil. Where else? She would go on to study French at Leeds University.

Ambition to learn and get on was widespread and by no means confined to young people just out of school or to those with aspirations to study at university. There was a hunger across the age groups not just for the rich experience of reading and learning but for information about classes and careers and all manner of stepping-stones to a better life. And the nerve centre for it all was the huge library in all its echoing grandeur.

There were of course moments during my time there which were rather less inspiring. Among the shelves were some set aside for what could be called 'popular fiction', including crime and westerns. One day a lady came in to ask me if there were 'any new murders.' I had read enough Agatha Christie to know that libraries sometimes contained bodies but this was rather disconcerting. Then I realised she was asking if there were any recent additions to the crime section. She came in regularly with the same question and I made a point of putting new additions aside for her. There was also the restricted section under the counter, including such works as Henry Miller's *Tropic of Cancer* and *Tropic of Capricorn*, now acknowledged classics, and also a large Medical Dictionary. Anything under the counter was available to adult readers on request, though obviously only to those who had the nerve to ask. But sometimes a book slipped under the radar. One day an elderly lady came up to me, clutching a short novel she had borrowed from the open shelves the previous week. There was a bright gleam in her eye. 'This book is an absolute disgrace,' she whispered to me in a confiding tone, looking round to make sure nobody could overhear us. I undertook to consider its future. As it was a quiet afternoon I sat down to read it. After consultation with the librarian on duty we decided it had better go under the counter. The librarian was far more concerned with the effect of the book on public morals than I was. My main reason for wanting it off the open shelves was that it was a truly terrible piece of writing.

We have seen that my Aunt Ida was a qualified and experienced librarian. It is a career I could well have taken up myself. On my very first day in a job which was intended to be only a chance to earn some money before university I learned that librarianship is so much more than cataloguing books and putting them on shelves, marking them out and taking them back in. As the chief librarian patiently explained to me as he showed me round the shelves, it is about the organisation of the entire stock of human knowledge, no more and no less. And with organisation, knowledge can always be retrieved and added to. The Dewey Decimal System, devised in America in the late nineteen century and used in libraries around the world ever since, classes knowledge not in an arbitrary fashion but according to how humankind developed from its very beginnings, long before anything like a book was ever dreamed of. Thus, philosophy, wondering about the world and our place in it, predates formal organised religion. Social science can only arrive once tribes are organised into societies. Pure science follows later, the arts later still, once societies have the leisure and surplus to invent and discover. History is among the latest, after events of worldwide import have occurred and could be remembered, recorded and interpreted. No array of library shelves would ever look the same to me again. And at last I had a philosophical and intellectual framework for my own deep inner conviction that art, music and literature are not idle and expensive distractions to be cast aside as soon as problems in society arise but essential rungs of that cumulative ladder of human knowledge and experience.

Sadly, the main library building has now been converted to offices. I sometimes wonder what has happened to the basement, which was always one of my favourite rooms, dusty and gloomy. It housed the library's share in the National Fiction Reserve, a scheme which still exists though its coverage is patchy. Its aim is to enable all published fiction to be available for inter-library borrowing. By chance, Bootle's share comprised authors with the initials BAL to BAN. That meant it included the great nineteenth century French novelist, Balzac, whose works I could devour down there in preparation for my university course. Once at college I would learn about Balzac first hand from my French tutor, Bruce Tolley, an internationally acknowledged authority on that author. (Bruce was an inspiring tutor and I was saddened to learn of his death a few weeks after I had completed the first draft of this book.)

Bootle covered a large geographical area, including remote estates then newly but poorly built. Those estates included some of the most deprived areas of the borough. To serve them there was a mobile library, including a section for children. I will never forget the one time I accompanied the 'mobile librarian' to one of the most desolate estates I had ever seen. Would we be safe? Would we be beaten up, the stock of books stolen and the van torched? The children who crowded into the van were noisy, scruffy and poorly dressed. But their hunger for the books and their anticipation of the joy they would derive from them was so intense that the cliché that we were swept off our feet comes very close to the literal truth.

Bootle is now part of the Metropolitan Borough of Sefton, which covers a huge and varied landscape. It extends east into the Lancashire countryside and as far north as the seaside resort of Southport, swallowing up Crosby and the commuter towns in between. Bootle no longer has its distinct identity, at least in administrative terms. As a result of decisions made by Sefton Council during austerity, the Borough has lost seven of its libraries, including not only the beautiful Bootle Central library but some of the branches where I would sometimes be sent to relieve temporary staff absences. I agree profoundly with David Crystal when he wrote in his autobiography[2] (p.30), 'Those who threaten any library service with cutbacks and closures are the most mindless of demons.' As of course are those who mindlessly carry out those threats.

The following October, leaving the library with considerable regret, I went up to Oxford, joined by several of my school friends who had secured places in different colleges there. I was not to know it at the time but my musical path was about to take a turn into yet another world.

EIGHT

BY THE WATERS OF THE CHERWELL...

We sat down and played Mozart

Bliss it was in that dawn to be alive.
Wordsworth, *the Prelude.*

Those were the days my friend,
We thought they'd never end,
We'd sing and dance forever and a day.
We'd live the life we choose,
We'd fight and never lose,
For we were young and sure to have our way.
(Gene Raskin, song as recorded by Mary Hopkin, 1968)

Mary Hopkin's recording of the song *Those Were the Days* came out in 1968 after I had been in college for a year. It was a huge hit worldwide, combining bittersweet nostalgic lyrics of Greenwich Village folk origin with harmonies and rhythms from Eastern Europe. It has haunted me all my life. I already knew at the time that it was about my own future. I knew that when advanced in years I would look back on those times of youth and hope and say to myself in the words of the song, 'Oh my friend, we're older but no wiser, for in our hearts the dreams are all the same.'

My college and the tumultuous times in which I had the great fortune to be there have since appeared in one of my novels (*Sisters of Fury,* Book Guild, 2015), so I will take the liberty of quoting myself. 'Our college had been built only a few years before, on a water meadow by the banks of a branch of the Cherwell. My window looked out onto the river, and on to the two lawns which separated it from my building. Every spring the lower lawn flooded for several days. At those times the college looked like a huge floating barge of gleaming glass...The summer of 1968 was not just any summer. Students had already rioted in France and Germany. In Oxford protests were mostly peaceful, apart from a few skirmishes outside the proctors' offices. But nobody could deny that there was something in the air. The older colleges in the centre with their enclosed lawns and quadrangles could insulate themselves from it. But not ours. On the outside it was wide open to the surrounding rivers and meadows. Within there were no enclosed boundaries or confined spaces. The buildings stood apart from one another, inviting the eye to reach beyond and above them. And up there, all around us, were the vibrations of the time, like a force from another universe, exhilarating and frightening. Our college could have been built as a receptor for them. We were helpless and vulnerable. We were all aware of the phenomenon. One man, hailed by many as a prophet for out times, had already found the words which would always define it. Huge home-made loudspeakers, probably extremely dangerous, were very much in vogue. Through the long afternoons of that endless summer from the open windows of the undergraduate rooms came the rasping voice of Bob Dylan. *The Times They are a-Changin'.'*

The architect, Arne Jacobsen, had thoughtfully provided for the music room to be located separately from the rest of the buildings out of consideration for those studying or giving or receiving tutorials. There were two pianos in the room, a grand and an upright. Whoever had donated the grand piano had clearly been unaware of a deadly danger lurking in the room, that of underfloor heating. The rising heat had fractured the soundboard, which in effect rendered the piano almost useless. The upright was in good condition, however, being less vulnerable.

The room soon became the focal point for students within the college with a practical interest in making music. It was ideal for chamber music. I was surprised to find that there were so many musicians in the student body, only a small minority of whom were actually studying music as an academic subject. I soon made the acquaintance of an excellent flautist and oboist, both in my year. With the flautist I played a piano reduction of the orchestral accompaniment of the first flute concerto by Mozart. The oboist's favourite piece was the Marcello concerto. We wondered if we could play together as a trio. But was there any music for that combination? We went along to Blackwell's Music Shop to ask. Certainly, said the assistant, producing some sonatas by Telemann. Those were the days (my friend!) when you could go into a specialist music shop, ask that sort of question and get an instant reply. The sonatas were a delight to play. Soon the numbers playing chamber music in our college began to swell. We put a group together to play Mozart's magnificent quintet for piano and wind. String players also arrived and we worked on the first piano quartet by Mozart and the quartet by Schumann.

Chamber music is essentially about the art of listening to what you and your fellow musicians are playing and learning to integrate your contribution into the whole. Sometimes you lead them and at other times they lead you. You need to know the difference. Though we never got around to putting on public performances of our efforts, those times in the company of congenial fellow musicians exploring some of the greatest chamber music ever written were among the most rewarding of my musical experiences.

Mozart was now my new musical god. I had already had some exposure to his piano music. Miss Penhall had given me his so-called (and miscalled) 'easy' Sonata in C K545, which he had written as a teaching piece though it is delightful music in its own right. Edgar Brown had tried me out on the first movement of his early Piano Concerto in E flat, the so-called *Jeunehomme*. But the problem for me was always bringing his music under the full control of timing, phrasing and expression which it requires. There are composers for whom that degree of control does not greatly matter, especially if they dress their musical ideas in massed clouds of notes. But as the great Austrian pianist Artur Schnabel is reputed to have said, children are given Mozart because of the small quantity of the notes while grown-ups avoid him because of the great quality of those notes. In my late teens and as a grown-up I did not avoid Mozart, but I came more and more to realise the truth of

Schnabel's words.

It was through playing Mozart's chamber music that I really began to get some of the measure of his true greatness. Immersion in the world of his great operas would not come until some years later. With fellow students who were interested in music but not musically active I began to explore recordings of his piano concertos and symphonies. With a fellow pianist I tackled a two-piano version of his Concerto in D minor, on which occasion we had to press into service the harsh-sounding grand with the split soundboard. So often pianists just have to make do and mend as best they can. There are many advantages to being a pianist, but a major disadvantage is that you cannot take your favourite piano with you wherever you go, unless of course you are Michelangeli or Barenboim.

Our college music society had the luxury of a budget which we could use to invite visiting lecturers and musicians to college. There was a lecture hall with excellent acoustics, though for occasions requiring a piano we had to hire one in. Our visitors included Antony Hopkins, not the actor but the musician and broadcaster, famous for his weekly programme, 'Talking about Music'. He arrived in a red open-top Alfa Romeo. We asked him to talk about ... Mozart, of course. His talk was witty and perceptive and I certainly gained many new insights from it. It was also largely improvised, a gift of which he was proud. Apparently his agent had forgotten to tell him we wanted him to talk about Mozart and he had prepared something more general. He only realised the misunderstanding when he saw the poster in the porters' lodge advertising his visit. The talk was so well attended that we had to let people in at a reduced price to sit on the steps of the hall as all the seats were taken. These days, that would be a serious breach of fire regulations. Hopkins continued with his radio programme until 1992. He died in 2014, aged 93. Other visitors included the sublime guitarist John Williams, still active to this day.

Our spacious dining hall was large enough to accommodate larger scale events. We collaborated with another college, St John's, in putting on a choral concert featuring Stravinsky's *Symphony of Psalms*. The event launched the conducting career of the then organ scholar at St John's, Peter Robinson. Among the soloists was Emma (now Dame Emma) Kirkby, who went on to have a magnificent singing career specialising in early music. At the time she was not studying music and did not plan a musical career. Other future 'stars' taking part in the event were pianists Andrew Ball and Julian Jacobson. I got to know Andrew well in later years when he was a tutor at a summer school in Hereford.

I was able in my final year to contribute to an all-student performance in the lecture hall of Stravinsky's *Soldier's Tale*. One of our music students conducted the small ensemble of seven instruments. As well as musicians, we needed a narrator, a female dancer and a male actor to play the devil. Our director, Nick, had recruited a dancer from one of the ladies' colleges to play the princess. Her name was Juliet, as I recall. In addition to learning her own role she was called on to choreograph a short, suitably diabolical dance routine for the actor playing the devil. The conductor asked me to assist him by playing with him a piano duet version of the relevant movement, so that Juliet could work with the actor on his routine. The movement had a very tricky rhythm but by the time we had played it a dozen times while various versions of the routine were tried out we had really got to know it. I determined there and then never to work as a rehearsal pianist for a dance company. Once the routine was settled my role was over. I had the privilege of attending the performance as a member of the audience while seeing my name in print in the programme. The performance was absolutely stunning. I do not know if Nick and Juliet went on to have successful careers in theatre but I am in no doubt they could have done so if they chose.

There was other music of course, a parallel river, where the words mattered more than the notes. Bob Dylan, Joan Baez, Joni Mitchell, the prophets of the sixties, still alive at the time of writing and in the case of Dylan and Baez still musically active though Mitchell's later life has been overshadowed by illness. Songs of protest and love. We listened to them in our rooms, alone or in company, late into the night. I recall someone saying that Joni Mitchell had taught him how to feel. I was no stranger to feelings. My mother had taught me pain and fear. My father's lesson in dealing with feelings was repression. Don't react, don't feel at all, don't resist, take it on the chin, be a man, a man like me. Mitchell and the others taught me about other feelings, anger about social injustice, hatred of evils such as racism.

And yes, love. I learned that not only was it okay to feel such things but okay to express them in ways which might be shared, whether through music or through the written or spoken word. That lesson of course meant that the gap between my parents and myself could never be bridged.

Love in particular was the great unmentionable, much more so than sex. Such feelings could never be of any concern to my mother while to my father they could only be an embarrassment. They had, for reasons only they could ever understand and probably not even then, contracted a loveless marriage and chosen to imprison themselves within it. Neither ever gave the impression of ever having been in love or understanding what that would mean to most people.

I was becoming an adult. It is a sad fact of life that many adults who learn the piano in childhood and adolescence, often to a high standard, give it up. The next interlude examines why that should be so and what can be done about it.

INTERLUDE V

WHY DO ADULTS GIVE UP THE PIANO?

I have come across quite a few adults who learned the piano as children, sometimes to a high standard, and then gave up. Some of them found in later life that they had time on their hands, wanted to take up the piano again but found great difficulty in reconnecting with their piano past. The reasons stated for giving up were usually twofold, work and family. Those factors affect nearly all of us at some time. Piano careers, amateur and professional, are often subject to interruption, sometimes for long periods. Many concert pianists were separated from their pianos for years as a result of the world wars of the twentieth century, but were able to resume afterwards. The questions I want to consider now, before resuming my narrative, is what are the underlying reasons for giving up and what prevents a successful resumption?

Some of the pianists I met who had given up had achieved good results at Associated Board Grade 8 (advanced) or its equivalent or gone even further. There is no doubt that this represents a very high level of accomplishment. But it does not necessarily mean that playing the piano has taken those deep roots in the psyche of the individual such that it remains there for life, whether or not a piano is ever touched again. Our practical music examination system has much to commend it and is used and respected worldwide. I will return to that subject later on, when I come to consider my own teaching experience. But one of its major flaws lies in its emphasis on the vertical rather than the horizontal. A piano student who has taken each of the eight grades in turn will only need to have learned to an acceptable standard a total of twenty-four pieces, many of which will of course be at the earlier, less demanding stages. The student will also have gained expertise in sight-reading, scales, ear-tests and theory. The choice of repertoire at each grade is wide enough to cater for a range of tastes and styles. But the system does mean that it is perfectly possible to achieve a distinction at Grade 8 without having learned a single piece by one of the composers who are generally accepted as great composers for the piano. No Bach, no Schubert, no Chopin, no Beethoven, no Mozart, no Schumann, no Brahms. If the student is focussed on achieving those grades alongside other accomplishments, in school subjects, sports and other hobbies, in order to present a well-rounded CV to an interviewer for college or employment, the grades then become a means to an end which in itself is not musical.

Given the pressures on the time of young people, especially today, their music exam successes may have been achieved through quick intense learning which allows the student to shine on the day but does not allow the music to penetrate deeply. When other life pressures intervene, giving up the piano may be no great hardship. It has served its purpose.

For some, that will be the case. But for others, especially those who try to regain their piano skills in later life, there may well be a sense of loss. I have seen and heard it with a number of my adult pupils and fellow pianists. In their case, something very real did indeed take root. But some thing or things prevented the fire being kept alive (if you will forgive the mixed metaphors). When the fire went out it left a space in their inner lives, perhaps also in their social lives if playing the piano had been something they had enjoyed in company. The demands of work and family would have played their part. But another factor might well have been that growing self-consciousness so characteristic of adulthood, particularly notable in fields of self-expression such as singing and playing and dance. Those activities are fine for children, so the stern inner voice tells them, but you are grown up now, time to put aside childish things. Perhaps it is indeed the case that to persist in playing or singing or dance into adulthood requires us to maintain and nurture an element of the child within. Letting that wither and die in the interests of achieving an emotionally inhibited adulthood is surely a recipe for later regret, even sadness.

Coupled with and perhaps allied to this self-consciousness may be a tendency to severe self-criticism. Pianists who return to the piano in later life after a long gap may not realise that a lot of patient hard work will be needed to regain their former fluency and command of the instrument. Lack of early progress and impatience with unexpected mistakes and hesitations lead to a self-castigation which may lead to the enterprise being abandoned altogether. Children are far more concerned to make music and enjoy the process than they are about mistakes and wrong notes. It will often be difficult for some adults to regain that sense of risk and adventure.

Children are also on the whole less bothered than adults about the quality of the music they play so long as they enjoy it. Adults have had a lifetime to refine and develop their sense of what is great music. That is the music they want to play, not simple pieces for beginners. If that is you, if your early musical experience has taken broad and deep roots, if basic techniques and disciplines have been embedded from an early age, if there are certain composers and styles of music that now live within you and will always be part of you, then I believe your pianistic career can and will survive the interruptions which life will inevitably bring.

How can that be done? The rest of my story shows only the way which I found for myself, and I have to admit that good fortune played a major role. If you are an adult anxious to maintain or revive your interest in the piano there are five 'finds' I can suggest which might help. But whatever steps you decide to take, remember not to be hard on yourself, especially if you are resuming after a long break. If you played a lot in your childhood and teens it is very likely that much of your technique was natural and spontaneous. It may now have to be relearned in a more deliberate and conscious way. Be determined, of course, but above all be patient.

(a) Find: a piano. That seems obvious enough but may not always be easy. I spent my early working life in London in various piano-less furnished rooms. But you can always beg, borrow or steal time at the piano of a friend, neighbour or work colleague. They may be delighted to hear their pianos used by someone who knows how to play. The pianos are out there. Sniff them out, until you can buy or hire your own.

(b)   Find: practice time, even if it is only a few minutes a day. I once went to a dentist who had an upright in his surgery. He took to the keys between patients or while waiting for an injection to take hold. When you add it all up it came to a fair chunk of daily practice time. Fortunately it did not seem to affect his concentration when he picked up the drill again.

(c)   Find: a sympathetic teacher. Most in my experience will be happy to engage with the special problems of the busy adult and will find your enthusiasm and commitment rewarding.

(d)   Find: others in the same situation and help each other. Join a local piano circle and/or attend classes at adult education establishments such as Morley College or City Lit.

(e)   Find: singers and players of other instruments with whom to make music in company. This is an excellent way to restore your confidence and enjoyment.

NINE

ALL THAT JAZZ AND SOME BIZARRE ENTERTAINMENTS

It's not the leaving of Liverpool that grieves me,
But me darling when I think of thee.
(Liverpool folk song).

After college I moved to London to work in the civil service. The process of application, posting and preparation was long and tedious, taking several months. Those months at home before my move passed in a curious twilight world. I did not play much, lacking the stimulus of my college musical environment. I was all too aware that when I did leave, which my parents expected me to do at the earliest possible opportunity, I would no longer have ready access to a piano.

My parents were bewildered. They had focussed so much on my gaining a place at Oxford and completing my studies there that they had no idea what would come next, any more than I did. I was haunting the house in a state of chronic indecision, armed with an apparently useless second class arts degree. I reminded myself of Benjamin in *The Graduate*, though without the consolation of his sexual

155

adventures. My parents and I rarely spoke. I kept out of their way and they left me alone. There was an atmosphere of mourning in the house, in sharp and poignant contrast to the celebrations which took place in the houses of school friends who had also completed their degrees. After passing my civil service interview I was posted to the local National Insurance Office in Brixton, South London. My father was content. A regular monthly salary and job security meant that I would not be any further drain on his meagre resources. My mother made no attempt to hide her shame. For her the civil service was a dead end and I had become the failure she had always dreaded.

Of all my mother's moods down the years her silence was the hardest to deal with. I would have preferred her to show her anger. It would have given me something on which to build a response. What response? How about the following. I had like nearly all my friends at college obtained a good second class degree in a demanding subject (first class degrees were few and far between in those days and almost unheard of for anyone taking French at Oxford). I had done what I thought she had wanted: got to Oxford and graduated. And what if I did now want a career in which I might give something back, make a contribution, help improve the lives of others, even if it meant I would never be rich? Was that not my choice? I could have said all that and so much more. That I now had a much deeper and wider appreciation of music from my association with musical fellow students; that weekly one to one contact with renowned tutors had deepened my understanding of my chosen subjects in ways I had never thought possible; that from my friends in other disciplines I had gained unexpected insights into history, politics, even physics (how I admire physicists, not just for their mastery of the science and mathematics of their subject but for their soaring imaginations!); that I had experienced the enrichment of mind, heart and soul that only time at one of the world's greatest universities can provide. I could not say any of those things at the time, because I did not believe them. I shared her belief that I was indeed a failure.

A few years later her anger did at last erupt. Neil and I were both working in London by then and we were paying a visit home together. During the visit she pointedly asked me how much I was earning. Foolishly, I told her. She tore into me about how little that was and the fact that I did not yet own property, though I was only twenty-four. But twenty-four was old enough for me to answer back at last, to tell her it was now my life, however much she might despise it. My father and Neil were both present. To my amazement they did not do what they would have done in earlier years, turn on me for upsetting her, a capital crime in that house. They were silent. They must have realised that this time she had gone too far. Not that they dared to speak up for me. That would have been too much to expect. But it was still a crucial moment, that silence, when something which had seemed eternal and indestructible suddenly bent and broke. For her, being a wife and mother had given her the power she had lacked as a child, to get back at those who had bullied and belittled her. They were no longer there but we could stand in for them. She could bully and belittle us and be confident we would not answer back, would never challenge her right, born as it was out of the divine gift of motherhood. Now the mirror had cracked from side to side. Her power had gone. She seemed suddenly diminished, almost pitiful, though I had no room or time for pity.

It would be a long time before I realised the full extent of her weakness. The dream of gaining her approval, not just for an hour or a day but definitively, still lingered in me. I visited her again some months later, having just passed the extremely rigorous three-stage selection procedure for the fast stream of the administrative civil service, the gateway to early rise to the senior ranks. As I had done all my life with my school prizes and examination results I brought home this latest success to lay at her feet and receive her blessing, or, if a blessing would be too much to ask, then at least a retraction of her former harsh words. Surely such enhanced prospects deserved something better than the scorn she had always poured on my career choice? But she was no longer interested in anything I had done or was likely to do. She ignored me. She had more important things on her mind. She had just been to America for the first time and her eyes had seen the glory. More of this later.

There was another reason I was ignored. By then, though I could never have pinpointed a precise moment because it had happened slowly, almost imperceptibly, a seismic shift had taken place in the family dynamic. I had failed as Chosen Child.[6] For a long time I had had no gifts to offer which could interest her. Moreover, I was no longer a safe target. She knew I had it in me to fight back. Aware at last of her own weakness, she needed more amenable prey. And my understudy stood ready in the wings. A light had come on in my mother's brain when

Neil began to talk and be talked of as a future lawyer. Our father was as seduced by the idea as she was. *Lawyer*. Law meant money, success, a big house and all that. The magic word 'law' attached to his degree conferred on it a corona of future glittering prizes.

For my mother this latest family reshuffle was also driven by a search for an acceptable form of masculinity which neither I nor my father could provide, one which would be hyper-aggressive and take no prisoners. My father looked and sounded the part. Everything about his manner and voice conveyed an aura of stern masculinity. But he was passive and lacked ambition. I had fallen between two stools, unable to be the daughter she had always longed for but too imbued with the female qualities associated with my musical pursuits to be a real man. My choice of career was another disqualification. 'Success' in the civil service is achieved more often than not through compromise and negotiation. No manliness in that. Legal activity often takes the same form, of course, but neither she nor my father would see it that way. No, in law, the winner takes it all, the loser standing small. She knew. She had seen Perry Mason on television, the defence attorney who never lost a case. Though Neil would never be a barrister in criminal courts, however much the idea might once have appealed to him.

Ironically – I apologise for using that word again and not for the last time, but it is undeniable that there is a great deal of irony in life – Neil had only been accepted to read law, at King's College, London, by chance. The idea had never previously occurred to him. He had gone for an interview to read English. The interviewer had obviously had his

159

doubts and suggested he pop down the corridor to see his colleague, the law tutor. It was the latter who offered him his place. Neil's academic record at school was at best solidly average. He got through exams by hasty last-minute revision, what he called his donkey's gallop. Yet he had a genuine love of and interest in English literature. During his O-level year he once borrowed a tape recorder and recorded huge chunks of *Julius Caesar* on his own, using different voices and accents for each of the conspirators. Despite that gift for mimicry he was certainly never destined to be any sort of linguist. His French teacher once told him he spoke French 'like a Spanish cow.' Compliments in that school were hard to come by but insults were always on tap. The start of his academic legal career was hardly more auspicious. In his first year at college he failed all of the first set of examinations and most of them again on the second attempt. He was close to being sent down. The dream of a dazzling legal career was on life support before it had barely begun. He hung on by the skin of his teeth, eventually securing enough passes to go on to get his degree. He could then do his solicitors' articles at Bootle Town Hall and qualify. Relief all round. Dream out of intensive care. While all this drama was being enacted I was left amid the dreaming spires to wallow not just in music but in the glories of French and German literature without a single thought given to that troublesome word 'career'.

For Neil, the glittering prizes would still take many years and a lot of hard work to achieve, requiring a self-discipline which did not come naturally. As he assumed his ordained role as family saviour his personality changed, grandiosity and arrogance taking pride of place. Rarely did his former natural sense of fun show itself. Self-oriented ambition took hold. After qualification he started his career in the legal department of the London Borough of Southwark, later joining a private firm specialising in commercial law. He could easily have continued in that way. A well salaried post in the public or private sector or a partnership with an existing firm would have been his and the burdens of responsibility as well as the rewards would have been shared. But that could never have been enough. There could be no sharing. He had to run his own practice under his own name, with employees but no partners.

He needed to borrow heavily to set up his practice, relying on persuading his bank that he had built up enough of a personal following among his employer's clients to take those clients with him. What he lacked was security for the loans. He had no property of his own. What he did, as I only discovered some years later, was persuade our father to put down the equity on the family home as security for the loan. Even now, after all this time, I find it astonishing that our father, who had only recently and late in his own career achieved homeowner status in a house in which he had invested no little effort, sacrifice and pride not to say relief after the precarious financial years of the Waterloo business, would have been prepared to take the risk of making himself and his wife once again without property. If the bank had called in the loan and repossessed the house they would have had no alternative but to rent a small flat for the remainder of their days, which they would have lived out in severely straitened circumstances. Given his declining health and our mother's always fragile mental state, I find it hard to imagine the quality of life which would have faced them. I find it just as hard to believe that they had discussed that possibility with Neil or even contemplated it. It seems that their faith in Neil and his in himself was absolute. The venture could not fail and so there was no reason even to entertain the thought. Needless to say, I was not consulted about the decision and only learned about it much later by chance. I would have been far less concerned about my own share of the inheritance from the family home being put in jeopardy than about our parents' situation should the gamble not pay off. Fortunately, it did pay off, at least during our parents' lifetimes. The fact that it did not occur to any of them to consult me is yet another sign of how far out of the loop of family affairs I was by that stage.

As Neil's business grew and success came, so parental adoration increased. This rather than the material wealth, which never particularly interested him, was what drove him on, becoming an addiction in itself. The pressures were immense. He had to make good not only the fortunes of his own parents but also the decline in the fortunes of both sets of grandparents. The removal of the stigma of failure from all three families was on his shoulders. The burden was huge and in time would prove intolerable. To help him to cope, he adopted self-destructive habits and these would eventually take their toll. In time, many years later, he too would fail and the failure would be his alone. Though by then our parents were no longer around. Our mother had lived long enough to see others come into his life, seeking, as she saw it, a share in the spoils which were rightly hers. So he too would betray her.

So much of the course of our lives depends on chance encounters. What if he had been accepted to read English at King's or another university? Might he have gone on to be a teacher, for example? So much of the natural charisma, kindness and generosity of spirit he later suppressed in the pursuit of his ambitions would have gone into making him a fine teacher. That comment is not merely fanciful. It was something he and I discussed, though only on a rare occasion when his guard was down and in any case long after the die was cast. Any such decision would have horrified our parents. He was too dedicated to the thankless and ultimately impossible task of trying to please them. And once he had decided to become a lawyer, an occupation for which despite his early academic struggles he undoubtedly had a strong practical aptitude, no moderately successful career would be enough.

At the time I first realised my family demotion I felt both relief and resentment. I could never bask in my parents' approval again but I was free to follow whatever paths I chose. But, as I was soon to discover, being no longer chosen did not absolve me from guilt or punishment. I had sinned against her commandments and there was still a heavy price to pay.

At the time of my departure for London I did not grieve to leave my home city. I loved London from the start, its size, energy and infinite variety, and have never seriously contemplated living anywhere else. It was only after some years that I realised I missed Liverpool. There really is nowhere like it and nobody like its warm-hearted, quick-witted people. Though of course no true scouser ever really leaves Liverpool. You take it with you wherever you go.

In my first posting I had an outdoor job which I loved, visiting local businesses and those working on their own account, usually to find out why they had not paid their national insurance contributions or to enquire into apparent irregularities in benefit payments. Brixton in those days had one of London's most concentrated African-Caribbean populations, from what we now know as the Windrush generation. Not only did I meet many in the course of my work, but several were work colleagues. My background up to then had been remorselessly white, even in multi-ethnic Liverpool. Liverpool has an African-Caribbean community which is even older than Brixton's. But it is concentrated in the Toxteth area of the city, later the scene of riots, as Brixton itself would be as tensions from decades of racism and discrimination exploded. While Bootle and Waterloo were always culturally mixed the ingredients were predominantly white, and Crosby exclusively so. In our school or any of the places where I had holiday jobs I saw nobody of colour and rarely saw any such while shopping in central Liverpool. Certainly not in audiences at the Phil.

My parents were anxious that those I have called people of colour, whom they never saw but for whom they had much ruder names than I can set down here, would subvert their white neighbourhoods and bring down house prices. They were of course disturbed to learn what my new job entailed, even more so when I told them of the warmth, humour and dignity I had found in the African-Caribbean community of Brixton, despite the pressures and hardships of their often appalling living conditions.

You cannot of course 'cure' racists by telling them that

their views are only born of fear of the unknown and would not be vindicated by contact with real people. My parents had already been exposed to 'colour shock' when I was still at college and insisted on bringing home for a short visit one of my best friends there. He was from India, name of Jaswant. They were of course polite to him. Why wouldn't they be? He was handsome, charming, educated at a public school in this country, and a brilliant physicist. Sadly, back in India many years later, he would fall victim to acute schizophrenia. In Brixton I would get to see the extreme end of the racist spectrum, the virulent, aggressive hostility of some of the white residents there. To say that my parents were never that extreme is not to excuse any form or degree of racism. So-called 'passive' racists might believe their private thoughts to be harmless, but from thought to speech to violence is a natural and inevitable progression, in wider society even if not in every individual. My father could be bewilderingly inconsistent on the subject of race. He supported apartheid South Africa, but believed 'the American Negro', to use his term, should have had complete equality long since. Maybe he thought the latter liberal view somehow cleansed the former of the taint of blanket racism. I was not convinced.

In my first year in London I lived in various furnished rooms while keeping my eyes and ears open for playing opportunities. I soon discovered which work colleagues had pianos I could visit. The office canteen had one, though only available to be played at office parties. On those occasions my preferred style was now jazz, in which I had taken an increasing interest in recent years, stimulated by contact with jazz-loving school friends. One of them persuaded me to join him in a visit to the Phil to see Duke Ellington. I still recall the stunning solos from stratospheric trumpeter, Cat Anderson, and lyrical tenor saxophonist, Johnny Hodges, all under the urbane and relaxed leadership of the 'Duke' himself. (The Duke was an accomplished, self-effacing pianist, the name of whose childhood teacher was Marietta Clinkscales, a prime example of nominative determinism if ever there was one.) The advantage of playing jazz for me at the time was that I could improvise according to the techniques I already had. I could play to my strengths and avoid my weaknesses.

Initially, my interest in jazz was focussed on where it interfaced with classical music: Dave Brubeck and his complex time signatures, Miles Davis and the searing intensity he brought to Rodrigo's *Concierto de Aranjuez,* the crystal clear counterpoint of the Modern Jazz Quartet (MJQ). I was an occasional visitor to Ronnie Scott's in Soho, and took a rare opportunity to see the MJQ perform live. During the interval, I went up to the bar for a drink and found myself literally rubbing shoulders with Milt Jackson, the quartet's vibraphonist and one of my all-time jazz heroes. I was too star-struck to utter a word. Just as I was about to pull from the back of my throat something totally inane which he must have heard a thousand times before, an American lady on the other side plunged straight into conversation with him as if she had known him for years, which clearly she hadn't. The opportunity was lost.

Above all, there was Jacques Loussier and his albums of *Play Bach.* Loussier opened my ears to a new understanding of Bach. Where Bach had apparently provided only harmonies Loussier wove a tissue of melody.

To Bach's melodies he added exotic harmonies. Always he remained within the spirit of the original. When I came to revisit the original music again for myself I understood what had been there all along. Loussier had only teased it out and spun his own magic around it. Bach's melodies imply a world of harmony and his harmonies a world of melody. That to my mind is the real key to understanding the infinite richness of his art. The progression of harmonies which at first sight seems to be all that comprises the opening C major prelude of the *Well-Tempered Clavier* in fact implies an infinite number of beautiful melodies. That added to Bach's score by Gounod in his *Ave Maria* is just one of them made explicit.

My exploration of jazz did not stop there. I discovered that there were true Titans of the piano who had come there by very different routes from those of their classical counterparts, notably Art Tatum, Oscar Peterson and Erroll Garner. When the final roll call is made of the greatest pianists who have ever lived, these names should if there is any justice in the world be up there with them.

The following year, 1972, I joined with some friends in renting a large house in Fulham. I had the front downstairs room, which had ample space for an upright. There was a local piano showroom, in which I found a solid-looking upright in excellent condition, the interior having been completely renovated. It was on sale for the princely sum of ninety-five pounds. I did not have the money but persuaded my father to guarantee a loan. So it was I bought my very first piano. As I write, that same piano sits in the house of my younger daughter, Pamela, in Bath, where I know it is being put to good use. It has had an extraordinary journey, which will unfold as I describe subsequent events. At no time has it been idle. Given that the Fulham house was always busy with the comings and goings of the six residents and their many friends and guests, I confined myself to my increasing repertoire of jazz and popular standards. I even played for a few nights in a local pub. (Don't knock it – so did Brahms!) I was soon told that my services were no longer required as I did not make enough noise.

Through a work colleague I met and became friendly with Claude, a singer and jazz pianist who had come to London from the West Indies. He had a basement flat in Pimlico. Claude did not have a piano of his own but he would play each week at a pub in the East End. I deputised for him there one Saturday night, having greater success than I had had in my local. It was the first and last time I ever had the exhilarating experience of playing with an expert jazz drummer.

At the end of that year the Fulham gang dispersed and I found new accommodation in an upstairs flat in Clapham. There would have been space for the piano except that it was impossible to contemplate manoeuvring it up the narrow stairs and around the corner at the top. It would not have survived the attempt. So I agreed to lend Claude the piano by having it moved into his basement flat. It was a heart-stopping moment watching it being lifted by hoist from an upstairs window and lowered down. Pianos have been dropped that way, but luckily mine survived. Thus did my piano begin its strange odyssey.

In 1974, newly married, my wife Joan and I moved to a rented ground floor flat in Streatham. It could accommodate the piano, so I was able to retrieve it from Claude's, after another nerve-wracking extraction. The piano later moved with us to our first house in the Kent countryside and later to our next house in Beckenham. Already my piano had had four moves. There were many more to come. After being reunited with the piano I took up once again my interest in the classical repertoire, though my practice time was confined to a few minutes in the morning and evening. My work was extremely demanding of time and energy and before long there were two young children in the house.

One of the stimuli for my renewed interest was the opportunity to attend some remarkable piano recitals in London. In later years I always tried to encourage my pupils and other pianists I knew to attend live performances. I know many would dispute the value of this. After all, none of us is going to play like Pollini or Barenboim, so what is the point? But I believe there is a great deal to be learned, and not just from the excitement of being in the room when live piano music is being generated by a single individual. For a start, live sound has a way of penetrating more deeply and making a more lasting impression than recorded or radio sound. There are fewer distractions. The physical presence and actions of concert pianists can also teach us a lot. Many amateur pianists focus so much on trying to move their fingers accurately from one note to the next that that becomes the sole objective, the lateral movements so slow that the music loses its shape and flow. The quality of the sound and the relations between the sounds of sequential notes are neglected. With the best pianists you are barely aware of their lateral movements, so rapidly are they made. Instead we note the movements they make down into the keys, with a combination of arm, hand and fingers. That in essence is how they produce their sound and make the music alive.

One of those live occasions which utterly absorbed me, though it was actually eight occasions, was a complete series of the Beethoven sonatas played by John Lill, a magnificent Beethoven pianist, at the Queen Elizabeth Hall. That was in 1981. The following year the Royal Festival Hall hosted the return after many years of the legendary Russian pianist, Vladimir Horowitz. He was seventy-seven and enjoying a glorious Indian summer in his incredible career. In those days tickets had to be bought in person or by phone. There was no advance booking for those signed up to some form of membership. I invented an excuse to take a day off work and joined the queue in the morning. By lunchtime all the tickets for both recitals had gone. I had managed to obtain tickets at the back of the platform with an excellent view of the pianist's back and hands. He started with exquisitely delicate Scarlatti and finished with Chopin's 'Heroic' Polonaise in A flat, which brought the entire audience to its feet with the final flourish.

I had no performance ambitions myself at that time. But I felt an intense need to work my way through much of the piano repertoire I had missed, entering fingerings and phrasing into my copies, perhaps against the day when I would have a chance to return to them. This was an epic task which, given the pressures on my time, would take some years. It included a detailed notation of all of Bach's forty-eight preludes and fugues, the so-called *Well-Tempered Clavier*. I was learning how the pieces were put together but had no chance to work on the finer aspects which would be involved in performance. What I was accumulating was a sort of half-repertoire, a set of notes on notes to be consulted at a later date.

Early in 1984 a performance opportunity did arise, though it was an unexpected and rather bizarre one. I was attending a week-long course in so-called administrative German at the University of Manchester Institute of Science and Technology. It was for civil servants who might find themselves in contact with their German counterparts. The course was total immersion, which meant that we had to speak German even among ourselves outside course time.

We soon discovered a widespread interest in music among those attending. It seems that whenever civil servants are gathered together for any purpose this will always be the case. Some were competent singers. A grand piano in good condition was available. One of those on the course, Christine, whom I had met previously on a course for trainee administrative civil servants and who later became a very close friend, had brought some choral music with her. We formed a small choir and met at lunchtimes to rehearse. We were not too deterred by the fact that we had to rehearse in German. I also had for the first time the chance to accompany solo singers, including Christine. Another singing member of the course was Michael Longford, who had served as a colonial administrator in Tanganyika before it became Tanzania after independence. Michael had worked in the same branch where I had taken up my first posting as an administration trainee. By the time of the course we were already good friends and would become very close over the next few years.

Together we formed the idea of putting on a concert after the final dinner. I wanted to include a piano solo but had no music with me. I asked if one of the organisers could look out for me a copy of Schubert's G flat major Impromptu, a piece which had always been one of my favourites. In it he floats one of his most heavenly melodies above a characteristic rippling brook accompaniment, both melody and brook being taken in the right hand. The organiser obliged. But I was dismayed when I saw that the version he had obtained was printed in G, a semitone higher than the original. This is easier to read if you are coming to it for the first time but harder to play. I was further dismayed when at the final dinner I discovered that the guest sitting next to me was the Dean of the Royal Northern College of Music. I decided not to tell the others who the guest was until after the concert. The concert was well received, perhaps because sufficient wine had flowed at the dinner. The little choir performed impressively. One of the singers, a baritone, offered a solo, Schubert's *Heidenroeslein.* It is a strophic song with three verses. He was very nervous and sang faster and faster as we went on. Thankfully, the accompaniment is one of Schubert's easiest and I was just about able to keep up. I managed to play the impromptu in the right key despite having the wrong key on the stand in front of me. Even the Dean was complimentary, or perhaps just polite.

After the course had ended, Christine, Michael and I continued to meet up for musical sessions. We were soon joined by a colleague of Michael: Julian, an excellent baritone. Like Christine and Michael, Julian sang in choirs, but was also often asked to take a solo. He sang regularly in

performances of Bach's *St Matthew Passion* at the Barbican Hall. I remember accompanying him while he practised his short solo lines, '*Bin ich's, Rabbi?*' and '*Ich habe Uebel getan.*' 'Is it me, Rabbi?' and 'I have done evil.' Yes, Julian had been given the role of Judas Iscariot! Between us we explored lieder, in particular the songs of Schubert and Schumann.

In German 'Lied' simply means song but lieder are not just songs. They are real duets for piano and voice, exploring in extremely concentrated form the full range of human emotion and experience. At school, Slade had given me a glimpse of the world of lieder by asking me to accompany my class in Schubert's *Trout.* Now I could go so much wider and deeper, even into the tragic depths of Schubert's *Winter Journey (Winterreise).* With Julian I also played Beethoven's song cycle *to the Distant Beloved (An die Ferne Geliebte).* I believe there is no more rewarding experience for any pianist than to play the great lieder with good singers. Christine was a deaconess in a Congregationalist church in South London, where a small choir regularly performed. I began to join them for their concerts, sometimes accompanying the choir as well as playing the occasional solo.

The piano Christine, Michael, Julian and I used for our informal sessions was a very serviceable grand we had discovered in one of the conference rooms of the department in which I worked. It was sometimes used for lunchtime concerts given by visiting pianists. We booked it for evening sessions after most of the civil servants working in the building had gone home. I would use it for my own practice as well. Michael had a special love for the lieder of

Schubert and the *basso profundo* Sarastro arias from Mozart's *Magic Flute (Zauberfloete)*. Christine particularly shone in Schumann. She and Michael memorably combined for a duet rendition of Schubert's *Death and the Maiden (Tod und das Maedchen)*, in which Michael was a terrifyingly sepulchral Death.

Michael, though one of the most intense and serious men I have ever met, had a mischievous sense of humour. For an office Christmas party he and Julian decided to put on an entertainment in the form of a version of Offenbach's duet, *The Bold Gendarmes*. The party took place in the canteen, where there was no piano. So with the help of Julian's tape recorder I pre-recorded the accompaniment on its own on the conference room piano. Michael's professional responsibilities at the time included arrangements for the medical inspection of immigrants at UK ports of arrival. So his adaptation of the duet replaced the refrain 'We run them in' with 'We keep them out.' This was long before the 'hostile environment' with which we are all now so sadly familiar. Michael's lyrics were intended as an operetta-style satire on a form of thinking which was by no means mainstream at the time and represented the polar opposite of his own deeply humanitarian instincts. These days the satire would be lost. I cannot remember all the lyrics but they were hilarious. For a section in the middle we abandoned Offenbach temporarily for the more expressive strains of Neapolitan song. Michael began this section in gruff tones to the tune of *Torna a Surriento*: 'It's a reasonable assumption, if we find you've got consumption, then with minimal delay, you'll be back home in Bombay.' When Julian then burst into full Italian opera-style mode with the following words, set to the music of *Santa Lucia,* 'If you've got gonorrhoea, then we don't want you here; if we find you've got trachoma, then you go home-a...' the whole room burst into laughter, such that the two singers were slightly unprepared for the Offenbach re-entry for the final verse. Julian glared at the tape recorder, then at me in the audience. I shrugged my shoulders as if to say that in a live accompaniment I would of course have been exactly in time with them.

By 1984 it was clear my marriage was failing and late in that year I moved out of the family home. Once again I was separated from my own piano. But I still had access to the conference room piano and to the company of those fine singers who were now firm friends.

About this time I conceived the idea of taking up piano teaching in a small way, something which I could then perhaps develop into a second career on retirement, though I was still only in my late thirties. I gave some informal lessons to colleagues on the conference room piano. But if I were serious about teaching later on I would need a diploma, one offered by one of the music colleges. I put in for the exam. This was held over two days. It comprised ear-tests (writing down from dictation passages of music in two parts), papers on harmonisation, theory and history, concluding with a practical involving sight-reading, scales and arpeggios, a short recital, and a viva on teaching methods. I had chosen the diploma offered by the Royal College of Music, which gave a free choice of recital items. I chose three pieces from my half-repertoire, a Scarlatti sonata, Schubert's Impromptu in G flat, and Debussy's *Cathedrale Engloutie* (Cathedral Beneath the Waves). My main problems were my lack of exam experience and my long absence from the guidance of a teacher. I had only the conference room piano for practice and it was not always available. One reason I had never done any grade exams was that I had changed teachers so much in my early years. By the time I was settled with Edgar Brown the pressures from school exams ruled out any ambition to add piano exams to the burden. I had always had a naturally good ear, but the ear-tests in the exam called for specialist tuition. I worked through a textbook on harmony in preparation but it was not enough. I had always been a useful sight-reader but the exam test was not in a familiar style (lots of discords and accidentals and no obvious musical character). I did well enough in theory and history, but not in the rest. The viva exposed my lack of teaching experience. My recital, in which I must have focussed wholly on just playing the right notes in the right order, lacked 'style and conviction'.

It will be clear from my description above of the components of the exam how little of it was actually concerned with teaching. It was built on the curriculum taught at the college, much of which could best be described as 'musicology'. The equivalent diplomas from the other colleges had the same basic structure. Musicology is a fascinating subject in its own right but its relevance to the actual processes of playing and teaching is somewhat tangential. Nonetheless I considered how to prepare to retake the exam in a way which would give me a greater chance of success. I discovered that Goldsmith's College in South London offered courses to help prepare for the teaching diplomas of the music colleges. When I went to enquire about those courses I found they had been withdrawn, as had the music college diplomas themselves. The reason was lack of public confidence. It seemed there had been persistent and growing criticism of diplomas which too often failed to turn out inspiring or even just competent teachers. Parents and pupils could not rely on them. The colleges would later adopt a wholly different system, one which was to suit me far better. I certainly never regretted not obtaining my old-style diploma.

TEN

BETRAYALS

Shortly after my abortive diploma attempt I made, with Julian's help, a tape recording of some pieces from my half-repertoire, using the conference room piano. I intended the tape for my father, who was by then in poor health, and gave it to him on my next visit to the family home along with a portable machine on which to play it. I also lent him a commercial tape of a recording by the great Jorge Bolet of music by Liszt. When a cousin of mine visited my parents from America my mother played him the Bolet tape and boasted to him that I was the one playing. This was of course totally ludicrous and a deliberate lie, but my cousin, being ignorant of such matters, believed her. When the cousin and I met soon afterwards he was distant and puzzled, until I told him my mother had made it up. My mother, I later learned, told quite a few lies about me to our relatives, some of which I did not discover for many years. The most cruel was that she had taken on the hairdressing business in order to pay for private schooling for Neil and myself. The truth, as we have seen, was that we had attended a direct grant grammar school after passing the eleven-plus examination and our education was paid for by the State. It seems all her lies were believed without question. All were damaging to my relations with those relatives, who could not understand how I could be such an apparently ungrateful son. But my mother lied to show herself in the best light and never cared about the consequences for others.

So why did I make that tape? Why did I not just go up to the house and play some pieces for my father at the piano rather than go to the trouble of making a recording? For the explanation I will need to go back some years.

In 1973 my mother made the first of several visits to America to stay with relatives there. (American relatives were all right, it seemed. Just don't mention Irish ones.) She returned full of dreams and excitement. America was the land of opportunity and unlimited riches. She would not listen to any remarks about the possibility of any darker side to American society. There was no poverty or inequality there; everybody was rich. It was certainly the case that some of her relatives had done quite well for themselves, while others who were never mentioned had most definitely not. But as I saw for myself on a visit of my own some years afterwards, none of them was particularly wealthy. The tendency of Americans who have managed the Dream to have bigger cars and houses than over here had dazzled her. America was where she felt she had always belonged. After a further visit, to Philadelphia to help out a niece with childcare, she talked to my father about moving there.

It was hardly practicable and at some point she must have realised that. She could not cope with the loss of her dream and the return to the drab reality of her Liverpool home, alone in that big house with a man she had never begun to understand and who in his turn had never appreciated her need for some excitement in life. She took refuge in an alternative plan, to move to a small house in the remote Lancashire countryside. They had seen it up for sale on a drive though the area. It was a chance encounter which was to have tragic consequences. The move was every bit as impracticable as the American plan. It took no account of my father's declining health which would be ill-served in such an isolated place, not to mention his removal from his drinking companions and a house to which he was deeply attached. Nevertheless, she began to plan in detail for the move, including disposing of items she thought would be an encumbrance in the new home.

I have no doubt that my father prevented the plan from going ahead, though without telling her. If he had had the courage to confront her and explain why the move could not happen things might have turned out very differently. She had inherited their first house, which was hers to dispose of as she wished. But the mortgage on the present house was in his name and his agreement to the sale would have been needed. The crushing of this second dream, only gradually becoming apparent when no potential buyers came forward, was too much for her. She had a breakdown which resulted in her admission to hospital and to her receiving the still controversial electro-convulsive therapy treatment (ECT). She emerged calmer and less aggressive, though memory loss soon began to become apparent, almost certainly as a result of the treatment.

The question of how critical and chronic mental conditions should be treated is beyond the scope of this book so I will make only a brief digression here. My mother was never 'cured' or effectively treated. The ECT had only dealt with an immediate crisis. At no point was she prescribed any form of cognitive therapy. Instead, after the ECT, she was prescribed benzodiazepines over many years, though they were only ever intended for short-term use. She had no idea about their side-effects or addictive dangers, believing them to be simply harmless sleeping pills. But if she had been offered any form of talking therapy she would never have responded. Nobody had ever questioned her about the underlying causes of her behaviour. We in her immediate family did not dare. How could we, when we were the ones she blamed? It would have been unthinkable for her to have sought help for problems she was convinced lay with others and not with herself. I have no idea what she actually did remember of her childhood or adolescence. But I have no doubt that she was in a state of deep denial which no therapist, however skilled or sympathetic, could have overcome. The walls she had erected were too thick and high. And as time went by, denial gave way to oblivion. Her demons faded away, never confronted, leaving only scars which would never heal.

Some time after her discharge she returned to America for a further visit. On her return she had already learned that my father had suffered a heart attack in her absence. His health declined steadily over the next fifteen years. He suffered stoically from a progressive muscle-wasting disease as well as heart disease and the effects of a stroke. My mother looked after him dutifully, perhaps conscious at last of the part she had played over the years in destroying his health and peace of mind. Though he could be an infuriatingly stubborn and impenetrable man he never deserved what he suffered at her hands. I had never heard her say a kind word to him, only words of resentment and criticism. She cared for him diligently as she would have cared for a sick stranger entrusted by circumstance to her care. Strangers indeed they had always been and would remain to the end. But perhaps that caring role gave her a purpose and direction which for the first time in her marriage was not focussed solely on herself. She resented it, of course. But on his death the absence of that or any other purpose in her life accelerated her own decline.

One of the items which my mother disposed of prior to the move which never happened was the family piano. The radiogram had also gone. My vinyl record collection which had once been housed in the radiogram survived this initial clearout. I had taken the records with me to college, where I had a portable record player. Both player and records came back with me and were installed in an attic room which I had taken over as my personal refuge. However, the collection did not survive the much more catastrophic disposal organised by Neil some years later when my mother, by then a widow, moved out of the house. Recently, thanks to the internet, I have been able to reconstitute most of my vinyl collection.

I was not too concerned about the loss of the radiogram. By then, I was building up an alternative collection on tape and compact disc. But her decision to get rid of the piano shocked me to the core. This was the piano on which Molly and Stella had learned, on which she had made her own abortive efforts to learn, which had been my companion and refuge throughout my childhood, a family heirloom full of memories to be treasured and passed on. It was in good condition. At some time during my university years my father had spent some money on repairs, money he could ill afford. There would surely have been room for it in the house to which she wanted to move. After all, we had managed to squeeze it into the kitchen at the back of a hairdresser's shop. There had to be some other reason, something deeper.

It was surely those very memories which were the problem. Though she often claimed her childhood was happy it was abundantly clear from comments she made at other times that it was full of frustration and disappointment. And surely much more, of which she never spoke and never could have done. No ordinary measure of frustration and disappointment such as we all encounter in life could have been the root cause of such intense lifelong emotional states, of so much enduring rage and bitterness. Who in her childhood was responsible? She always spoke of her parents with affection and respect. Were those her true feelings? What about her siblings? She had never been close to any of them, from what I had observed. She was closest perhaps to the mother of Pauline, the niece born out of wedlock, though she had to keep her distance from a sister guilty of such a sin, at least until that sister was dying of cancer. Her relations with other siblings have been described already. She did not seem ever to have placed any trust in any of them.

My long association with the piano would only have made matters worse. For years she had encouraged me, often severely, to persist with my playing and was able to boast of my successes to friends and relatives or to bask in the reflected glory of Speech Day applause. But sooner or later it was clear that I was never going to be a household name. Even worse, I had left home at the age of twenty-two and married three years later. Neil had also left, but she was still able to live through him and his successes as a lawyer. He had pledged never to marry, a pledge he later broke, and was able to divert a portion of his earnings to her. He also promised to spend more time with his parents later on, expecting that by the time he reached his forties he could retire and live off the income of his firm and share his wealth with them. (The future did not exactly turn out like that for him, as will be seen.) I, on the other hand, was still a junior civil servant, an occupation she always despised since being for a short while a clerical assistant in the Inland Revenue, with a still modest salary and the responsibilities of marriage. I had prospects since my success in joining the fast stream of the administrative civil service, but prospects were no use to her. Such a career takes a long time to mature and rewards remain modest compared to those in more glamorous walks of life. However high I would rise, my work would always in her eyes have that aura of Dickensian clerical drudgery about it. There would never be any glory or success or riches to reflect back to her.

She already had a history of betrayal at my hands. It had started when I emerged from her womb the wrong gender. But at least I could plausibly argue that that was not my fault. But after finishing university I had told her I could no longer continue in the practice of the Catholic faith in which I had been brought up. She took it as a personal affront, never accepting that I had a right to make that choice, though when Neil had abandoned the faith years before I did it did not bother her in the least. Nor could she accept that I had a right to choose my career and to get married. She nurtured those grievances for years.

Before my father's illnesses became too serious for him to travel, he and my mother were able to take some holidays abroad with Neil's financial support, which went some way to meet her craving for novelty and a degree of excitement. One of those holidays was to Tenerife. The climate suited them both, especially my father. Neil, who had joined them on this occasion, decided to buy them a holiday home there. They were proud and pleased, not realising that he had had to borrow heavily to finance the purchase. They visited the Tenerife flat each year for several years, escaping the Liverpool winters which adversely affected my father's health. During one such visit I had occasion to visit Liverpool. I stayed overnight in the family home, which was empty at the time. I could not help but notice that photographs of me which had been on display in the house had been removed, though other family photographs remained. I got the message. Once I had reached early adulthood she was no longer able to avenge my betrayals in person. And since that pivotal moment when I had for the first time answered her back she was now wary of challenging me directly. She avoided confrontation. But she had not forgotten and certainly not forgiven. She found other ways to get back; the damaging lies told to friends and relatives, the removal of the photographs, and now the disposal of the family piano and all the memories which went with it.

In later years, by which time the ECT treatment had softened her aggression and begun to erase some of the early memories which had produced it, I regained a measure of favour in her eyes when her first two grandchildren arrived and she could enjoy spending time with them. If there were not to be daughters in her family there could at least be granddaughters. I did become rather concerned when she once described my daughters as her 'possessions', though I do not think she had any real plans to kidnap them. But my divorce was yet another setback to our relationship. As the Catholic she still claimed to be she could not condone it. It was not just a matter of religious doctrine. It would reflect badly on her. People would judge that she had brought her children up badly. This was despite the fact that we had sacrificed much of our childhoods to homework, and in my case also to music and the church, got to university and graduated, established ourselves in promising careers, all without ever running away from home despite the temptation to do so on many occasions, taking drugs or getting into trouble with the police. But somehow the failed marriage of a son well into adulthood would mean fingers being pointed at her. It was a strange way of looking at the world, many decades out of date. But it suited her lifelong conviction that the only feelings which mattered were hers. Of my surviving aunts only Fiona understood that there are two sides to every marriage breakdown and never criticised me for what had happened.

My mother eventually came to terms with the divorce as best she could. But we were never able to be close. I could never feel any affection for her. She had loaded her huge burden of unhappiness onto our shoulders, where it had transmogrified into life-long guilt for some thing or things of which we had no knowledge or understanding. And each of us in our different ways and at different times paid the price. Without doubt, harm had been done to her as a child of which she never spoke, the worst of which perhaps was to have been told that she was special, superior, that life would give her everything she wanted simply because she was who she was. When real life came along with its inevitable disappointments she decided that her husband and children would be the ones to pay. Then there was her disastrous business venture into hairdressing, for the failure of which she never accepted any responsibility. It was entirely because of that failure that the family had been left struggling at a time when it would have been reasonable to expect a measure of comfort and security. Inheriting the Crosby house with no mortgage attached could not have given her a better start to her married life, but she had thrown it away.

Did I also blame that decision for the fact that I had such limited practice opportunities during those essential developmental years of the early teens? It was no doubt the major factor. On the other hand I had because of those unforeseen circumstances developed abilities I might not otherwise have, including that of sight reading and rapid learning, of getting straight to the heart of a piece, of never becoming musically bored. Surrounded by so many distractions and with so limited time, I had to experience my music intensely or not at all. Fortunately it was the former.

One of the major regrets of my life is that I did not try to find out where the piano had gone and try to recover it. After all, the move did not go ahead. The piano could so easily have been restored to its former place. But I doubt if

I could ever have traced it. I suspect it had been put into the hands of the same local dealer who later disposed of the remaining contents of the house. I hope that the piano found a good home and was put to good use.

It is time for another interlude. This one will deal with the fascinating subject of touch at the piano; what it is and how to cultivate it.

INTERLUDE VI

TOUCH

Sometimes you hear a pianist described as having a fine or sensitive touch. Surely all aspiring pianists would want to hear themselves described in those terms. But what does it mean? And how can you go about acquiring such an attribute?

Touch at the piano is about two related things which have already been covered in this book. So take a bit of time to revisit the first interlude. There you learned that when you play a note on the piano you can control (a) how loud or soft it sounds and (b) how long the sound lasts. Loudness and softness depend on the speed of key descent. Length depends on when you release the key and let the damper stop the string vibrating.

Detached and Staccato

In the last interlude you learned how to count and subdivide beats. You are now armed with techniques to control precisely how long you want a note to last. Play our tune again (*Twinkle, Twinkle, Little Star*). It should be very familiar to you by now. Remember that the tune has two beats to each bar. This time, the challenge is to play it with precise lengths for each note. Firstly, instead of trying to make each note fill a whole beat, aim for each note to last for exactly half a beat. This means that each beat needs to be divided into two, with your finger coming off the key at the half-way point, leaving the rest of the beat silent. Silences in music, however brief, are called 'rests'. So this can be illustrated as follows:

C rest C rest / G rest G rest / etc

Play this on the piano as you did before, but make sure you are counting and feeling two precise half-beats to each beat before you start.

Now try to play the same notes, but give each one a length of three quarters of the beat, leaving a rest of one quarter beat. This is more difficult, because you will need to count and feel four quarter beats to each beat. Then, also counting four quarter beats, aim to make each note last only one quarter beat followed by three quarter beat rests. A word of warning: subdividing beats in this way is only feasible if your overall pulse is slow enough. Mentally subdividing beats at faster speeds takes a great deal of practice and experience.

This sort of touch is usually called 'detached'. This is when notes are given a specific and intended length which can be expressed as a fraction of the main beat.

Sometimes a composer will ask, or you as performer will decide, that a note or notes should be played so short that the length is not measurable to the ear or perceptible as a fraction of the main beat. This sort of touch, like so much of piano terminology, has a fancy Italian name, *staccato*.

There are two main ways to play a note *staccato*. The

first is to keep the finger firm and let it bounce back as soon as it has made contact with the key. A useful tip is to imagine the key is red hot. Withdraw fast enough and you will not burn yourself. But withdraw too quickly and your note will not sound. Remember that you will not get a sound until the key descends to the point where the hammer is thrown against the strings. This sort of touch takes a lot of practice to get right. If you let your finger stay too long in the key the note will have a perceptible length and will not be *staccato*.

Another way to produce *staccato* is to hold the hand above the key and flick the finger towards you so that it travels quickly across the surface. The flicking action will ensure the key goes down and comes up quickly out of the bed, all in a single motion. This technique can produce a very light *staccato* but can be unreliable. It needs a very responsive piano mechanism.

Legato

The opposite of *staccato* has another fancy Italian name, *legato*. This is where notes are joined together the way a singer or a string player will usually do. *Legato* means moving smoothly from one note to the next, with no audible gap between them.

A moment's thought will make you realise that you cannot play *legato* with one finger. So this means we need to move on to another important milestone in our exploration of piano technique. It is time to use more than one finger. Indeed, why not go mad and use all five of them?

191

Our tune will not serve this purpose. Most of its notes are played twice in succession, so the finger needs to come out of the key and go back in again, making it impossible to join the sounds together. Even if it were possible, the syllables of the lyric call for a musical setting with a detached touch. Speak them slowly and clearly and you will hear a distinct gap between them (*twin-kle-twin-kle-lit-le-star*).

So what we need to start our exploration of *legato* is a simple five finger exercise. Find middle C again. Don't worry for now about sound or touch. Just play middle C with your thumb and then the four notes above it (D, E, F, G) with your other fingers in turn. Then come back down again.

Piano manuals and teachers have a peculiar system for identifying fingers by number. You would no doubt say that on each hand you have one thumb and four fingers. Piano teachers say otherwise. We call the thumb the first finger. The others in order away from the thumb are two up to five. This fingering system is now universal, used in all printed scores which indicate fingerings. It takes some getting used to. Practise touching the fingers by random number as quickly as you can. Try these numbers: 1,4,3,5,2. Or get someone to call out numbers one to five at random while you point to the corresponding digit with your other hand. Try it at first with your right hand, then with the left.

Now you have the hang of it, you are ready for the following exercise. Play the notes of the five finger exercise with the fingers in sequence, one to five. First of all, get used to the sequence and to using all your fingers by playing the notes detached, as indicated above. I suggest half the length of each beat. Then try it *staccato*. Now you are ready to try *legato*.

The important thing to remember about playing *legato* is that it is not easy. It is in fact quite an advanced technique, and one some quite accomplished pianists never fully master. It involves ensuring there is no gap in sound between the notes, nor any audible overlap. Place your first finger (remember that that is actually your thumb!) into the key and while the note is still sounding start to lower your second finger into place. Only lift the thumb out when the second finger reaches the key bed. The only way to test whether you have achieved a good *legato* is by listening. Do the notes move smoothly one into the next, or can you hear a gap? Is there an audible smudging where both sound together before the first is released?

The ability to play smooth and effective *legato* takes a lot of patient practice. But it is essential to achieve the sort of *cantabile* (singing) style which comes so naturally to singers and string players. Most piano pieces call for *legato* playing at least to some extent. You cannot aim to play the piano music of the Romantic period, or Beethoven, Mozart or Haydn, without this ability. This is also true of Bach, though there is a school of thought, mistaken in my view, which is that because he did not write for the piano Bach's keyboard music for instruments other than the organ should all be detached or even *staccato*. I believe this is based on a misunderstanding of the nature of the instruments for which Bach did write, including the tiny clavichord, which is the very essence of *legato*! It is also based on a failure to understand the melodic and vocal inspiration for much of his keyboard music. But these are deep waters, so we must move on, quickly!

As you go up and down with your five fingers you may notice that some sounds are weaker than others. *Legato* requires more effort from the fingers than other touches, and this can expose a characteristic weakness of some fingers, especially the fourth (just a reminder that this is not the little finger but the one next to it!). This problem is to a large extent anatomical. The fourth finger has deep connections to surrounding tissue and has less independence than the others. No finger has complete independence. Exercises which claim to develop such independence should be avoided as they can cause physical damage. There is no reason why you cannot play as effectively with the fourth finger as with the others, certainly in slow *legato* passages. Remember to keep the knuckle joint firm and curved in. This may take more practice than with the other fingers but it is worth it. Very young children often play with a flat fourth finger because the joint has yet to develop the necessary strength. As they get older this flatness can become a habit long after it is easily curable. Playing firmly with the fourth finger should be cultivated as soon as it is strong enough.

Legatissimo

In certain pieces especially of the Romantic period calling for a high degree of *cantabile* playing some pianists will slightly exaggerate the *legato* effect so that there is a slight, barely perceptible overlap between notes that are adjacent in time. This is called *legatissimo*. Only pianists who have thoroughly mastered all aspects of *legato* should think of tackling it. It requires the utmost sensitivity and precision. For present purposes we will take it as read that *legato* playing should avoid both gaps and audible overlaps.

Shaping your Sound

With a good *legato* you are well placed to introduce tonal shaping into your playing. In the case of your five finger exercise this would normally mean getting gradually and smoothly a little louder as you go up and softer as you come down. The result may come as a pleasant surprise to you. Though it is still only an exercise it will sound like music. It will have that sense of direction and purpose which is the essence of musical playing. Combining this sort of tonal control with smooth legato in a simple five finger exercise, while of course keeping steady time, is the start of your journey to becoming a really musical pianist. You will be developing a quality which will make your playing of even simple pieces stand out from that of those who have never bothered or been taught to cultivate it.

ELEVEN

RECITALS AND COMPETITIONS

By the late 1980s I had bought a flat of my own in Haringey in North London, and after a subsequent improvement in my finances was able to purchase a new upright piano. It was modern and compact, able easily to fit into my sitting room. It had the advantage of having a silencer pedal, useful when there are neighbours below and to the side. This pedal does not silence the piano totally but muffles the sound. This did not stop me getting complaints from the neighbour below, especially when I started my practice early in the morning before setting out for work. In the meantime the original piano I had bought in Fulham had embarked on a northern odyssey, moving to two addresses in Scarborough and a further two in Scunthorpe. I continued my musical associations with my singer friends at the office and Christine's church.

Haringey in those days was sometimes known as Little Cyprus, for good reason as a large and lively Greek Cypriot community had been rooted there for many years. Along Green Lanes, just a few yards from my flat, fruit and vegetable stores open until late at night overflowed onto the pavements, the scent of their exotic contents mingling with the warm wholesome odours from numerous pastry shops. The sounds of chatter in mixed Greek and English and the strains of Bouzouki music provided the sonic backdrop. The area is now more mixed, with Turkish residents moving up from Stoke Newington as the more successful Cypriot business owners move north to Cockfosters. For fresh air and space, locals haunt Finsbury Park, spacious and undulating, with views to the skyline of Central London. It is equipped with a circular jogging track. It was there that the next surprising chapter in my musical life began. That was where I met Asterios.

We were both out jogging one Sunday morning, approaching each other from opposite directions along the track. He crossed my path with a friendly 'hello', then turned round to join me, having decided that we were running at about the same pace and could help each other. After that chance encounter we met for jogging each Sunday. He told me he and his family were from mainland Greece, near Athens, and that his name meant 'the stars.' I was invited to their house for their regular Friday gatherings and was delighted to find that they had a piano. The family was intensely religious as well as musical. Those Friday evenings were devoted first to discussion of a passage read from the Bible, chosen by his wife, Anna, and then to music. Nearly always, as is the Greek way, we were joined by many of their friends and relatives.

Asterios was a competent enough pianist, but the instrument at which he really shone was the accordion. The instrument itself was a shining thing of beauty and the sounds he produced effortlessly from it were drenched in romantic nostalgia. Anna, a local doctor, was an excellent singer. With the help of their friends and relatives they performed Greek songs, full of passion and intensity.

Asterios was also a composer, and therein lay a difficulty. He did not read music and did not have recording equipment. Sometimes he would play a beautiful new song he had just composed. By the following week a new one would be ready and the earlier one forgotten. I decided to rescue some of his work from oblivion. I brought along a pen and some manuscript paper and asked him to play his new song again and again while I frantically jotted down the notes. At home during the week I would arrange the song in my own way and bring it back. I arranged two of his songs that way, and still have the manuscripts. Usually he would only compose the melody, Anna later adding words in English. In return, I composed a piece myself to play for them, a song without words, inspired by their friendship and warmth. In homage to their Greek background I called it *On the Wine-Dark Sea*, borrowing the phrase from Homer. The piece does have a kind of Mediterranean feel to it, I like to think. It remains my favourite among the small number of my own surviving compositions.

Though I was not to know it at the time, the early nineties was the start of what would prove the busiest time of my life, musically speaking, since my schooldays. 1993 in particular was a pivotal year. It was the year in which my father died, an event to which I will return along with its sequel, and in which I remarried. Valerie and I had known each other for several years, since before my separation from my first wife. She has at the time of writing recently retired after forty-four years working for the Ministry of Defence. We first met on a course for civil servants who could speak German and were expected to spend time visiting their opposite numbers in the German Civil Service. The aim in those days, which now seem many centuries ago, was to encourage contact and mutual understanding between the administrations of the Member States of the European Union including the UK. Yes, it may seem impossible to believe now, but that really was the case! We are one of what must be many thousands of couples who would never have met were it not for our membership of the EU. The cost of Brexit is not just to be measured in economic or diplomatic terms. We maintained contact through her chairmanship of a ballroom dancing club (she was always a much better dancer than I would ever be) and later in Bonn where she went to work in the British Embassy. Throughout our marriage, while pursuing her own career to the most senior ranks of her Ministry, she has patiently encouraged my musical and literary pursuits, enjoying my successes and sympathising with my failures, always putting the latter into perspective. As the century ebbed away and the shadows which had followed me for so long receded, so the sun of Valerie's warm and joyful personality rose and has shone into my life ever since.

The immediate catalyst for the new musical era was the opening of a shiny new open plan office for my department and the replacement of the old conference room piano with an excellent new model in the atrium of the new building. I do not know who first thought of the idea of lunchtime concerts in the atrium but it was to take off in spectacular fashion. There was ample space for choral as well as instrumental events, and a captive audience in the form of those taking lunch in the office canteen, which occupied one corner of the ground floor. Those wanting to listen more closely could take a seat after lunch, while those passing through to the offices overlooking the space could use the event as background music. No doubt we irritated many as well entertaining others, but on the whole the concerts were welcomed as a major contribution to the maintenance of morale in the department.

I was astonished to discover the wealth of musical talent available among my fellow civil servants and how much of it was concentrated in the branch of which I was by then head. The initial inspiration came from Jeremy, a former Cambridge organ scholar who assembled and trained a very competent choir from our ranks. There were also singers and instrumentalists, some of whom could have had professional careers. The instrumentalists who would take part in atrium performances over the next few years included two clarinettists one of whom led a saxophone quartet, a classical guitarist, a cellist, a violinist and a trumpeter. There were three pianists including myself and Jeremy.

And then there was Colm. Colm played the flute, though that bald statement gives no hint as to the quality of his musicianship. Colm worked in my branch and we got talking about music during an office party. He was aware that the atrium was by then available as a venue for performances. Somehow after a few drinks we had agreed to put on a flute and piano recital, an experience which would be wholly novel to me. I had had some experience of playing with a flautist at college but we had never gone as far as to perform to an audience. In the cold light of day I wondered about the wisdom of what I had agreed to take on, even more so when my copies of the music arrived. Certainly the programme was very attractive: sonatas by Handel and Hummel, and French music by Fauré, Ibert and Gounod. But none of it was familiar to me. It represented a real challenge to one whose only performance experience since school was that scratch concert put on at the end of the German course nearly ten years before and the occasional much more informal event at Christine's church.

It was a revelation to hear Colm for the first time in rehearsal. His tone had a sweetness and purity which reminded me of his idol, James Galway, and there seemed no limit to his virtuosity. He was more confident than I about the likely success of the event, though my doubts were entirely about my own contribution. If something did not go quite right in rehearsal he would declare that it would go all right on the day and I gradually learned to believe him. It worked. The concert was well received.

We began right away to plan another such event. But soon we were visited by the spectre of a new virus which was already claiming thousands of lives across the world. Colm was rapidly becoming physically weaker and his playing was suffering. Only a few months after our recital he told me he had decided on medical advice to give up playing. I had suspected the truth for some time. He had been diagnosed as HIV-positive some years before, and was now developing full-blown AIDS. There was no cure or effective treatment at the time. Colm died in Westminster Hospital later that year, still only in his forties.

He was remembered with huge affection by his friends and colleagues, and not just for his musical abilities. I sought the help of those of his colleagues who were musical to put on a memorial concert for him in that same atrium space where he and I had given our first and last performance. There was a magnificent response, everybody whom I invited agreeing to take part. My own contribution was a solo, Mozart's poignant Adagio in B Minor. The choir also contributed Mozart, the Introit from his Requiem Mass and his *Ave Verum Corpus.* Schubert, Handel, Mendelssohn and Fauré also featured.

I had by then formed another musical partnership, this time with Paul, an excellent clarinettist. Like Jeremy and Colm he worked in the same branch as myself. I found playing with a clarinettist a very different experience. The clarinet has a more robust tone and range than the flute and can be heard through even quite complex and challenging accompaniments. This is particularly the case with what are generally accepted as the greatest works in the clarinet and piano repertoire, the two sonatas by Brahms, models of eloquence and concentration. We included the first of the sonatas, the one in F minor, in our first atrium concert. Though Paul played with expressive tone and control I did not feel that I had given him adequate support. The truth is that the work demanded far more time to understand and absorb that I had had time for. A few months later, we performed the second sonata, in E flat; mellower though scarcely less difficult. I took to it much more readily. This time we achieved a real mutual understanding. We would go on to perform this sonata on two further occasions. Over the next few years we would also perform sonatas by Saint-

Saens and Poulenc and the sonata-like Fantasy Pieces by Schumann. Such works are the serious core of the clarinet and piano repertoire, deeply challenging and rewarding. But this repertoire has another side. It includes pieces by lesser composers in lighter vein designed to show off the clarinet's flexibility and versatility. We would regularly incorporate such pieces in our programmes, which Paul would perform with great panache.

By the end of 1995 I was beginning to get some feel for what life must be like for professional musicians on a busy schedule with limited time for practice or rehearsal. That year we put on twelve lunchtime concerts in the atrium space, including a summer concert with mostly lighter music on the menu, plus three public concerts in the nearby St John's Church, Waterloo, an impressive neo-Grecian building dating from shortly after the Napoleonic wars. All of us involved in the performances were busy civil servants with many other demands on our time. It was a heartening and at the same time exhausting and sometimes bewildering experience, learning new repertoire quickly and responding to the different needs of singers and instrumentalists, all with different qualities and preferences.

And then, to cap it all, it was our turn that year to host a vocal competition. Our departmental sports and social club ran a competition for soloists every October, vocal in odd years and instrumental in even years. Each region was responsible for putting forward the candidate who had won a local eliminating round. Our eliminating round took place in St John's, and I was the accompanist. I knew some of the participants and their chosen songs but not all. One of the competitors worked in a distant office and we would not have a chance to get together to rehearse. He had sent me his music, but it was in an unfamiliar style and I had no idea how fast or slow it was meant to go. He rang me up the day before and sang his song down to me over the telephone. It must have been an extraordinary experience for his colleagues in that office. It was as well he did so. The song went much faster than I had thought, and I needed to get up to speed quickly.

The competition itself was held in St Giles, Cripplegate, in the Barbican, one of the few mediaeval churches in the City to survive wartime bombing. It had a superb Steinway piano. The lady vocalists performed in the morning and the gentlemen in the afternoon, about ten performers in each half. While that does not sound too bad, each singer had a programme of up to three songs each! We provided two accompanists, myself and Jonathan, a very fine pianist with whom I would later put on a recital for piano duet. I persuaded Jonathan that it would work best if I took the ladies and he the gentlemen. Being himself a gentleman, he readily agreed. While all the contestants were expected to provide copies of their music well in advance not all did so. Quite a few of the scores arrived at the last minute. Some of the music was familiar to me but not always in a familiar key. I had to play Schubert's *Standchen* (Serenade) once in D minor and again half an hour later in B minor. Arranged accompaniments for opera arias were complex and difficult. Some last minute simplifications were inevitable. There was only one chance to rehearse, on the day before. One of my singers never made it to the rehearsal because of transport difficulties. She was a confident performer with an ebullient personality so somehow we made it through on the day. Such experiences are no doubt part and parcel of everyday life for professional accompanists, whose qualities are surely severely underrated. Certainly my respect for them was growing all the time.

The final musical event of the year was memorable indeed. I had come across an arrangement of Aaron Copland's *Quiet City*, one of the most atmospheric pieces I have ever heard and featuring a deeply expressive trumpet solo part. He wrote it for a play by Irwin Shaw about 'the night thoughts of many different kinds of people in a great city.' The arrangement was for trumpet, cor anglais and piano. I was very keen to put the piece on. David, our resident trumpeter, agreed to tackle the trumpet part, though he reminded me that it is a piece which most trumpeters approach 'with some trepidation.' There was still a problem. We had nobody to play the cor anglais part. I persuaded Paul to play the part on the clarinet, which would have to be transcribed for him. I did this in a cottage in a remote part of Cornwall, where Valerie and I had taken a late holiday.

We had another problem. Some of the rhythms were complicated such that we decided we needed the services of a conductor to help us over some passages. We called on Simon, who had taken over from Jeremy as conductor of the choir, Jeremy having left to work in the NHS. The programme also included Haydn's Trumpet Concerto, a Concertino by Weber for clarinet and piano, and the Dance Preludes for clarinet and piano by Polish composer, Lutoslawski. It was a demanding programme for all of us, but all except the Copland was familiar and had been performed before. The rehearsal for the Copland – there was only time for one – was difficult at first. I began to wonder if we had bitten off more than we could chew. Then suddenly it all came together. At that point I called a halt. A further go and it might all fall apart again. At the performance it went far better than I dared to hope. For the final echoing trumpet passage as the music faded away, David dramatically took his trumpet and music stand into a far corner of the space and played from there, exactly the distancing effect the music required. And so the sounds of the city at night faded away. It was unforgettable.

The next year we continued in the same vein, with regular performances in the atrium space and at St John's. Our two soprano soloists, Jan and Pat, our contralto, Margaret, David on trumpet and our two clarinettists, Paul and Angela, gave several performances, in most of which I took part. Margaret described herself as a contralto and mostly performed music for that voice. But she had an extraordinary vocal range, and regularly sang tenor with a choir specialising in Renaissance music. Jonathan and I gave a piano duet recital, while in a programme of French music Paul distinguished himself at the piano as well as on the clarinet.

With changes in personnel and the departure of Jeremy, the choir was much diminished in numbers but still featured in the summer concert alongside a smaller vocal ensemble. All the regulars took part in a programme of mixed classical and popular music, including the saxophone quartet, one of whose pieces was entitled *Handel's Waterworks* [sic]. For the choir's rendition of Rutter's *The Lord is my Shepherd* I was joined by an oboist from outside. I had never met her and she had not been able to join us to rehearse. We went straight into the performance on the day, without any hitches. Jan and Margaret performed a duet for two mewing and spitting cats, once thought to be by Rossini, satirising the quarrelsome divas of his time. For the finale, for which we had found no fewer than three solo tenors, the audience was invited to join in a medley from the musical *Les Misérables*, which had recently celebrated its tenth anniversary on the London stage.

I now had more time available for study and practice, having moved to new duties which enabled me to work part time, and at one stage to take an unpaid break of several months. I was also building up a real repertoire of solo pieces, as opposed to my former half-repertoire. Largely this was as a result of the solo singers and instrumentalists asking me to fill in with solos during their recitals so they could take a breather.

That year it was the turn of the instrumentalists and pianists for the annual competition, which took place in Birmingham. Paul decided to enter the instrumental section, with me as his accompanist. As the piano section of the competition took place later the same day at the same venue I decided to enter for it. Paul played some of Finzi's charming Bagatelles. For my solo programme I offered Mozart's B minor Adagio, which I had played at Colm's memorial concert, and Liszt's transcription of Schumann's wonderful song, *Widmung* or *Song of Love*.

At the previous year's vocal competition I had been impressed by the cordiality, generosity and fairness of the adjudicator. Expecting the same this year, I was shocked at the rudeness and impatience of the instrumental adjudicator. He abruptly dismissed all the competitors' efforts, telling them that they suffered from the usual amateur defects of being unable to play through a line and communicate with an audience. He took no account of the fact that all were busy civil servants without the time and training which had placed him in his own privileged position of being asked (and paid!) to judge them. I sometimes wonder if some professional musicians resent amateurs for the way they can enjoy the music without the pressure of needing to make a living from it and perhaps find something fresh in what to the professional may have long since gone stale. Where that is the case, they surely should not agree to adjudicate amateur competitions. He did however say that he had quite enjoyed the performance by an accordionist and awarded her the first prize.

By the time the piano session was over and we were awaiting the results I was naturally apprehensive. The piano adjudicator was far more genial than his colleague. He said of my performance of the Mozart that I had a sensitive feel for the style and some lovely tonal qualities. The Liszt had some excellent playing though I needed to bring out the melodic line more. All fair enough. I was however rather bewildered when he awarded first prize to a lady who had collapsed with nerves, and the second prize to a burly young man who played Liszt's second Hungarian Rhapsody with such aggressive force that the full size concert grand actually shook on the stage.

After the competition and in the light of it I began to reflect on my pianistic future. There was a lot of solo repertoire I wanted to explore and perform if possible. But I was clearly missing something. I had failed to find that particular quality of communication which might have helped me secure a better result in the competition. I had to admit that I needed help. But where to find it? I was forty-eight and had not had any lessons since I was sixteen. Most piano teachers make their living teaching in schools and/or giving private lessons to children who want, or whose parents want for them, to move through the system of grade examinations. How could I find someone who would understand and help an adult pianist like me, one with a lot of performance experience under his belt, with a good memory and enough technique to tackle most of the pieces I wanted to learn but who was looking to find that missing element, that wow factor that had somehow got lost?

I had joined an informal organisation of amateur adult pianists in North London called the London Piano Circle, which hosted meetings in members' homes where we could play to each other, talk about music and generally socialise. At these meetings I would hear talk of a lady who taught some of the members. She was referred to only as Ricci. She was clearly held in something like awe. I asked Andrew Cockburn, who had co-founded the Circle and who I knew was one of her students, if he thought she could help me. He promised to pass on her details to me. It was Ricci who contacted me, sending me her brochure through the post. I rang her to arrange a consultation.

So it was that I came to another crossroads in my musical life, as I stood outside the door of Ricci Horenstein in Hampstead, thirty-two years after my last piano lesson. If I had changed my mind at that moment and walked away the course of future events would have been very different.

But it is time for another interlude, for a major step forward. Yes, it is time to use *both hands*.

209

INTERLUDE VII

LOOK, BOTH HANDS (AND FEET, TOO?)

This interlude comes with a health warning. You have already come across it earlier, but it is worth recalling. *Failure to progress with the piano usually comes at a later stage, when the two hands are called upon to play different notes at the same time and in a coordinated way.* That is the stage we have now reached, and it is indeed a challenge. But if you have worked steadily and conscientiously through all the preceding exercises, taking no shortcuts, you stand a good chance of overcoming it. The failure to which I referred usually has its cause in persistent weaknesses in the basics of technique which have been explored in the earlier interludes.

Time for the left hand to join in

Go back now to our tune, which should be very familiar to you by now. Indeed, you may be a little tired of it. But that feeling should soon dispel as you work through what follows. First of all, you will need to get used to playing with the left hand alone, prior to using both hands. So find the C below middle C and play the tune with one finger of your left hand. (Remember that C is immediately to the left of each group of two black notes.)

How will you play it? That is up to you. Armed with what you have learned so far, you will choose a speed (tempo) which suits the tune, not too fast and not too slow, and you will count out loud to make sure you play in time. Your playing will be neither too loud nor too soft. It is after all a nursery rhyme, in the English version. As you listen, notice how the register, meaning the range of notes, in which you are now playing is naturally louder than when you played with your right hand. Piano strings get longer and thicker and so louder the further down you go. All pianists need to bear that in mind and adjust their touch accordingly. What about note lengths? Again, that is up to you, but I suggest you aim for a detached half-length throughout.

Our tune with all the fingers

In the last interlude you learned to use all the fingers of your right hand in order to play a *legato* exercise, that is, to join notes together. Our tune is not to be played *legato*. But if you have seen even a preliminary stage pianist in action you will know that they usually use all or most of the fingers. So why not do so now with our tune? Once you have got the hang of it, you will find it helps with note accuracy, especially when you want to go a bit faster, and avoids tiring sideways movements of the hand and arm.

Go back now to using just the right hand. The first

problem you will notice is that our tune covers a span of six notes and we only have four fingers and a thumb (or five fingers in the case of pianists, but either way there are not enough digits to cover the notes). So one finger has to do duty for two adjacent notes. You now have to make what is called a fingering decision, something all pianists do all the time though not all do so as a conscious process. You need to decide, because there are many possible solutions to this problem. By all means, try out different ones. To save time now, I will suggest a fingering which will serve the purpose. These are the finger numbers for the first eight bars, one number per note sounded. I have placed each fingering below the note to which it applies.

C C / G G / A A / G / F F / E E / D D / C
1 1 / 4 4 / 5 5 / 4 / 4 4 / 3 3 / 2 2 / 1

Remember that pianists have only fingers and no thumbs! So 1 refers to what most people call the thumb, and the other numbers to the fingers counting away from the thumb. In this scheme of fingering the fourth finger plays both the Gs and the Fs.

Life is complicated for the pianist, not just because both hands are used but because the hands are mirror images of each other. When you play our tune in the left hand you are playing notes which have been exactly transposed. But left hand fingers go in the opposite direction from those of the right. So a different set of fingerings will be needed to play the tune in the left hand. This is what I suggest.

5 5 / 2 2 / 1 1 / 2 / 2 2 / 3 3 / 4 4 / 5

Here, it is the second finger (yes, the first finger next to the thumb!) which does duty for two adjacent notes. You will see that the jump with one finger from one note to the next occurs at the same point in each hand. This will help coordination when you come to play the tune with both hands at the same time.

Which is what you will now do, after taking a deep breath. To avoid discouragement, it is essential to move cautiously and take one step at a time. So go back to using just the one finger in each hand. Take your time. Listen carefully to ensure that the hands match, meaning that the notes start and finish at the same time, that they are at about the same level of loudness or softness at each point, and that a steady pulse is maintained. If you break down, start again at a slower speed, but keep it steady.

Though you know how tricky this is, anyone watching who has not travelled the same road may scoff that you still look like a total beginner, using just one finger per hand. But you know you are not a total beginner and are well prepared for the next step, which will surprise them and may well make them envious. Now you will play the tune with both hands, using all the fingers as set out above.

First of all, go back to separate hands. This is a basic principle for all the piano playing you may do in future. *Always learn and practise the hands separately first.* If you have difficulty with a piece or a passage, take each hand at a time, ensure you have a fingering which works for both you and the music, and practise patiently through careful and listening repetition. The listening bit is very important. Practice will become tedious and may even be harmful if you do not listen carefully to what you are doing and make the adjustments your ears tell you to make. Only put the hands together when you feel ready. It may not work the first time. If it does not, take each bar at a time. Then put larger sections together, then finally the whole tune.

This is a real step forward. Do not move on to the next step until you have mastered it.

Tune with accompaniment

So what is the next step? Remember that with the piano there is always a next step, no matter how advanced you are. Our next step is to play the tune in the right hand but with an independent bass, or accompaniment, in the left. This will add depth and colour to the tune, in the same way that a voice added below one singing a tune enriches the tune with depth and colour, provided that the two voices form a coherent whole.

What does that mean? You will probably be aware that the tune on its own sounds a bit thin, as if something is missing. That applies even when you play the tune with both hands, because it is the same notes that are sounding in each hand. A separate accompaniment can add two things, rhythm and harmony.

Rhythm and the associated issues of timing have been dealt with at some length in a previous interlude so I will put them to one side here. Suffice it to say that the accompaniment can help to reinforce the rhythmic patterns of the tune. Once both hands are mastered and put together, it is easier to play in time and with a strong rhythmic sense a tune which has a strong rhythm in the accompaniment.

As for harmony, its theoretical basis is far beyond the scope of this volume. But harmony will be very familiar to you as an experience, even if not as a concept. Almost every piece of popular music you hear consists of a tune or melody with an accompaniment which adds harmony. Listen to a song with guitar accompaniment, or better still, watch the performance. You will see that the guitar player adds what are called chords by strumming across the strings, a different note to each string. The whole effect is called harmonious, provided the sounds complement each other and support the tune. Why some notes add harmony and support to the tune while others seem to clash with it is a complex issue, requiring some knowledge of acoustical physics. Interesting in its own right but not essential to the enjoyment of music.

As before, you will learn the new left hand separately, before trying it with the right. It is simpler than the tune itself. These are the notes, beginning on the C below middle C. Note that there is only note per bar, or to put it another way, one note for every two beats, or, to put it yet another way, one note for every two of the tune except where the tune has one note with two beats.

C /E /F /E /D /C /G /C / [repeat]

The G can be either the G above your starting C or the one below it. Try both and decide which you prefer. Don't forget that you have to decide on fingerings. You know now how to do that for yourself. It is always a good idea to stick to the same fingerings, once you have decided and you know they work for you.

The accompaniment notes for the middle eight are as follows:

E /D /C /B / [repeat]

However long and short you choose to play the notes of the tune, try to make these accompaniment (or bass) notes as long as possible. If they are cut too short the tune will lack support.

Feet as well?

Using the pedals in a truly musical way is without doubt an advanced technique. But I believe that from an early stage you should know what the pedals do and how they achieve their effects. I will assume that your piano has two pedals, left and right. Some pianos have three. Ignore the one in the middle. It might be a practice pedal, if your piano is an upright, meant to dampen the sound so much that while your neighbour will not hear what you are playing neither will you. On a grand it has a specialised function not worth bothering about here.

The right pedal is best described as the sustaining pedal. What does it do? You will recall from the first interlude that pressing a key lifts the damper off the strings for that note. Press down the sustaining pedal and the dampers are lifted from all the keys. This means that all the strings can vibrate in what is called 'sympathy' with the sound of the note you are actually playing.

You won't actually hear the individual sounds of the other strings, not directly. But they are sounding and they enrich the sound of the note or notes you are playing. Try it with middle C. First without pedal, then with. Listen to the difference.

How do we know other strings are vibrating? We can't see them, and we can't hear them individually. But the effect can be illustrated in what can seem like a magic trick to your non-musical friends. Ask them to challenge you to sound a note without playing its key. Maybe they will be willing to bet you cannot do it. If they put money on it, they will lose.

This is how the trick works. With your right hand press down the key of middle C very slowly so that there is no sound. Keep it down. Then with your left play the C below very loudly and come off quickly. Your right hand will still be pressing the key of middle C. But now that C can be distinctly heard. Try it again, this time with the G above middle C, again using the lower C to start it off. The G will sound, quietly but clearly. Depending on your piano, this should also work with the C above middle C. What is happening is that the silent pressing of the higher keys releases the damper from the strings for that note. When the lower note sounds, the strings of the higher note vibrate in sympathy, but the effect cannot be heard until the lower note is released. The reasons why this works only for some notes and not for others has to do with the complex acoustical physics to which I referred above.

Don't bother to try this trick on an electric or digital piano. If you do and invite your friends to bet on it, you will lose. It doesn't work, because there are no strings to vibrate. All the more reason to have a real piano.

As well as enriching the sound of your note the right pedal also sustains it. If you release your note but keep the pedal down it carries on sounding, because the damper does not return to damp the note. So you can sound a lot of notes together, far more than by holding on to notes with your fingers. Try it and have fun.

This enriching and sustaining effect is essentially a colouring device. More often, the right pedal is used not for colour but to achieve *legato* (see the interlude on touch) when the fingers cannot do it on their own, for example, when you want to join the sound of a chord (several notes together) to another chord. Achieving a smooth *legato* through the use of pedal can indeed be described as an advanced technique.

The left pedal has different effects, depending on what sort of piano you have. With a grand piano, it moves the entire keyboard, and with it the hammers, slightly to the right so that only two out of the three strings are hit. This produces a veiled effect of great beauty. On an upright a similar but far less successful effect is attempted by moving the hammers closer to the strings. Both left and right pedals can of course be used together.

TWELVE

HAMPSTEAD LADIES FROM VIENNA

'I don't play accurately – anyone can play
accurately – but I play with wonderful expression.
As far as the piano is concerned, sentiment is my
forte.'
Algernon in Oscar Wilde's *The Importance of
Being Earnest.*

The photograph of Ricci in her brochure showed a dignified
lady in middle age seated at the piano, her hands raised in
the air as if summoning spirits from beyond, thick hair
framing an intense gaze. It could have been the portrait of a
fortune-teller or medium. By the time I came to her, she
would have been about seventy (accounts of her life differ
on the question of her exact year of birth). Born in Vienna,
she fled ahead of the Nazis, eventually reaching Palestine in
1941. After further extensive travels she arrived in London
in 1965, where she settled.

She let me into her semi-basement flat without a word
and I followed her into a large, elegantly furnished room in
which, unsurprisingly, the main feature was her grand piano
up against the window. She invited me to sit down and

explain why I was there. I told her some of my background, and in particular why I thought she could help with my problems of projection and communication. I mentioned that I had never done any grade examinations. 'Oh good,' she replied. I played her the two pieces I had performed at the competition. Of the Mozart Adagio, she said that while my intentions were there they were not fully coming across. After I had played the Liszt, she told me, 'You are not an amateur; amateur pianists do not do what you have just done.' We agreed that I would come to her every fortnight for an hour's lesson. At that point we seemed to be on friendly, even warm terms. Then we returned to the Mozart and she made some suggestions. When I was getting ready to go I sensed that the atmosphere had become distinctly chilly. Her goodbye at the door was peremptory. Had I said something to offend her?

The mystery was cleared up when I returned for my first lesson. She told me that the consultation had turned in its later stage into a lesson and I should pay her for that. She wanted half of the agreed weekly fee. Not wanting to provoke a rift between us before we had even started I consented. But I was uneasy. In the light of my own subsequent teaching experience I am now in no doubt that in demanding this retrospective fee for what was still officially a consultation she was behaving in a totally unprofessional manner. A consultation should always be free of charge. Fees should only be levied once there is mutual agreement to proceed with a subsequent course of lessons and after the fee has been agreed. Had she felt at the time that she was going beyond a consultation she should have stopped and said that from this point on this is really a lesson and I will need to charge for it. We could have agreed that, or not, at the time. I learned later of another strange practice of hers, of charging different fees according to what she thought her pupils could afford. Another member of our piano circle had enquired of her about lessons and been asked for a higher fee than the one she charged me. She knew that this other member was a dentist. This is also unprofessional. The same hourly rate should be charged to all. Of course a teacher may at his or her discretion allow a discount for a pupil who may be in difficult financial circumstances, but the basic fee should be the same. But in such matters Ricci was a law unto herself.

Ricci enjoyed her life among the Hampstead intellectuals who were her friends and neighbours. One of these was R D Laing, author of *the Divided Self* and renowned as a guru of the anti-psychiatry movement. I do not know if he was ever a pupil but he certainly was aware of her qualities as a teacher. In his words as quoted in her brochure, 'She acts as a catalyst, inspiring her students to break through limitations and reach heights of which they did not know they were capable.'

That was certainly the case with me. She taught me to free up my sound by eliminating tensions in the arms and wrists and by using arm weight. She did not adhere to any particular school or philosophy such as the Alexander Technique. Her knowledge of the way physiology affects sound production at the piano was profound and derived from many sources, but above all from her own experience and that of her own teachers.

As a teacher she was perceptive and consistent in the promulgation of her values of expressive freedom and

221

intense communication. She had no time for the inhibiting concern which I, like so many adult pianists, had developed about playing wrong notes. 'Play your wrong notes with conviction,' she would say. Of course we should not, like Algernon in *The Importance of Being Earnest,* abandon all attempts to play the right notes in the right order. Wrong notes may be the result of inaccuracies in reading or ineffective fingerings, problems which can be easily rectified. But note slips will occur under the pressure of live performance, even, or sometimes especially, with the greatest of pianists. While Slade at my school was preparing me to play Weber's *Invitation to the Dance* at Speech Day he told me he had seen those legendary greats Rachmaninov and Vladimir de Pachman hit 'fistfuls of wrong notes, all due to nerves.' He would shake his hands to demonstrate. It was not exactly the encouragement I was looking for. But I would have gladly gone a very long way indeed to hear Rachmaninov's wrong notes.

Whatever her undoubted qualities as a teacher, Ricci in her personality could be inconsistent and unpredictable. At times she was warm and emotional, at others cold and distant. After her apparent initial meanness over a half-lesson fee for what I had understood to be still a consultation, she proved to be extremely generous with her time and attention. Our lessons often ran well over the scheduled hour. After a lesson was coming to its end, she would often ask me if I had brought anything else to play. Exhausted by then, I would promise something new for the next time.

Ricci was often invited to meetings of the London Piano Circle, which generally took place within no more than a mile or two of her home. She loved to drive her own car to these events. But as parking spaces were often hard to find she would drive around until she found one, often nearer to her own home than to that of her host. After the event some of the party would be deputed to accompany her as she searched the streets for her car.

I at last felt free to explore and perform many of the pieces I had longed to bring into my repertoire. Among those I studied with her were Schubert's G flat Impromptu and Sonata in A (the so-called little one though only by comparison with the huge later one in the same key), Mendelssohn's brilliant Rondo Capriccioso, Beethoven's big early Sonata in D, Chopin's Nocturne in D flat and Fantasy-impromptu, Schumann's Arabesque, Rachmaninov's Prelude in G sharp minor, and several Scarlatti sonatas.

And then there was what she came to call just 'the Brahms'. I always knew what she meant. It was his Rhapsody in G minor, a big-boned, tragic piece, with all that composer's expressive power and tautness of construction. I had loved Brahms intensely since childhood after coming across a recording of his Violin Concerto. But I had always been nervous of tackling his piano music, which however glorious it might sound always looked crabbed and awkward on the page. Edgar Brown had tried to interest me in this very work, telling me, quite rightly, that it was one of the great pieces. But I could not come to terms with it then. It needed a greater technical and musical maturity than any I could aspire to at that age. But now I was ready for it. My work with Paul on the two clarinet sonatas had brought Brahms' challenging piano writing into my sphere and prepared the ground. Ricci's words as I offered my first attempts were an uncanny echo of Edgar's, though her emphasis was slightly different. This will be one of the great pieces for you, she told me. It was hard work, but slowly it began to yield its sombre, majestic secrets. At the end of the year Ricci organised a pupils' concert at Burgh House, Hampstead, and invited me to play 'the Brahms.' I readily agreed.

The activities of our civil service music society continued much as before, in our two venues of the atrium space and St John's Church. One of the highlights was a concert in the atrium in June 1997 in honour of the 200th anniversary of the birth of Schubert. We assembled the usual suspects, namely our sopranos Jan and Pat, Margaret our contralto, Jonathan and myself on piano, a violinist, and Paul on clarinet. Jonathan and I shared two of the impromptus and combined for a piano duet while the vocal soloists contributed lieder, including the always popular *Trout*. For the grand finale Paul, Pat and I combined for *The Shepherd on the Rock*, a large-scale song with a brilliant clarinet obbligato.

That autumn I joined the weekly piano class of Katharina Wolpe at Morley College, a further education establishment in South London renowned for its musical pedigree. Holst and Tippett had taught there. It is fascinating to reflect on how much Ricci and Katharina had in common. Both lived in Hampstead. Katharina's spacious house in Well Walk was a few yards from the Heath. It was home not just to several grand pianos but at any one time to a collection of orphaned cats, often with injuries, whom she had taken under her wing. The cats always formed part of the audience when she invited her class members to her home for an informal concert and afternoon tea. Ricci and Katharina were both born in Vienna and were refugees from the Nazis. Both travelled widely before settling in London. For both, music was the inner home which took the place of the external one they had lost, and there was therefore a special intensity in their commitment to it. Katharina has been quoted as saying that she did not feel like a stateless refugee because she had Schubert.

Of the two, Katharina's life was the more colourful. She moved throughout Europe, working as a cleaner, waitress, model and singer before being recognised for her pianistic abilities. To a large extent she was self-taught and discovered her own ways of learning and teaching. There was a deep and passionate eloquence to her playing, especially of Schubert, whose dark side she would always capture. But there was a lighter side to her. She had mentioned in class her admiration for the jazz pianist, Erroll Garner. When once she was absent from the college through sickness I sent her a gift of a compact disc of Garner's famous live album, *Concert by the Sea*. She wrote back to me: 'Nothing could have given me more pleasure than the Garner CD, which I have been playing most of the time since its arrival. I really do think he is a genius and I have never heard a pianist who has such complete independence of hands, and that's just for starters, not to mention his fantasy, imagination and beautiful sound.' I agree with every word. It has always been one of my favourite piano recordings.

Exceptionally, she was as at home with the music of

Berg, Schoenberg and Webern, the so-called Second Viennese School, as with the classics. Her breakthrough had come when she learned the Schoenberg concerto at short notice. People use many different words to describe the music of Schoenberg, not all of them complimentary. She is the only one I can recall who called it 'gorgeous.' A salutary reminder to listen to his music as music and not as examples of a system. Let her develop her thoughts on this subject in her own words, from the sleeve notes to her 1991 recording of the complete solo piano music (Symposium, 1107): 'It was inevitable that the extended chromaticism of the 1900s would eventually lead to the democratisation of the twelve chromatic steps in the octave that came to be called twelve-tone composition. It would have been better for Schoenberg had he either not noticed or not mentioned this; then the whole twelve-tone chimera would never have raised its head. Even so it is a mystery why this became such an issue: never before had people been so inordinately interested in the purely technical and personal matter of how a composer translated his vision into reality rather than what that vision was...To my mind he is the greatest composer of his era and all we have to do is to stop talking and listen and listen again.'

Listen and listen again. Very wise and important words. Though for those who with the best will in the world find such listening difficult I would like to add a suggestion of my own, one of which I think Katharina would have approved. I want to make a compare and contrast point about two composers who to the best of my knowledge have rarely if ever been brought together in the same sentence, namely Schoenberg and Mozart. Surely no two composers could be more different. What have they possibly got in common? What I believe they have in common is the need for the listener to devote full attention to the underlying meaning rather than the surface sound of their music, which is essentially what Katharina is saying in the passage just quoted. Schoenberg's sound is still widely regarded, sometimes but by no means always with justification, as difficult so we do not try to listen to what he is saying. Mozart on the other hand mostly wrote within the conventions of his day, which called for easy listening. So his deeper meanings passed over the heads of his contemporaries, as they still tend to do today. If we are repelled by Schoenberg's sound but charmed by Mozart's we are doing neither composer justice. A useful maxim might be to listen to Schoenberg as if he were Mozart and to Mozart as if he were Schoenberg.

Though Ricci and Katharina knew each other, they were not friends as far as I could tell. Indeed, Ricci seemed rather taken aback to learn that I had signed on for Katharina's class at Morley College. Perhaps their lives and their backgrounds were too similar and their personalities too strong, forged in adversity as they were, to be able to accommodate each other in friendship, though each had a wide circle of devoted friends.

Morley College runs a number of piano classes at different levels, all organised on the master-class principle. Each week some class members play one piece each and then the tutor comments on the music and the performance, with other members joining in the discussion. It is an excellent way to learn not only how to present a piece to a small and well-informed audience but also to observe a great teacher in action. Katharina was certainly that, original and inspiring, always willing to impart the secrets she had learned for herself on her long and difficult journey.

The first piece I played for her in the class was 'the Brahms.' While Ricci had focussed my attention on bringing out the passion and the drama in the piece, especially towards the end, Katharina's particular interest was in the way I was playing a very quiet section in the middle. Put simply, I was playing it much too loudly. 'Play it again,' she said, 'and this time try to lose about half the notes.' I did so, not actually losing any notes but achieving the desired sound level. I wonder who had taught her that trick, or if indeed she had found it for herself. On a later occasion, I played for her the Prelude in G sharp minor by Rachmaninov. I was having difficulty with a passage where chords were spread widely. She advised me to rearrange one chord so that the same number of notes making up the same harmony were within reach of my hand span. 'Do you want to be the only pianist in the world who tries to play exactly what Rachmaninov has written?' she asked me. It is of course well known that that composer, one of the greatest pianists who ever lived, had exceptionally large hands. It was a perfect illustration of one of her favourite maxims: if you have a technical problem, find a musical solution. This has come to my aid many times.

Generally I would not take a piece to the class until I had done the initial work with Ricci. Sometimes Katharina would have a different view of a piece from Ricci's. That in itself was a useful lesson. However well-informed any teacher's view on a point of interpretation may be, it will not be shared by everybody. At the end of the day you need to make up your own mind, so long as you have taken into account all the relevant considerations. There was a danger I was able to observe with each of these two great teachers, that of pupil over-dependence. Having both of them teach me almost simultaneously, I was able to avoid this danger. But still Ricci was uneasy, and that perhaps should have been a sign of problems that lay ahead in our relationship.

The Morley class was friendly and good-humoured. I was only really nervous on one occasion. One of the new class members was a large Polish lady, fiercely proud of her country's heritage in the music of Chopin and particularly in the mazurkas. She joined after I had started to prepare a mazurka for Katharina. When it was my turn to play, the Polish lady stood up and pronounced in her thick accent ringing around the room, 'I want to hear the mazurka.' She pronounced the word with heavy Polish intonation and several more syllables than we use in English. I recalled how jealously Polish people guard what they see as their national spirit embodied in this particular art form. I need not have worried. After I had played she was warmth and generosity itself.

In the autumn a new venue became available for our activities. With the temporary closure of St John's for repairs, the choir had secured the services of a smaller church nearer to the office in which to rehearse. This was called St Matthew's at the Elephant, a perhaps less than picturesque title but one which simply reflected its location near the busy Elephant and Castle roundabout. The church organised a service in memory of Diana, Princess of Wales, and invited the choir to take part. There was a very serviceable Bechstein grand, so I offered to contribute

Mozart's Adagio, as I had at the memorial concert for Colm.

St Matthew's is a small modern church, an intimate space, well-lit with excellent acoustics. In all those respects it is the opposite of St John's. I could not help thinking even as early as the service itself what a perfect venue it would make for chamber music and recitals. With the connection between the church and our music society already established I decided to contact the church's director of music, Stuart Whatton, to see if they would be interested in becoming a host venue for lunchtime music, as several local churches already were.

Stuart was yet another musical civil servant, in one of the central departments, and had a growing reputation as an organist. I later heard him give some outstanding recitals in City churches, including one at St Stephen Walbrook, where he was introduced by the Reverend Chad Varah, founder of the Samaritans. Varah was then well into his eighties and would not retire until he was ninety-two. Stuart and I met to discuss the arrangements. As a good civil servant he was anxious to work through all the details and possible problems but I could tell he was enthusiastic. The proposal needed to be ratified by what he solemnly called 'the Church Fathers', but their agreement to a series of monthly concerts was soon forthcoming. Paul and I put on the inaugural concert in the series that November.

I found the venue much more congenial than either the atrium or St John's. The atrium was a busy space full of echoes through which people were constantly moving in the background. St John's is a beautiful church but more suitable for big choirs or orchestras. At St Matthew's, intimate communication was not only possible but positively invited. It would perfectly suit an idea which had been forming in my mind since I had begun my time with Ricci, that of performing my first ever solo recital.

I arranged to play the recital there the following May. I opened with what that great Soviet pianist Emil Gilels would have called a bouquet of Scarlatti sonatas, then the Schubert A flat Impromptu which had first opened my ears to Schubert when I was twelve. At the end came the Chopin D flat Nocturne and Liszt's *Widmung*. In the middle, providing the centre of gravity, was of course 'the Brahms.' I played an early Chopin mazurka as an encore. The recital was well attended both by local people and members of staff from the office. Ricci came as well, braving the wilds of South London away from her comfort zone of Hampstead. The reception was enthusiastic. Ricci was delighted, sending me a letter the next day to say the recital had been 'splendid, and full of wonderful surprises.'

I repeated some of the programme the following August at St John's, adding another Scarlatti and the G flat Impromptu of Schubert, and replacing the Brahms and the Liszt with Chopin mazurkas and the Fantasy-Impromptu. Concerts at St John's were advertised in a lively weekly what's-on journal called *Time Out*. I was slightly perturbed to read in the entry for my recital that 'Keith Jacobsen tickles the ivories' (that phrase again!). I sensed a hint that neither I nor the event were to be taken seriously. Should I take offence and complain? Then I saw in the same issue that Alfred Brendel was due to perform at the Royal Festival Hall later that week. According to the advertisement for that event, 'nobody tickles the ivories more beautifully than Alfred Brendel.' Quite so. Well, if Brendel could tickle ivories so could I.

Meanwhile we continued with our performances in the atrium and at St Matthew's. Jonathan played a solo recital at St Matthew's in April including Schumann's complete *Scenes from Childhood.* Jan and I put on a programme of English song there in June. The summer concert in the atrium featured the usual mix of light and classical with a 'grand Puccini finale', where Pat and one of our tenors, Keith, gave a moving account of the final scene of the first Act of *La Boheme.* By September we had added a cellist, Ruth, to our ranks. We put on a trio concert at St Matthew's in September, including Beethoven's trio in B flat opus 11. This is usually played as a standard piano trio with violin and cello. We were pleased to be able to present it with cello and clarinet, as Beethoven originally intended.

With two solo recitals under my belt I was gaining valuable experience and confidence as a soloist. The next instrumental and piano competition was scheduled for the following October and I was sure that this time there would be a better outcome.

Sadly, that did not prove to be the case. The event took place at the Leeds College of Music, with two adjudicators provided by the college. I had chosen to play two pieces from my May programme, a Scarlatti Sonata in B minor and, of course, 'the Brahms.' I was the last to play. During the break while we awaited the results, I was congratulated by some of the other participants, and also by Sir Geoffrey Otton, a Permanent Secretary who was then chair of the organising society (its official full title was the Health and Social Security Sports and Recreation Association,

HASSRA for short). Sir Geoffrey told me he had found my playing of the Brahms 'stunning.'

However if I had managed to communicate to at least some of those present, that did not extend as far as the adjudicators, whose manner was grim and surly. First of all, they criticised my choice of Scarlatti, who in their view should only be played on a harpsichord. If played on a piano, it should not have any of the tonal shading which only the piano can produce. I have to say that that was the only time I have heard anyone, let alone a professional musician, express that absurd point of view. They had obviously never heard Scarlatti played by Gilels or Horowitz or any other of the numerous pianists for whom he is staple fare. They had heard that Scarlatti wrote for the harpsichord, clearly not knowing that he had access to early pianos at the Spanish court where he worked and could well have intended his piece for such an instrument. In any case, what they also did not know is that Scarlatti has been an integral part of the pianist's repertoire since Chopin's enthusiastic advocacy. Any pianist tackling his music will use the resources of the piano to bring out the extraordinary range of colours contained in the music. The only exception would be the sustaining pedal, which certainly can be used but with restraint and discretion. I assume the embargo of these adjudicators would also have extended to all the keyboard music of J. S. Bach. It would, to say the least, have been helpful to have known their views in advance.

The best they could say about 'the Brahms' was that I 'seemed to know where the piece was going' (to the end??) and commended my use of arm weight. About the piece itself as music or my interpretation they had nothing to say. Finally, one of them made a snide comment about the fact that I had played from memory. I was the only one who had done so, not to show the others up but because I was more comfortable without the score before my eyes and without the distraction of a page-turner waiting beside me for the signal to turn.

On later reflection I was certain that neither of them knew my pieces at all. They were not classical pianists. One taught jazz and the other was a cellist. My main mistake was in the choice of repertoire. I had not chosen entertaining pieces, as the winners had. Both of mine were in minor keys. 'The Brahms' ends tragically, not what they wanted to hear after a long day. But it was painful and humiliating to hear misinformed comments like these announced to an audience. This is one of a number of areas where amateur pianists have it worse than professionals. To the best of my knowledge, in no professional competition do the adjudicators read out their adverse comments to the audience. While the outcome was not in itself a setback, a competition prize being ephemeral, it did have one sad result. I have not touched 'the Brahms' since, nor any Scarlatti.

I later secured a commitment from Sir Geoffrey that future HASSRA piano competitions would be judged by professional pianists or teachers with a professional background as pianists. But the whole fiasco did raise the question, which I also put to Sir Geoffrey, as to whether a competition is the best way to showcase the musical talent within the department. The adjudication of both of the competitions I had entered had been marred by subjectivity and lack of clear criteria. It is fine to award cups to those who win races by crossing a line ahead of others, but hardly to those who for obscure reasons find favour with at best unsympathetic and at worst unqualified adjudicators. Surely when it comes to music something more like a festival, where participants are not set against each other, would be far preferable.

Again I had cause to wonder about the ethical standards of professional musicians who take on the role of adjudicating the work of amateurs without the necessary commitment to fairness, impartiality and, in this case, without even the relevant knowledge and background. It would surely take a much larger fee than the one they earned on this occasion to make it worthwhile selling their souls in that way.

That up and down year ended in the freezer. Almost literally. Ricci's end of year pupils' concert took place on a freezing December Sunday afternoon at the Belsize Music Rooms. There was a flicker of heating available but I suspect the owner was simply too mean to heat the space properly. There seemed no way to generate more warmth except through the music. My hands are sensitive to cold and I came very close indeed to walking out. The only reason I did not leave was that I did not want to let Ricci down. I was scheduled to play the Mendelssohn Rondo Capriccioso, which requires fingers in good condition, not stiff ones straight out of the icebox. I sat in coat and gloves until my turn, only taking them off at the very last moment. I managed to get through the piece. I then had just enough movement of blood through the fingers to join another of her pupils on a second piano in the slow movement of

Mozart's G Major Piano Concerto. It was another occasion when I thought to myself that professional performers never have to put up with anything like that. But maybe they sometimes do. Richter's tours of remote towns in Siberia come to mind.

The next year, 1999, was to prove momentous in a number of ways. Before I get to it, I need to retrace my steps and catch up on family history.

THIRTEEN

ENDINGS

SIR THOMAS MORE:
Why not be a teacher? You'd be a fine teacher;
perhaps a great one.
RICHARD RICH:
If I was, who would know it?
SIR THOMAS MORE:
You; your pupils; your friends; God. Not a bad
public, that.
Robert Bolt, *A Man for all Seasons*

After my father's heart attack, my mother had to accept that she could make no further visits to her American relatives. She had often urged me to visit them and I agreed to do so some time in the mid-1980s. They were based in Philadelphia. I took in the opportunity to visit Washington and New York as well. My relatives were welcoming, though I was unable to endorse my mother's verdict of America as a land flowing with milk and honey for all its inhabitants. I have never returned.

I brought back with me a particular musical memory from New York. Exploring Central Park on my own I found myself close to the huge Cathedral of St John the Divine. I entered to find it dark and deserted, or so I thought at first. There were flowers placed at the end of each pew, as if in readiness for a service later that day. I sat down. Then I heard from the organ loft the sounds of a glorious voice singing Purcell's *Dido's Lament*. The voice was in the soprano range though it defied that sort of easy classification. It was so reminiscent of the voice of Jessye Norman that I had to sit and listen, spellbound. She has a great career ahead of her, whoever she is, I thought. I continued to listen. The organist was accompanying her, though I could see neither performer. I was still as far as I could tell the only other person in that huge space. Yet the doors had been open and I had seen no notice forbidding entry. I continued to listen and was no longer in any doubt. It *was* Jessye Norman. That was confirmed a few moments later when she stopped singing. A man in the loft asked her if she was comfortably positioned or wanted to try somewhere else. He had addressed her as Miss Norman. I waited until the end of the rehearsal, for such it clearly was, then tiptoed out. I felt blessed. Though she had not known, and if she had I might have been asked to leave, I had by chance attended a performance by the legendary singer just for me. I have never been able to hear that music since without recalling that occasion.

The time when my parents could take holidays together and visit their holiday flat in Tenerife was short-lived. While Tenerife suited my father's declining health by keeping him away from British winters, the sun and relaxed atmosphere could not mask the continuing and never confronted tensions between them. I visited them once while they were there. My mother was increasingly irritated with the Spanish habit of speaking Spanish, and annoyed with the time it took to get repairs done to her cooker. My father took petulant umbrage when a travel company made a late alteration to the itinerary of a boat tour we were due to take. He sulked and refused to come along (the trip was a delight). In their childishness and selfishness they seemed to have forgotten the sacrifices Neil had made to get them the luxury of a holiday home in the sun. When my father fell ill there on a later visit they decided they would never return. The flat was put up for sale.

Back home, things did not improve, my mother becoming increasingly resentful of my father's growing dependence on her. Absurdly, she demanded changes in his behaviour and attitude he could never have delivered even when in good health. On my visits there I sometimes brought tapes of music I thought he would enjoy, especially of Schubert songs. The tape I had made of my own playing had long since left the house. My mother had sent it off to various relatives, still never missing any opportunity for reflected glory. It had apparently never occurred to her that I had made it for him and it was not hers to dispose of as she wished. She had of course long since ensured there would be no more live music in the house. My father must have realised he did not have long to live. He asked me to send him a tape of Tchaikovsky's *Pathétique* Symphony, always one of his favourite pieces. By then he must have seen it as a personal requiem. But why that most emotional of music for this apparently least emotional of men? It is not the paradox it seems at first. He was not unemotional, quite the contrary. But he needed the music of a man who wore his heart on his sleeve to find some expression and release for the emotions he had always kept hidden.

The saddest thing about my father's final years was not his physical decline but the loss of his belief in the values by which he had lived, those for which I had most admired and respected him. He had found teaching an increasing burden in the years before his heart attack, rejecting innovations in the practice and conduct of his profession which he regarded as trendy and counterproductive. His relations with his headmaster, never easy, became ever more sour. But more distressing was his disaffection with the whole idea of teaching.

Now I have always held the teaching profession in the highest regard. I revered those of my own teachers who had inculcated in me a love and knowledge not just of music but of language and literature. I will always regard the modest and self-effacing Christian Brother who taught us English literature in the sixth form, Brother Carey, as one of the greatest men I have ever met. Nobody could surpass his understanding of the works of Shakespeare and the great English novelists and poets or his ability to communicate his love of them. Never once in class did he raise his voice or impose any form of punishment. His quiet voice, rich in wisdom and knowledge, held us spellbound, not an easy thing for a class of restless teenagers. I will always cherish his memory in particular for his unexpected choice of John Steinbeck's *The Grapes of Wrath* as one of our set books for A-level. It is one of the greatest novels of the twentieth century, a work of blazing anger and compassion for the plight of the dustbowl farmers of Oklahoma forced out of their homes and encountering as refugees in California the hostility reserved for despised outsiders. Why an unexpected choice? The book was always controversial not just for its radicalism but for the earthy realism of its language and treatment of sexuality. A Christian Brother might have been expected to make a safer choice, from the mainstream tradition of the English novel. But Brother Carey was not in the least daunted or embarrassed. He conveyed to us all the book's richness of language and structure and its deep humanity. And he was able to bring to it a perspective not available to many readers, an understanding of how deeply Steinbeck was influenced by the Bible.

Brother Carey enriched my life beyond measure and he was not the only teacher in my school of whom that was true. My father taught in an even more challenging environment, which made his achievements all the more remarkable. I know there are many of his former pupils still alive who have every reason to be grateful for the life chances he gave them. But in his final years he took no pride or satisfaction in what he had done. He caught, as one catches a virus, my mother's selfish materialism and her envy of all those who were better off. He said he wished he had never become a teacher but had gone into something more lucrative such as dentistry, a career for which he would never have had the aptitude or the personality. Nor would he have known what to do with the ample material rewards available to practitioners of that profession. He spoke with envy of a dentist he knew who owned a large house and a yacht. What use would a yacht have been to him, who had no interest in sailing? If he had wanted a more lucrative career to do more for his family, that maybe would have been an acceptable form of regret. But by then he spoke only in terms of himself. Though I know I would never have lasted more than a few seconds in front of a form class, I had formed an ambition in my middle years to take up teaching in my own way when or if the chance arose. It was his example which helped to inspire me to that ambition. But the flame of that example and the beliefs which had kept it alive had expired. My parents, having started off their marriage life at opposite ends of the universe in terms of values, finally came together, sadly at her end of the spectrum.

In some ways my father represented at an individual level trends clearly visible in wider society over the period of his life. I will make no secret of the fact that they are trends I deplore. He was, I was given to understand, sympathetic to communism in his youth, no doubt as were many young people of his generation, before disillusionment with its external manifestations set in. After the war he shared the idealism which put the post-war Labour Government into power and saw the birth of the welfare state and National Health Service. There then followed a long steady move to the political right. The Daily Express became his regular source of their version of 'news', all of which he swallowed without question. He loathed the Labour Government of the late 1960s and all its social reforms. Long before Thatcher pronounced her immortal words he decided there was no such thing as society. Neil took up the mantle of his individualism in an even more extreme form, resenting any form of state or governmental intrusion into the business of making his fortune. He paid taxes with great reluctance and in as small a measure as possible. How ironic (again!) that he is spending his declining days wholly supported by the state and funded by the taxpayer.

In February 1993, by then extremely weak, my father suffered the latest of a number of falls in the house. Those called to attend him suggested he be taken to hospital. But he knew his time had come and he preferred to die at home. At last he was able to say what it was he wanted, or rather what he did not want, which was to die in hospital. Surprisingly for a man who had always given every appearance of hating his life, he had long feared death and fought against it. Now at last he was able to accept the longstanding invitation to peace from the herald who had stood at his elbow during all those long years of illness. His heart gave way a few hours later. In a final ironic twist of the knife, my mother persuaded her local parish priest to give him a Catholic funeral, the form of send-off this confirmed atheist would have detested most of all.

That was the year I remarried, as we have seen. Neil also married in the same year, breaking his longstanding pledge to remain a bachelor. Relations between him and my parents had become distinctly cooler in recent years. He must have resented their ingratitude for what he had done for them. Nor did they ever show the slightest understanding of the adverse changes in his personality wrought by the pressures they had put on him, though to me those changes were obvious and tragic. He nevertheless did what he could for her, as her own health as a widow declined rapidly.

She was desperate to leave the house. It had been a constant feature of her life that wherever she found herself she had always wanted to move elsewhere, failing to realise she would only take her anger and bitterness with her. Neil arranged for her to move to a newly-built flat in Windsor, a very long way from her native Liverpool. Her only association with Windsor was that one of Neil's former girlfriends, Andrea, lived near there. Andrea had found the accommodation and suggested it might be suitable. She had been fond of our mother and no doubt was acting with the best of intentions. But the move was to prove a disastrous error.

Neil put the family home on the market. He gave the go-ahead to a local dealer and odd job man to clear out the entire remaining contents of the house and pocket whatever he might make from selling them. This included not only furniture but all of my books, manuscripts and records which were still there, worthless to the dealer but a priceless treasure to me. Also gone was my academic dress, consisting of cap and gown. The gown was especially precious to me because it was not the gown I had first worn at college. It was a scholar's gown, which I became entitled to wear only after my tutors had nominated me for an honorary scholarship in my third year, a rare privilege. As it was honorary, the award carried no financial benefit but the Master of the college, Alan Bullock, was kind enough to send me a cheque to cover the cost of buying the gown. So its value and importance to me far outweighed any question of its monetary worth. I never had the chance to save any of these possessions. I only found out about the clearout after it had happened. Neil no doubt saw it as the easiest and quickest way to clear away his painful memories of times in that house, a sort of mental cleansing of the Augean stables.

If only it were that simple, I might have told him though by then I saw no point. In time he would realise it for himself. For me, the clearout meant the loss of much that had helped me to cope with those difficult times.

My mother's new accommodation was sheltered but still required a degree of independence of which she was no longer capable. I thought at the time that it was a huge mistake, contrary not only to common sense but to accepted professional advice on coping with dementia, to remove her from a familiar environment when her memories were already fading. It was for example impossible for her to learn to use an electric cooker for the first time in her life, having always been used to a gas one. I recall a telephone call from her to me from the new flat, soon after her move there, in which she complained that Neil 'had put her into an old people's home.' It was one of the most grotesque and wounding of all her distortions. She owned the flat. Neil had purchased it for her. It did not remotely resemble an old people's home except that fellow residents tended to be elderly and there was a warden on hand to keep an eye on them and deal with their requirements. What could I have said to her? 'Neil bought the flat for you because you insisted on it. Moreover he has totally screwed up his own life in a vain effort to please you, you ungrateful old ...' The word I would probably have used if I had said any of this would have been the one preferred by my generous-minded Aunt Fiona: '... so-and-so.' But I did not waste my breath. We only have so much breath in life and I had wasted too much on her as it was.

She soon moved again and this time it was indeed to an old people's home, or rather a secure nursing home in the

Midlands. She died there a few years later, still full of that same anger and bitterness but now unable to remember whence they came or any of the good times in her life. There had been good times. During her extravert phases she could readily attract other women to her as friends, though with men she always kept a cautious distance, and some of those friendships lasted for years. But each of them eventually failed as a result of her chronic habits of envy and of taking offence at any slight, real or imaginary. And once offence was taken it would be nurtured for life.

The loneliness of both my parents had from early on taken a physical as well as a mental form. Her distrust of men and longing for a more rewarding form of female companionship than her sisters were ever able to provide must have had their origins in early experiences of which she never spoke. Once her family was complete, after my birth, my parents used no form of contraception other than abstinence, though both were only just into their thirties. Neither had affairs or contemplated divorce, though only my mother had an ostensibly religious justification for this self-repression. The Catholic Church forbids divorce, all sexual relationships outside marriage and all so-called 'artificial' means of contraception, including the pill, condoms or any form of cap or IUD. My father was not subject to any such external constraints. But he never showed any apparent interest of a sexual nature in women or girls, though his generally low regard for the opposite sex would not in itself have precluded such interest. He may have been homosexual by nature, notwithstanding, or perhaps consistent with, his regular outbursts of homophobia and his exaggerated aura of traditional masculinity. But if so, that aspect of his personality would have remained as suppressed as any other, maybe unacknowledged even to himself. He may have been at some level aware of it at the time of his marriage, in common with those thousands of men for whom in those dangerous times marriage provided a protection from suspicion. It is a bizarre thought, but a very real possibility, that Neil and I were only brought into the world to provide him with cover against the prejudices of the society of the time. But we would by no means have been the only ones of which that was true.

Did marriage also provide protection for our mother? If he was indeed a covert homosexual, did she realise it and if so when? I have described their marriage as loveless, as it was in any normal sense of the word. But loveless marriages often have compensating factors which sustain them, such as wealth or at least material security. Their marriage, constantly frayed as it was by persistent financial insecurity, offered no such compensation. I have speculated on what it might have offered our father, castigation for his survivor guilt, protection from questions, internal or external, about his own sexual nature. For her, she would have known at least instinctively that her choice was safe, protecting her from forms of male aggressiveness or even just the attention of physical attraction and closeness which at the deepest level she had learned or been taught to fear.

But there would be a price to pay for that safety. Once Neil and I had emerged from the awkwardness of early adolescence, our complexions cleared and our physiques developed by regular games of squash and tennis, she began to replace her earlier cold distance, and in my case an

247

unmistakeable sense of physical disgust, with a physical interest which can most tactfully be described as inappropriate. We were beginning to be men, but in her eyes we were 'safe' men, products of her own womb and thus her possessions, no danger to her, there to meet her unmet needs. But of course we could hardly react other than with revulsion, which served only to accentuate her loneliness and constant sense of betrayal. Always lacking insight into her actions and their consequences, and having done all she could over the years to create distance between herself and her husband and children, she could yet complain about that distance as if it were our fault that she did not spend her middle to late years comforted by the warmth of family love. Though she died in the professionally caring environment of her nursing home, in a very real sense she died alone.

I could not grieve for my parents as they were, though I did grieve for the lives they could and should have had if they had made different choices. It was never inevitable that they would always carry with them the shadows of anger and self-pity which they hung over the lives of Neil and myself. For me the process of separation and self-definition which is a universal part of growing up and reaching adulthood should not have taken so long or been so painful. At the cost of much anguish, guilt and soul-searching I did eventually free myself from my mother's control and the spectre of my father's nihilism. Ironically – that word again – it was the music which had been so much part of my mother's means of control which in the end provided me with the means for escape. Neil never did fully escape, lacking sufficient sense of an identity separate from that which both parents defined for him. For me the end of the process of separation meant that I could never see my parents other than as strangers who could never know or understand me any more than I could fully know or understand them. Quite a few of my mother's nephews and nieces had received a kindness and concern from her she had never been able to show her immediate family, though of course those relatives had their own families and could not reciprocate with the attention she would have wished or expected. I knew some of them would be at her funeral. I did not want to hear them praise her, however much the praises were justified in their eyes. I did not go to the funeral.

Her dream that Neil would have supported our parents from the income of his law practice could never have been, even if he had not married and had children of his own. He would divorce as well, while his business went much the same way as our mother's. In her tiny shop she had charged five shillings for a shampoo and set and a guinea for a perm, a few pounds in the till at the end of the day. In comparison huge sums of money went through his business each day. But the final result was the same. Nothing left, after depression and alcohol abuse had taken their toll. Even if she had lived to see it with her own eyes she would not have believed it. Or maybe she would. Maybe she would have been proud. After all, slow self-destruction through alcohol is a traditionally hyper-masculine way to end your days, far better than to go gently into that good night. By comparison our father's weekly pint or two with his mates in the pub was the sign of a wimp rather than the real man he always held himself out to be.

I hardly need to spell out the fact that family life as I was growing up was very difficult. Music provided an emotional world into which I could escape. But that does not fully explain why I continued to pursue my pianistic interests for so long, in such depth and in so many different contexts, continuing down to this day (I am now in my seventies). With time and perspective to reflect on this I have concluded that the clue is in the word 'family.' It was never enough for me to take solitary refuge in music, as many do and are content in so doing. For me music was a way to find alternative families. That would explain why when still very young I would go on long bus-trips on my own to visit my musical Aunt Ida, and later why so many of my friendships and associations were based on music, as with the chamber groups in college and the numerous forms of collaborative music making in the office. Morley College, the London Piano Circle, the circle of Ricci's pupils, and, as will be seen, the various groups and classes I attended at a piano summer school, all provided an opportunity for sharing, collaboration and reaching out to an audience, however small. It is no exaggeration to say that these experiences provided, even if briefly, a family sense of security which had never been there in the past.

Others have noted the sense of family which derives from close musical association. String quartets must be very 'familiar' with it. Once when I was attending Andrew Ball's class at summer school a rather heated disagreement broke out between two of the class members. The class had had more or less the same membership for a number of years and we all knew each other well. Andrew, noted for his wit and wisdom as well as his brilliant musicality, commented, 'We're a family here and families have their differences from time to time.' I have no doubt both Ricci and Katharina saw their classes and groups of pupils as to some extent replacing the early family life which had been disrupted in ways far more traumatic than any which had befallen me.

So does this idea of family replacement explain my lifelong musical obsession and the various paths along which it took me? No, not wholly. It is a start, but other factors played a role. My mother's attitude to my development was, to say the least, ambivalent. In my early years of learning, as we have seen, she insisted that I devote time for practice. But in later years she did not like to hear me practise. She appeared to think that if I needed to practise I could not really be any good after all. By then she could no longer use my musical talent as an extension of herself, as she had also used my and Neil's successes in other fields. Her real fear was that my continuing development would take me down paths which would remove me from her sphere of control. Which, of course, is what inevitably happened. This would lend a certain logic to her brutal decision to remove the piano from the house. My father could certainly take pride in what I achieved, but could also appreciate what I played as music for its own sake, something my mother never could.

My attempt to restore something like direct musical communication between my father and myself by recording and sending him that tape proved abortive when that too left the house. He could of course have found music he liked on the radio, or I could have sent him more commercial tapes I thought he would enjoy. But by recording my own playing

I had intended another, perhaps deeply uncomfortable message for him: that releasing and expressing emotion through music never had the attendant dangers he always feared, that a family or group with its own music-making, whatever tensions may be tearing at its heart, is the richer for it. It would be my last attempt to communicate with him. I will never know if that message got through before the tape went on its way for a purpose for which it was never intended. There would have been time enough, but more than time would have been needed. A gateway to the heart which had remained closed for far too long would have had to open, just a little, just for a moment. It is at least possible that it did.

I can never know, any more than I ever really knew anything about him. At some time in his youth or early adulthood, as I have observed earlier, he had switched off the taps that feed the soul. I was referring then to literature and music. What of love? What of friendship? Towards his mother and sister, both admirable and loveable people, he showed no affection, only a sense of duty to the former. Towards his own family he was for the most part cold and distant, anger erupting occasionally and with frequent misdirection. To Neil and myself he could respond with pride but that always came at the price of our achievements, a price that called for regular payments. He had had a close childhood friend, the son of a neighbour in Walton. They had explored North Wales together. And he always had his regular drinking mates. But about all of them, family and the rest, he could be critical, often cruelly, though never to their faces. I shudder to think what he said about me in my absence. His childhood friend, though brought up in even greater poverty than he had been, went on to have a very successful career in the civil service unions. Jealousy of that success would erode and finally end that friendship. He made no new friends at all during his adult life. He did not mix socially with any of his teacher colleagues and never spoke of them, always excepting his headmaster, whom he hated and despised. As for his two regular drinking mates, they were lively, loud, extravert, hyper-masculine, self-made, successful men, a good decade younger than he was. They were good-natured and amusing company, though my mother disliked them, finding probably that they reminded her too much of her overbearing father and brothers. For my father they were a mirror into which, once a week in their favourite pub, he could look and see himself as he wished he might have been, not as he knew he really was. Close friends they certainly were not. They were of a different generation and mindset. To nobody was he close, in nobody did he confide. Of all the people with whom I have come into contact in my entire life he was the one I knew and understood least. Small consolation that nobody else knew or understood him, either.

FOURTEEN

CHUTZPAH

At the start of 1999 we were delighted to take delivery of a new grand piano at home, our first such purchase. I say 'our' purchase because Valerie and I shared the cost. We have since had light-hearted conversations – at least, I think they are light-hearted – as to what would happen if we split up. Who would get what half of the piano and how would it be divided? Black keys for one and white for the other? Or the upper half for one and the lower one for the other? As for the cost, it was an excellent value Petrof, just under nine thousand pounds, from Jaques Samuel Pianos on Edgware Road. Terry Lewis, the managing director, whom I had got to know during the time when he ran the London Piano Circle, reduced the cost still further by taking my Kemble upright in a generous part exchange, and, even more generously, provided an excellent adjustable stool free of charge.

I had managed with the Kemble at home up until then, having access to the grand pianos at the office, Morley College and Ricci's. When I needed private practice on a grand I would hire a practice room at Jaques Samuel's. But since the Petrof entered our lives I have barely touched an upright. I sometimes wonder if I compromised too long to the detriment of my technique. Some uprights are on their own terms quite satisfactory in touch and sound quality and will do well enough when a grand is not a practicable proposition. The Kemble had served me well in my North London flat.

But for the serious pianist, regular access to a good quality grand is not a luxury. With an upright the pedals are usually located higher off the floor than with a grand. This is not only physically awkward, it also makes it hard to develop the heel-on-floor technique necessary for sensitive degrees of pedal depression, unless you have very long feet and arms, and impossible to achieve such special effects as rapid changes and half-pedalling. The so-called 'soft pedal' mechanism on an upright whereby the hammers are moved closer to the strings is far inferior to that of the grand, where the keyboard moves laterally to enable only two of the three strings per note to be struck. I did not really begin to develop a properly refined pedal technique until I had left uprights behind me. On an upright the music stand will be lower, which suits some but makes it difficult when they come to play on a grand. But above all a grand has a range of sound sensitivity even the best uprights cannot achieve. The soundboard of a grand is horizontal and spread out before you as you play, letting the whole instrument resonate, especially if you lift the lid. It sends the sound out into the room, helped there by the angle of the lid. Even if you leave the lid closed the sound board remains exposed below. On an upright the vertical soundboard is imprisoned within the structure. Lifting the lid only sends the sound upwards. It is rather like the old coal fires which sent most of the heat up the chimney. (You could of course make the best of a bad job, take the whole front off your upright, harden the hammers, let the string get out of tune and become a honky-tonk pianist! It's an art form in its own right.)

My reference above to hiring a practice room at Jaques Samuel Pianos has reminded me of something which happened during one of those practice sessions. When you have paid your hire fee for an hour's practice you do not expect to be disturbed. I was therefore rather annoyed when, halfway through my session on a Bach fugue, someone burst in. I was on the point of remonstrating with him when I realised I knew who it was, though I had never met him or seen him play. It was the Australian pianist, David Helfgott, who was in London preparing for a performance at the Royal Albert Hall of Rachmaninov's third piano concerto. He was by then world famous as a result of the film *Shine*, in which he was portrayed by Geoffrey Rush. The film portrays in harrowing detail Helfgott's descent into mental illness and his slow and inspiring recovery. We chatted for a while. He was a delight to meet, full of manic charm and energy. I had seen the film. The accuracy of Rush's portrayal I can only describe as uncanny. At one point he looked at the music on my stand and saw what I was attempting to play. 'Ah yes,' he said. 'Chutzpah, chutzpah, that's what you need.' With that he rushed off to resume his own practice.

That last remark from him – and I apologise for the chain of associations; normal service will be resumed shortly – reminds me of a story I like very much, though in no way can I vouch for its veracity. It concerns Mascagni, the composer of the popular one-act opera, *Cavalleria Rusticana*. At the time of the story Mascagni had already written the opera, which had brought him fame and secured a place for his melodies in the hearts and minds of all Italian music-lovers. One of those was an organ-grinder plying his trade in the street below Mascagni's lodgings. Unaware of who was listening in from above, he played an extract from the opera, repeatedly and far too slowly. At last Mascagni could bear it no longer. He went down to the street, told the organ grinder who he was, and showed him how the passage should go. Later, on returning from the shops, he was pleased to hear the organ grinder playing his music the right way. But he was taken aback to see that the organ grinder had placed a sign on his organ, 'Pupil of Mascagni'. Might those few words of encouragement in that practice room justify my advertising myself as a pupil of David Helfgott? After all, he had urged me to show chutzpah, and wasn't that exactly what the organ grinder had done?

Round about the time of the delivery of our new piano, tensions began to emerge in my relationship with Ricci. They were not just musical. She invited me to join her in a visit to the Royal Festival Hall to see Ivo Pogorelich give a Chopin recital. She knew him, having interviewed him and written an article about him. Pogorelich is surely the only pianist of the first rank to have been catapulted to fame as a result of having been eliminated from a major competition at an early stage, in this case the 1980 International Chopin Competition. Martha Argerich, a former winner of the competition, resigned from the jury, claiming bias on the part of other members and declaring that Pogorelich was a genius. I agree with her, though for some his genius is marred by excessive eccentricity. Afterwards we went backstage to meet him and get his autograph on our programmes. There was quite a bit of milling around and I saw that Ricci had inadvertently joined the queue at about the halfway point. I tried to guide her to the back of the queue, thinking perhaps that she might still not appreciate what a heinous crime queue-jumping is in this country. She failed to understand what I was trying to do and took serious offence. It would be some time before I would have a chance to explain to her.

In the meantime I was becoming aware of musical differences between us. I had long wanted to explore and learn some works by Haydn and Mozart. She was clearly unsympathetic not only to that repertoire but to my interest in it. It is worth pausing here to ask why that repertoire is so challenging, such that even virtuosos of the first rank often either shun it or struggle with it. It is not just a matter of technique. It is rather about those small quantity/high quality notes to which Schnabel famously referred. The pianos of Mozart and Haydn were not equipped for the heavy, pedalled sonorities of later instruments. Mozart's profound musical thoughts are often conveyed through single lines which must, in his own words, flow like oil, or, in the case of his slow movements, be shaped with all the refined loving care singers devote to his opera arias. Haydn, whose piano solo works are every bit as expressive as Mozart's and often more so, calls for minute attention to the details of phrasing and colour. Pedal in this music plays a vital but subordinate role and requires great subtlety to avoid blurring of musical lines. It cannot be relied on to boost sound or drive the music forward (or to hide mistakes!). Clarity, concentration of meaning and economy of means are the key features. There are those who believe that our techniques and our ears have become so immersed in the richer and louder sonorities of later music that we simply cannot now appreciate the solo piano music of Haydn and Mozart for the great art it really is, hearing it as thin and even trivial. I have heard even very fine pianists say that they believe Mozart is simply 'too difficult' and should be avoided. Sviatoslav Richter, one of the greatest virtuosos of all time, once asked in a television documentary, 'Can anyone play him well?'

Well, of course, there are pianists past and present who play him very well indeed. The greatest Mozart player I ever had the privilege to hear was Clifford Curzon. I was still at school when I saw him at the Phil give a sublime performance of the Concerto in A major, K.488. Among pianists still before the public, Mitsuko Uchida stands out as a profound interpreter of his music, digging deep into his emotional world and drawing her audiences into it. I do not agree Mozart should be avoided, or that we cannot now listen to him as he intended. But we have to work at it. Our ears do need adjustment, if only to screen out the sounds of later times and let the deep and rich meanings within the pure classical style come through.

For any pianist tempted to dismiss Mozart's piano writing as 'thin' and his emotional world as too polite I would always recommend his magnificent Fantasy in C minor, K475, sometimes but unnecessarily paired with his sonata in the same key. The Fantasy takes us through multiple keys, moods and emotional worlds in the way I am sure he would have improvised, a skill for which he was renowned in his lifetime. What I find particularly fascinating about this piece, quite apart from its technical and interpretative challenges, is that it ends in the same dark mood in which it begins. It is not the only time Mozart defies the convention of his day requiring even minor key pieces to end on a positive note.

Ricci would sometimes arrange for a group of her pupils to play informally at the house of Samir Saleh, another of her pupils. He had put at her disposal his excellent Bosendorfer piano and the beautifully furnished and spacious room in his Chelsea flat where it had pride of place. Samir is originally from Lebanon and a leading international jurist. An author and poet, he has a passionate love of literature and music, especially the music of Brahms. With one of these occasions coming up I told her that I wanted to play Haydn's late masterpiece, his Variations in F Minor (a work which like the Mozart Fantasy similarly defies the expectation of a happy ending). It still needed work, but I was sure an informal play-through among musical friends and colleagues would help. Ricci however vetoed my choice, telling me the piece was not ready even for informal exposure. I therefore boycotted the event, not wanting to choose another piece which might be even less ready. Our final split was inevitable and imminent. (I later discovered that Ricci fell out sooner or later with most of those of her adult pupils whom I knew personally, for a variety of reasons.)

There had certainly been misunderstandings between us but at the end there was no animosity. In the words of R. D. Laing, she had been a catalyst for me, freeing up my sound and enabling me to rediscover my communication abilities. I had had the joy of exploring and sharing some wonderful music with her. But after three years I needed a more patient and workmanlike focus on details of technique, tone and touch. Ricci was wonderful with the broad sweep of interpretation but rather impatient with detail. It was detail I now needed. Her own strong taste and preference was for the Romantic repertoire. I now wanted not to neglect that repertoire but to extend my own into the classical and beyond. Apart from Haydn and Mozart, there, waiting in the wings and waving to me not to forget him (as if I could), was J. S. Bach, my first and always greatest musical love. Indeed Bach was already firmly back on my radar screen, thanks to Katharina Wolpe and an extraordinary event she had organised at Morley College. That story will be taken up again later. Right then I knew I needed a new teacher. And, just as had happened with Ricci, the right teacher came along at just the right time.

INTERLUDE VIII

INSTINCT AND MEMORY

In this interlude I want to digress a little into the question of technique, not the basic technique set explored in the previous interludes, but the sort of instinctive technique which can operate right up to advanced levels. I will also examine the role of memory.

Playing 'by ear'

It is likely we all know someone who can play very well 'by ear', as it is commonly known. They have never learned to read music, and they may never have had a lesson in their lives. But they can hear something and instantly find the notes on the piano, if not all the notes actually heard then ones that can make up a convincing enough rendition. I believe that the so-called classically trained pianist will, if he or she is to be a convincing performer, always have a strong element of this 'natural' technique. For a full concert career playing classical music, this element will need to be married to a rigorous and continuous technical training. But in the case of some jazz pianists the ear will evolve all the technique they need. In the case of Errol Garner, for example, the marriage of ear and technique was so perfect as to enable a true giant of the piano to emerge.

How does this natural technique evolve? A good ear is the first prerequisite. It should be developed from the start by the child being sung to and then encouraged to sing. In my experience very young children need no encouragement to sing but they can certainly be discouraged. I was fortunate in that school and church provided intensive exposure to the singing of hymns and well-known songs. There is far less singing in schools now than when I was growing up and this is a national disgrace. When I started to teach I was shocked to find how few of my young pupils ever took part in singing at home or school. The value of this early experience is that it lays down neural pathways in the young brain which enable music to be heard internally. The transfer of this what I like to call an aural image to singing is usually easy and natural. It is less so when it comes to transfer to an instrument, where the sheer physical difficulty of producing a sound from a recalcitrant metal or wooden tube may prove an insuperable barrier. As we have seen, it is easy enough to get a noise of some sort out of a piano. But you do not need to be an experienced teacher or musician to tell the difference between a child who is trying to reproduce musical sounds heard in the head and one who is simply playing around with what may seem to the child (and the desperate parent!) just a noisy big toy.

From the earliest days, and before I had any lessons, I was able to pick out on the piano tunes I had heard on the radio. The connection was already made. I am in no doubt that it was the sounds I heard from Miss Penhall when she played me a new piece that were in my head when I took the piece home. Later, when Jimmy Firth gave me that Schubert impromptu, which he must have played to me first, I found that the transfer from head to fingers was so natural and fluent that I was not aware of any technical difficulties. Now there are no doubt some fortunate pianists for whom this happens with everything they hear and decide to play. The case of that mighty natural genius, John Ogdon, for one, comes readily to mind. I was certainly not one of those. I still struggled with many pieces, then and since. For music that came naturally to me I found that the associated techniques came easily and spontaneously. For pieces that did not immediately 'click' I did not, in those crucial teenage years, have the time or patience to develop the required techniques. The music was abandoned or left in a half-finished state.

Memory

Memory plays a crucial role in this instinctive or natural technique. Memory is much more than 'playing without the music'. A fluent and finished performance of a piece with the score on the piano will still involve a great deal of memorisation. If there is no memory of the music present then what you are doing is playing by sight, a different but still valuable skill.

I have described (Chapter Five) how when I auditioned for Edgar Brown he knew that I had memorised the Schubert impromptu even when I did not know it myself. In young pianists, memorisation often happens without conscious effort. Older pianists such as I am now can still memorise, though it needs to be done systematically and deliberately. It is also the case that as you age the brain does not always retain what it memorises, whereas pieces memorised in your early to mid-teens may still be there decades later. That impromptu is still there, sixty years after I had subconsciously memorised it.

There are several components to musical memory. Visual memory means a mental image of how the score looks on the page. Aural memory is how the music sounds in your head. Kinaesthetic or muscle memory is a largely automatic process whereby the muscles involved in playing learn to do so of their own accord. The same form of memory is involved in many other daily activities such as playing sports or driving a car. Then there is what could be called cartographical memory, whereby you have a mental map of the shape or direction of the piece based on its structure. I like to call this your musical satnav.

Let's consider each in turn. Visual memory is likely to play a small part in any musical performance, even if you have a photographic memory. Relying on how the piece looked the last time you played it from score is only another form of sight-reading but without the physical presence of the score. The image is likely to fade altogether under the pressure of performance. Aural memory will be needed to guide your interpretation. How, in your mind, should the piece sound? Loud or quiet? How fast or slow should it go? What mood do you want to convey through it? Muscle memory will look after the precise movements of fingers, hands, wrists and arms. The more automatic the process the more secure the memory. Practising blind, so that your fingers have to learn where the notes are without visual direction, is a good way to reinforce this sort of memory.

For some short pieces, a combination of aural and muscle memory may well suffice. But for longer works such as those in sonata form you also need your satnav. When you start on a long car drive you have made many times already you do not need to consult a map, nor indeed to switch on your satnav, because you have a map of your route in your head. You know when to turn off one road into another. You have a pretty good idea of the length of your journey and your likely arrival time. Similarly, when you embark on a long musical journey such as a sonata you need to know the way ahead. For example, in a movement in sonata form the exposition will usually take you from the tonic (home) key to the dominant (nearest related key). When the material is recapitulated after the development it will remain in or return to the tonic. There will be a pivotal moment like a signpost pointing either to the dominant or the tonic. This moment – it may be a single note or chord or a more extended passage – will obviously be different in the recapitulation because the subsequent route is different. Your muscle memory will know both versions but it will not know which to use unless you tell it, and you won't know what to tell it unless you apply your inner satnav. Which are you in, exposition or recapitulation? This may all seem obvious, but recapitulations are often where so-called memory lapses occur. It is not actually the memory which has lapsed but the sense of overall direction from the mental map. To have a satnav in good working order you need to study the structure of your piece, its sequence of themes and harmonic changes. This is where the scholar and the natural instinctive musician meet.

FIFTEEN

NEW TEACHER, NEW DIPLOMA

In March of the same year in which I had welcomed our new piano into our home I took early retirement from the civil service after twenty-seven years. I was fifty. My department was downsizing, as the new jargon would have it, and there were favourable terms available for those who wanted to go early. It had been a varied and rewarding career, challenging, at times frustrating, but always rich in friendships and not just musical ones. In recent years it had become increasingly hard to reconcile the demands of my job with the musical claims on my time and energies. I could now devote as much time to music as I wished.

Despite my retirement I continued my association with the departmental music society, playing three times at St Matthew's during the year. In February, Paul and I gave a programme of Weber, Vaughan Williams and Poulenc, including the latter's magnificent sonata for clarinet and piano. The following month I played my second solo recital there. Ironically, given my wish to work on more classical repertoire and the rift this was already causing with Ricci, the programme was advertised as and consisted of piano music of the Romantic era, with pieces by Schumann,

Mendelssohn (the Rondo Capriccioso), Grieg and Rachmaninoff. In April, Paul joined Pat and myself in a song recital including two songs by Spohr with clarinet obbligato. For me the highlight was the opportunity to accompany Pat in two of Benjamin Britten's wonderful folk song arrangements. One of them was *Sweet Polly Oliver*. In the words of the programme note: 'The piano part is extremely independent, so the singer needs to hang on tight to the tune!' Which she did.

Two other occasions of note in the first half of the year took place outside our usual venues. In March the choir at Christine's church performed Fauré's Requiem Mass and I was asked to accompany, playing a piano reduction of the original orchestral score. Regrettably, I have never found the time or inclination to tackle any of that composer's piano music, which is unjustly neglected. But with its combination of polyphonic complexity, ultra-subtle Romantic sensibility and constant kaleidoscopic harmonic shifts it surely requires a specialist, someone who has made it their lifetime's study. Such specialists include the French pianist, Jean-Philippe Collard, and, to prove that this is not an exclusively French concern, the British pianist, Kathryn Stott. The Requiem is more direct in its appeal and musical language, though still it was a joy to experience through my own fingers that unique, heartfelt though understated blend of late Romantic harmony and melody. The choir, though small, had an excellent conductor and were well-rehearsed. Christine herself gave a moving account of the soprano solo, *Pie Jesu.* However, the baritone soloist had not been able to make it to rehearsals. At the beginning of the performance he had still not turned up. The time came for his solo, *Libera Me*. I played the opening two bars very slowly, wondering if I would have to improvise. Then suddenly he was there, only slightly out of breath, ready to pick up his cue. (Do professional accompanists have to put up with anxious moments like that? Yes, I suppose they probably do.)

Round about that time, Christine invited me to a rather more informal musical occasion in the hall of another of the churches where she served. I had the honour of accompanying her grandmother, whom she always called Nan, in some Edwardian ballads. Nan had a warm, rich voice and it was a pleasure to play for her. Oh and by the way, Nan was ninety-nine at the time. She was still fit and lively and would live another five years.

In May, our trio of clarinet, cello and piano played at another local church, St George the Martyr. This is a historic church with a close association with Dickens. The north side of the churchyard adjoins the surviving wall of the Marshalsea Prison, where Dickens' father in real life and William Dorrit in his novel *Little Dorrit* were both imprisoned for debt. The church, like St Johns', had a longstanding tradition of lunchtime music. I was therefore dismayed to find that one of the notes on the piano had a broken string. Unfortunately that note was a B flat in the centre of the keyboard and the main piece in our programme was the Trio in B flat by Beethoven! The piano part was difficult enough without my having to remember to avoid that note, which seemed to occur in every bar, and if possible to substitute another B flat from above or below. I raised the matter afterwards with the ex-military chap who had secured the job of organising the music despite having not the slightest appreciation of the needs of those who came to play it. He told me loftily that he was aware of the fault but that it was 'not a priority' to repair it. I told him not to expect any pianist to come back and play there.

In August I followed the suggestion of several fellow class members at Morley College to attend the annual residential Summer School for Pianists, held at that time at the College for the Blind as it was then known in Hereford. The core of the college is a school-type building in traditional gothic style, to which numerous extra wings and extensions in a bewildering variety of styles have been added over the years. I wondered if the maze-like confusion of the layout was part of the training for blind and partially sighted students in finding their way around complex environments. One of the areas in which blind musicians have tended to specialise over the years is piano tuning, which means that pianos of different qualities and sizes lurk in corners all over the estate. While most of those pianos could be used for practice the best quality grands were in the rooms reserved for the tutors, all of whom were highly qualified and dedicated. The timetable consisted of classes on the master-class model familiar to me from Morley, with plenty of time in between for practice and socialising.

I joined the school at the last moment, after dithering for a long time as to whether I should go. I would be away from home for a week and Hereford is not easy to get to by train from London. I was also concerned that all the participants would be far ahead of me in ability and I would spend the entire week being put to shame. In the end I rang the organiser, expecting and perhaps secretly hoping to be told it was fully booked. She told me that the classes of the regular tutors were all booked up. I was about to sigh with relief. But, she went on, there was still a vacancy in the class of a tutor who was attending the school for the first time, Raphael Terroni. She assured me that he was really very good, perhaps suspecting that the fact that he still had vacancies meant I would think otherwise. Yet again fate had taken a hand. It was Raphael's only year at the Summer School. If I had come a year later I would never have met him.

Raphael was at the time head of keyboard at the London College of Music. He had a particular reputation, as I later discovered, as a champion of English music, though for his recital at the Summer School he chose Rachmaninov and Chopin, playing with great sensitivity and musicality. He had studied for many years with the famous British pianist and pedagogue, Cyril Smith. Smith, who died in 1974 after a stroke, had an unrivalled reputation as a teacher. The roll-call of his eminent former pupils is impressive. As well as Raphael it included David Helfgott, my surprise meeting with whom is recounted in the previous chapter. In the film *Shine*, of which Helfgott is the subject, Smith is portrayed by John Gielgud under the thinly disguised pseudonym of Cecil Parkes, though I am assured that Gielgud's pompous, aristocratic depiction could not be further from the blunt Yorkshireman of real life. Another such Yorkshireman taught by Smith was John Barstow, director of the Hereford Summer School at the time of my first visit and for many years afterwards. Smith also taught Fanny Waterman, founder and director of the Leeds International Piano Competition. She died recently at the age of one hundred.

Smith formed a four-handed duo with his pianist wife Phyllis Sellick, which became three-handed when Smith lost the use of his left arm as a result of a stroke.

I liked Raphael from the start. The pieces I had brought with me to play for him in class included the Haydn F Minor Variations (the source of so much grief with Ricci), Schubert's B Flat Impromptu (also a set of variations), that long-standing favourite, the Liszt *Widmung*, and a piece of a wholly new character for me, one I had only recently come across. This was the toccata by the Armenian composer, Khachaturian, famous for his *Sabre Dance* and the ballet *Spartacus*. The toccata requires a lot of rhythmic bite and well-coordinated hands, but is not especially difficult. It sounds much harder than it is. And it is great fun to play, full of colour and excitement.

Raphael, a warm and genial personality with a wealth of anecdotes, instantly saw the problems I was still having with the Haydn and straight away I was able to start to put them right. The Schubert proved a tougher nut to crack. I booked a private lesson with him to work on it. Again he was able to home in on my difficulties and suggest solutions. After that lesson I asked him if he would take me on as a private pupil. He readily agreed. He was a Steinway artist, which meant that he could use the teaching and practice rooms in Steinway Hall in Marylebone whenever he wished. It was very easy for me to catch the tube into London to attend lessons.

The Summer School ended with the traditional pupils' concert. We were each allowed to play just one piece. My own preference would have been the Liszt. Raphael persuaded me to offer the Khachaturian, on the grounds that the Romantic repertoire was already well represented in the programme and the toccata would be a refreshing change. The concert took place in a gothic style chapel where the tutors had all played their individual recitals. The Steinway grand in the room was a big beast, sonorous and hard to tame. I had already sneaked in after dinner the evening before to have a go on it. To my dismay I saw that I was not due to play until nearly the very end. That was not Raphael's fault but the decision of the organisers. I had to sit through nearly one and a half hours while the others played, trying to listen politely while focussing the other half of my mind on my upcoming performance. (Another ordeal only reserved for amateur pianists?) I am not generally a nervous performer but this time I was really beginning to have sweaty palms. I could not get out of my mind that this was not a normal audience. Everybody was a pianist, some of a very high level indeed. When my time came it was with some relief that I was able to attack the opening chords and dispel my nerves. At the end I could not wait to get to the back of the room where I had been sitting. Then I realised that the applause was continuing. Raphael turned from his seat to give me an encouraging smile and nod. I had to go back up to the front to acknowledge the applause. I had expected the audience to have traditional tastes such that they would hate the piece, which has its fair share of dissonance. I had underestimated them.

A particular lesson I learned from that baptism of fire was that if you put yourself down to play Bach or another early composer at the pupils' concert you were likely to come on at or near the beginning, after which you could relax and listen to the others. That was one reason, but not the only one, why in later years at Hereford I often chose Bach.

The next month I played a recital at St John's which featured all of the pieces I had played for Raphael at Hereford. The same month I began lessons with him at the Steinway studios. The first piece I took to him was one I had dipped into several times over the years, Bach's French Suite in E Major, a delightful sequence of tuneful dances with an exquisite sarabande at its heart. He worked hard with me on sound production, especially how to achieve sufficient brilliance through fingerwork. I will not say fingerwork alone, because fingers never work in isolation. They are always backed up by flows of energy from the hands, wrists and arms. But Bach in particular requires a sonority in which firmness, clarity and flexibility of the fingers are paramount. The big chordal, pedalled techniques of later composers are alien to him, for the simple reason that he was writing for instruments such as the harpsichord or clavichord which did not possess those qualities. A dance feel is also often needed in Bach, especially in the suites. 'If it doesn't make you want to get up and dance, then it isn't working,' he told me, as we worked on one of the movements. I could tell he was not inclined to dance so clearly it wasn't yet working. The following August at the Summer School I put myself down to play three movements from the suite at the pupils' concert. I was delighted to see that I was put down to play first!

Other pieces I studied with Raphael in my first couple of years with him included Schubert's big F Minor

Impromptu, the first of his second set of four, and two pieces by Debussy, a composer to whom I was becoming increasingly attracted. I had always been fascinated by his evocatively free-standing harmonies released from classical progressions, his ability to create pictures and moods in sound. One of the pieces I had enjoyed working on with Edgar Brown in my teenage years was the ever popular *Clair de Lune*. I had played one of the arabesques at the office atrium concert when Paul and I had presented a programme of exclusively French music. Now with Raphael I revived one of my favourite preludes, *La Cathédrale Engloutie*. It had failed to impress the examiners when I had played it at my first diploma attempt, but I had never lost my fascination with it, especially with the extraordinary range of sonorities, from the mysterious opening of bare fifths evoking the cathedral under the waves, through the outburst of the full organ at the climax, down again to the final ebb of the echoes in the depths as the waters close over once more. By contrast I worked on a more extravert, brilliant Debussy piece, *Jardins sous la Pluie*, a vivid evocation of childhood games interrupted by showers of sparkling rain.

By then the programme of concerts at the office atrium had ceased, though they continued for some time at St Matthew's and St John's. The flourishing state of music in the office atrium from 1993 onwards was only possible as a result of a happy coincidence of three factors: the availability of the space with a good quality piano, the galaxy of talent ready and willing to take part, and the support of senior staff right up to the highest level. Our permanent secretaries often attended, sometimes even

Ministers. But the culture had already begun to change. An iniquitous system of performance bonuses and personal objectives had set civil servants against each other and exploded the concept of teamwork. Nobody wanted to be seen to leave early or even on time, for fear of being denounced for lack of commitment. As for lunch ... well, lunch, as we all now know, is for wimps.

With the extra time available since my retirement I began to focus once again on an earlier ambition I could now revive and pursue in earnest, that of becoming a piano teacher. This meant looking again at the vexed question of diplomas. In this country you do not need a qualification to teach piano privately, though unless you happen to be a household name it is very helpful in marketing the availability of your services to have those letters after your name. Since my earlier abortive attempt at a teaching diploma the bodies entitled to award diplomas, that is, the conservatoire-level music colleges and the Associated Board, had thoroughly revamped their system. Performance and teaching diplomas are now separate, the latter to be taken any time after the former. The new teaching diplomas have the advantage of focussing on the actual processes of teaching. They require candidates already to have some teaching experience so their qualities as teachers can be evaluated as part of the examination process. Of the available performance diplomas those which attracted me most were offered by the Guildhall School of Music and Drama (GSMD). While the syllabus for other performance diplomas still included items such as sight-reading and written work, that for the GSMD required a short recital, pure and simple. Well, not quite so simple. There were conditions. Though I had already given a number of solo recitals, as well as numerous performances as accompanist and chamber music partner, I was still not ready to apply. I knew a lot of hard work lay ahead.

It was a full year after my retirement from the civil service before I applied for the licentiate level performance diploma at the GSMD. I was aware that it was an ambitious aim. The licentiate diploma was an external qualification equivalent to the standard expected of students who had been studying for two years full time at what is one of the country's top conservatoires. Though open to anybody wishing to apply it was surely not intended for a fifty-two year old amateur who had never taken a single grade examination. I did not see it just as a passport to a teaching career. A lower level diploma would have done that job just as well. But I had other motives. I wanted to subject my progress to reputable external evaluation and what more reputable than that of the GSMD? Was that all? No, if I am to be honest with myself. Though she was already some years dead, my mother's attitude continued to rankle. In the days when I was still in a position to play at home she was always ready to insinuate that I was not really that good, that I obviously found practice a struggle and was clearly never up to the challenges of a concert career. She never understood that such careers are not all glitz and glamour but incredibly hard work, and that many very fine pianists make the conscious choice of a career away from the platform spotlight. Later on she could still show me off via the tape I had made for my father, but, as with everything else I and my father and brother did, it would never be enough for her. I could no longer reassure her, and in retrospect I know I never could have done. The truth is that I wanted the diploma to reassure myself.

While the only requirement for the GSMD diploma was a short recital – no sight-reading, ear-tests or theory – I would need to play five pieces from five different composers each representing a different style. One of the pieces had to be at least fifteen minutes in length. Normally in a recital I would never have chosen five different composers. Moving from one style to another so many times within a short programme is bound to show up not only the composers for whom you have an affinity but those who are likely to expose your weaknesses. This was obviously a deliberate strategy on the part of those who had designed the requirements.

For my programme I chose the Bach French Suite in E as the longer item, followed by the F Minor Schubert Impromptu, Debussy's prelude *La Cathédrale Engloutie,* the Khachaturian toccata and Liszt's transcription of Schumann's *Widmung*. By way of preparation I played three of these pieces, the Bach, the Schubert and the Debussy, at a recital at St John's in September, finishing with Debussy's *Jardins sous la Pluie.* St John's had recently acquired a new Yamaha which was really too small for the space. Working hard at the big chords in the organ section of *Cathédrale* I was aware of an uncomfortable sensation. The piano was moving away from me. By the time the passage had given way to a quieter section my arms were as stretched out before me as they could be while still enabling me to play. Another lesson. With an unfamiliar piano on a smooth floor check first that the castors have been locked.

The examination itself took place in a large lecture theatre in the Guildhall School's Barbican home in the City of London. It was an unsettling experience, to say the least, playing to a hall which was entirely empty apart from the two examiners. From the keyboard I was barely aware of where they were. When the results came through I saw that I was five marks short of a pass. They had liked the Khachaturian and the Liszt. But it was the Debussy which had particularly let me down. In my anxiety to communicate across the empty spaces of the venue I had projected it too much. The two pieces which had gone down well were the noisier ones. Later, I picked up a valuable lesson from watching Stephen Kovacevich give a master-class at the Queen Elizabeth Hall. He advised a student struggling with a very quiet passage not to worry about projection. 'Don't project to your audience,' he said. 'Draw them in.'

Paul and I had continued to explore the clarinet and piano repertoire during that year. In March at St Matthew's we added two substantial works, the Sonata by Saint-Saens and the three Fantasy Pieces by Schumann. The following year saw both our last recital together at that venue and my last solo recital there. At my recital, after intensive work with Raphael, I played one of Beethoven's lesser known sets of variations, the Thirty-two Variations in C Minor. Though Beethoven himself apparently did not think highly of it, and the work is dwarfed by his later Variations on a Waltz by Diabelli, it is a powerful piece with an astonishing range of moods and styles concentrated in each of the very brief variations. It deserves to be much better known. I followed it with two of the lovely *Moments Musicaux* by

Schubert and concluded with Chopin's melancholy Waltz in A Minor (an early favourite from my teenage years with Edgar Brown) and his rousing Polonaise in A. I had found the performance particularly enjoyable, both in terms of the venue and the programme. The mother of St Matthews' director of music, Stuart Whatton, was present. Afterwards, she told me, 'You have lifted our spirits.' This generous comment has remained with me. What else is performance for? What else justifies all the hard work of preparation?

The last time I accompanied the department's most gifted soprano, Jan, was about this time and in none of the venues thus far mentioned. She was active in her local church in Harrow and asked me to accompany her in a recital of sacred song as background to a festival taking place there. We performed discreetly in one corner of the church while parishioners came and went with various offerings such as flowers. When we started there was scarcely anyone in the building. I assumed that would be the case by the time we had finished. From my position behind the upright piano I could see Jan out of the corner of my eye. When accompanying you have to see as well as hear your singer. That way you know when they are drawing breath and you learn from experience to judge to the fraction of a second when the sound will emerge. I had no view at all of the pews. When I rose after our final piece I was delighted and surprised to find that a sizeable audience had gathered to listen and were warmly applauding. Jan of course had seen them all arrive but I had had no idea. I was surprised only because Jan had given me no hint that an audience was gathering. But for other reasons I was not surprised. Her voice was the sort that compelled overhearing passers-by to enter and those busy with tasks inside the church to stop and listen. She was always a joy to accompany. I never felt that I had to follow her and adjust my understanding of the music to hers. We always seemed to share the same understanding from the outset.

I applied for a further attempt at the Guildhall Licentiate Diploma the following year, and made two strategic decisions. Reluctantly, I decided to drop the Debussy. I substituted the Chopin D flat Nocturne. The rest of the programme was unchanged. The other decision was to make the diploma performance the third of three in fairly quick succession. The first would be an uninterrupted presentation of the programme to Raphael, who would then offer his comments and suggestions. The second would be a public performance at St John's. There was a risk that the programme would get stale, particularly as most of it was a repeat of the earlier attempt. But the advantage was that I would know it so well that I would be able to continue despite the pressures of the exam situation. For any periods when my concentration lapsed I would be able to proceed on autopilot.

The exam was scheduled for November 2002, at the end of what would prove to be a very difficult year as a result of family illnesses. I had very limited time for practice. Raphael was then no longer able to use the Steinway studios because of refurbishment and finding a time and venue for our lessons proved problematic. Once, I went to Ealing to see him at the London College of Music, another time to his home in a remote part of rural East Anglia.

The exam itself was a very different experience this

time. It took place in a small room, with the examiners near enough for me to feel I could communicate with them without straining. They applauded at the end and I felt at the time that I had won them over. But the result was a long time coming. I knew my performance had been recorded and that the views of the examiners in the room had to be validated by secondary markers on the basis of the recording. By the time the envelope arrived I had convinced myself that I had not made it and was already beginning to make plans to attempt a lower level diploma.

The nature of the communication from Guildhall was bizarre. There was no statement at all as to whether I had succeeded or not in obtaining the diploma. There was a general statement to the effect that while a lot of work and preparation had been done to prepare the programme I required 'at this level' a more developed level of pianistic and musical understanding. The marking system itself can best be described as byzantine. For each piece separate marks had been given for musical awareness, quality of sound, accuracy, communication and control of the instrument. Those marks were then tallied to give a mark out of fifty. The totals were then added up, divided by five and multiplied by two. While I took in the gist of the general remarks and was happy to accept them – they were after all intended as signposts to future development – my eyes were drawn down to the figure which had emerged from the maze of calculations. Fifty. But what was the pass mark? Was it more than fifty, or did fifty mean a pass and if so why couldn't they just say so? It was there, in very small print, under the mark. Fifty was a pass. I still did not believe it until the certificate itself arrived a few days later.

This time it was the noisier pieces which found less favour, while the Bach and the Chopin were comfortably in the pass zone. It seemed that I had still projected too much, not having expected that the venue would be so intimate. But my decision to replace the Debussy with the Chopin had been vindicated. It was by some margin the most successful part of the programme.

With the letters at last after my name I could now focus on starting my teaching career, while continuing to develop my own playing through attendance at the master-classes at Hereford and Morley College. After a further occasional lesson with Raphael I decided it was not really practicable to continue. He was rarely in London by then. But I have no doubt that without his careful and patient guidance I would never have achieved the level of musicality which not only had secured me my diploma but given me a platform on which to build even further.

With one exception I had given my last performances at St Matthew's and St John's. The exception was in July 2003, when Paul and I collaborated with another clarinettist known to Paul from their partnership in the East Grinstead Sinfonia. There are no other wind instruments, in my view, which make such delightful duets. By then I had already started to teach. Paul had moved to a new office in Croydon and had less opportunity to get into London to rehearse or perform. After a long, fascinating and rewarding partnership in which Paul had fulfilled a longstanding ambition to perform many of the major works of the clarinet and piano repertoire we decided to call it a day. It was time for a new chapter.

SIXTEEN

TEACHING AND DOING

He who can, does. He who cannot, teaches. *He who can do neither becomes an educationalist.*
George Bernard Shaw (my addendum in italics)

My diploma result had arrived in February 2003 and it was some time before I could begin to build a teaching practice. I advertised locally in the usual way. Eventually two charming young American brothers of Iranian descent came my way and showed promise. A lady came for one lesson and then was heard of no more. I still do not know what I did to scare her away. By the autumn of that year I still had only a few pupils. But then, as so often, a chance event came to my aid. A piano teacher who unbeknown to me lived in the next street retired to Devon and, without consulting me, sent over to me those of his pupils still interested in having lessons. My practice more than doubled overnight. Some were unhappy with the change of teacher and did not stay with me. But I now had a foundation on which to build.

I found teaching rewarding and frustrating in about equal measure. I have already mentioned how very few came with any musical background in the form of singing at home or at school. Some, or rather their parents, were only interested in climbing the grade exam ladder. But others had a natural musicality which made them a joy to teach. For those whose parents were keen that they do the grade exams I tried to counteract what I have criticised as the excessive verticality of the system by ensuring that after each exam success they learned some wider repertoire before tackling the next level. For some pupils, including adults, the exam system does provide a useful framework for a far more systematic learning process than any I experienced myself. And for a teacher it is valuable from time to time to have your teaching methods and approach validated externally.

In the early years of my teaching, economic conditions were favourable and a number of adults approached me with time and money on their hands. Some were complete beginners while others wanted to revive a career cut short years before by family and work pressures. At its peak my practice had sixteen pupils a week. Interestingly, about two thirds were from ethnic minority backgrounds. I was not surprised. It is well known that immigrant communities traditionally set great store by learning and I was pleased to see that this extended to music. Sixteen a week was plenty for me, given that there is a fair amount of work to be done additional to the actual lessons. Repertoire has to be chosen carefully to suit each pupil. For those taking examinations I needed to obtain and learn the pieces I would teach them, many of them by composers unknown to me, and for the more advanced grades this was not always easy. I had to keep up to date with new teaching materials as they became available and attend lectures and conferences. Then there was always the tedious business of invoicing, accounting and tax returns. I knew teachers whose practice consisted of seventy or more pupils per week. I could understand the pressures which led them to take on so many. I had another source of income. For those relying on their income from teaching alone my practice size would never have been remotely enough. I wonder if those parents who complain about the fees charged by private piano teachers, often a fraction of what they would happily pay a plumber or electrician for a knowledge obtained in a fraction of the time, realise how tough life can be for those teachers and how dedicated they have to be.

One of my pupils was a young boy of Chinese parents. They had come to this country to work in the NHS. The boy had had some piano lessons in China. With his scales and arpeggios he could race up and down the keyboard with astonishing speed for an eight-year-old. But the refinements of musicality which would be required if he were to do well in his grade examinations as his parents wanted were still unfamiliar to him. I explained to his parents what his priorities should now be. His mother was always present during his lessons. Although not musically trained herself, she participated actively and seriously in the study of his pieces, once catching me out when I miscalculated the number of quaver beats in a particular passage. Her son learned to play musically enough to gain a distinction at Grade 1. I found myself wondering about his early lessons in China, which had seemed to focus solely on speed and agility at the expense of control and musicality. Some years later, James Lisney, a longstanding tutor at the

Hereford Summer School, told us of his experiences with some young Chinese students who could polish off the notes of Chopin studies with ease but struggled with even simple Bach, such as his first two-part Invention.

All my pupils behaved well, but I could not say that of all the parents. I stopped one course of lessons because the parents, who were by no means badly off, repeatedly failed to settle accounts. Another, who could not stay with her daughter for lessons, was once nearly an hour late in picking her up. Luckily I did not have another pupil in that time. But I told the parent that next time I would charge my rate for the extra hour and that she could find a much cheaper and better qualified baby-sitter elsewhere. Other parents were inspiring. One was clearly struggling financially but desperate for her daughter to learn the piano. In her case alone I waived my usual rule of asking for ten weeks' payment in advance. I let her pay weekly. She never let me down. I once came across her delivering leaflets in the street. So that was how she found the money for her daughter's lessons. Her daughter was an excellent pupil.

Some teachers only ever put their pupils in for grade exams when they are sure of success. That way they can boast that they have 'a one hundred per cent examination success record'. In the case of one of my pupils – I shall call her Alberta though that is not her real name – I was ready to sacrifice my hundred per cent record. Before she came to me she had secured a good result at Grade 7. I was convinced Alberta had the musicality to pass Grade 8 (advanced), which for anybody is a considerable achievement. She also had great strength of character and determination. She failed three times, despite having in my view improved each time. It seemed the bar was persistently being set higher. At her fourth attempt she passed very comfortably, ten above the pass mark. Some pupils just take a little longer. I remembered how long it had taken me to achieve a diploma pass.

Alberta was also a very competent violinist. A couple of days before her Grade 6 violin exam her accompanist let her down. She asked me if I could help her out. We had a quick run through her pieces the night before the exam. The following day I found myself for the first and last time in the waiting room for those taking grade exams, surrounded by nervous pupils and their parents. When Alberta's time came I went into the room with her, reminding myself that I was not the one being examined. She played her pieces very well and secured a merit mark. My experience in learning accompaniments at very short notice had stood us both in good stead.

For parents whose children are musical or who would like their children to be I would offer this advice, again remembering my own experiences: their successes are theirs, not yours. The same is true of their failures, which may, as in the case of Alberta, just be stepping-stones to success. Encouraging them is what loving parents do in response to the child's wishes and needs. These may take time to unfold, during which you need to be patient and supportive. If a child is in the end no longer interested that must be accepted. The parents of a pupil who did well for a year or two with me were annoyed when he declared he was no longer interested and preferred to focus on cricket. I pointed out that there were plenty of pianists about, but we had at that time a serious shortage of good cricketers.

Although I was no longer taking private lessons, and determined to prove to the spirit of George Bernard Shaw that I could both teach and play, I continued to develop my playing through the master-classes at Morley College and Hereford. Since the diploma result I felt a new sense of liberation. I had got a monkey off my back. I no longer had to prove anything to myself or anyone else. Any performance which is intended for an examiner or adjudicator involves a trade-off between a personal interpretation which may not fit the examiners' view and a common denominator rendition in which the main focus is on getting through without a major disaster. From the moment I had played Bach for an audience of parents at the age of nine I had always focussed on communicating the music as I felt it. Feedback from my audiences, be it from the seventeen hundred in the Phil when I was sixteen to the very small and select audience who were there for my so far final performance (more about this event later) had always encouraged me to believe that I had done so, to some if not always to all. Not even the world's greatest pianists will get through to all their audience every time. In that experience of communication lies the reward for all the hard work of preparation and the stress of performance. Just playing to amuse myself has never interested me. But examiners and adjudicators, with the best will in the world, and that will not always be forthcoming as we have seen, have a different agenda. They are there to measure how you come up either against a prescribed standard or by comparison with others. They cannot experience the occasion in purely musical terms and neither can you. This helps perhaps to explain why I was less successful in competition and diplomas than in recitals. I took fewer risks in programme choice for the former and no doubt some of my pieces had gone stale or lost their edge. The sense of exploration, even danger, which can put the 'live' into live performance, was missing.

I have often wondered about the effects of the competition culture on young professional pianists. Those who go from one competition to another, and it seems that these days success in one is not enough, are constantly compromising, moulding their programmes and performances to what they think will work in the eyes and ear of the judges. Major competitions have, it is true, secured breakthrough results for some of the finest pianists before the public. But as a rule those had either fully developed their pianistic personalities beforehand or had the wisdom and opportunity afterwards to take time out, perhaps some years, to concentrate on that development. The pianist who secures premature success and is thrown into the arena of performance and recording while not yet ready or who spends many years searching for that elusive success to find that their originality and musical personality have slipped away has not been well served by the system. And neither has the music-loving public.

Around this time I moved from the intermediate to one of the advanced classes at Morley College. The tutor was the Australian pianist, Gwenneth Pryor. Morley was fortunate indeed to have at the same time such inspirational pianist/teachers as Katharina and Gwenneth. Gwenneth had moved to London in her teens to take up a scholarship at the Royal College of Music, from where she had gone on to have a distinguished career as a soloist and chamber musician. I had changed classes mainly to take advantage of the opportunities for solo performance at Morley, which were reserved for members of the advanced classes. As a teacher Gwenneth was outstanding, frank, outspoken, intensely practical, ready to be critical when we deserved it, delighted when we showed good progress. The class itself I found less congenial than the one I had just left. Perhaps because it bore the label 'advanced' it had its share of egos, some of which were in inverse proportion to ability. Certainly it had some excellent players, but also some who did not really belong and who had gained entry when standards were less demanding. When I first approached Gwenneth about joining her class she assured me that in terms of my playing standard I would be comfortable there. But she admitted that there were some whom she 'would not now have.' Unfortunately those longstanding members had formed cliques who did not welcome newcomers. They were particularly suspicious of those like myself who had come up from a less advanced class.

At the annual Summer School at Hereford a new arrival among the tutors was Andrew Ball, an Oxford contemporary of mine. Andrew, along with his fellow music student at Queen's College, Julian Jacobson, had played at one of the concerts put on by our college society. They were the pianists in Stravinsky's *Symphony of Psalms*. Andrew was a witty, charming tutor and one of the most natural musicians I have ever met, with an amazing breadth of repertoire. His class was very popular and I felt privileged to be a member of it, though like Gwenneth's but to a much greater extent it suffered from a startling range of abilities. That would not necessarily have been a problem if the class had been designated as mixed ability. Such classes can work very well if students choose pieces according to their standard. But it was classed as advanced. Those few members of Andrew's class whose abilities were very far indeed from advanced took that to mean that they were there to attempt very advanced pieces, often with disastrous results. Andrew was far more polite than I would have been. His own recitals at the School caused some alarm among the more traditional participants. One of his programmes opened with his operating the strings from inside the piano. It ended with a very exciting piece, whose name I forget, which involved him using his fists and elbows. There was never a dull moment when he taught or played. But I must not give the wrong impression. With more traditional repertoire he was as sensitive and refined as the music demanded.

I found these master-classes immensely helpful to my own teaching. As I watched Katharina, Gwenneth and Andrew at work I realised how intently they listened to what was being played and how skilfully they came up with solutions to the problems that emerged. One particular advantage of the master-class format for participants who are themselves teachers is that not only can they sensitise themselves to what the tutor is doing but can also offer their own solutions and join in the discussion. Thus they became part of a communal teaching process.

I still did not have a teaching qualification as such. I needed one more diploma to complete the set. I applied for the postgraduate Diploma course in Music Teaching in Private Practice, the first award-bearing, distance learning course for those working in the field of private music teaching. It had been developed by the Incorporated Society of Musicians and the School of Education at the University of Reading to promote and raise standards in private music teaching. By the time I enrolled it had been renamed as the Diploma in Music Teaching in Professional Practice, to take account of the needs of those who work within institutions such as schools but are not seeking to qualify as classroom teachers. By then the model from my own school days whereby schools directly employed music teachers had largely been abandoned. Now schools opened their doors to peripatetic teachers paid by the parents, sometimes with financial assistance from the better-off schools. As with so many aspects of music teaching in this country, and despite the dedication of the teachers themselves, it is another example of several steps backwards, especially for poorer pupils.

The course on which I enrolled was rigorous and demanding, both in its content and its formal entry requirements. The latter were a professional qualification in performance or equivalent ability established through a tape audition, and an honours degree or equivalent. Sadly, the course no longer operates. The University now offers residential MA courses in Music Education, a model which does not serve the needs of those with established private teaching practices. Fortunately, there are now alternative diplomas available which do cater for those needs, from the music colleges and the examining bodies.

Initially, the course was very heavy on educational theory. I found the subject tiresome and some of the educationalists who lectured to us patronising. It was during a conversation at a dinner with some fellow members of the course that I added those rather spiteful words about educationalists to the well-known dictum of George Bernard Shaw quoted at the head of this chapter. I also rather resented having to attend classes on how to write an essay. I had been writing essays since I was eleven! And how do you get an honours degree, which all course members were supposed to have as a condition of admission, without knowing how to write an essay? To judge from the anxiety and paranoia on the part of some members about the prospect of writing that first course essay, either their so-called honours degrees were no such thing or the requirement had been quietly waived in the interests of keeping up attendances and the income that came with them.

But by the time the second year was in full swing the focus was very much on the teaching process itself. Course members were required to watch other members as they taught, either by direct presence in lessons or by observing video recordings, and to write up their conclusions and recommendations. Each member was assigned a professional teacher as a mentor. The mentor also observed the teaching of the mentee and vice versa. This final segment of the course was both stimulating and very challenging and not all had the necessary finishing power. Of about a dozen who had enrolled in my year only six actually finished the course and secured the diploma. Only two of us were awarded distinctions, myself and the colleague with whom I had collaborated on the final project.

While I have had the good fortune to experience a wide of range of musical activities, I have never played a concerto with an orchestra. Gwenneth's class did however offer the next best thing, a concerto project in which we would play the solo part of our chosen concerto while she would accompany us on the second piano in the room used for the classes. I chose a longstanding favourite, Mozart's Concerto in G major, K453. Mozart's concerti work wonderfully well in two-piano arrangements and the experience was a delight. The excellent support from Gwenneth freed up my hands and fingers so that by the time the performance came round I found that passages which had at first seemed awkward and cumbersome flowed smoothly. Because several members were taking part, either with a complete concerto or a movement, there was very limited time for preparation, just one session per movement. But Gwenneth seemed to know instinctively exactly how I understood the piece and how I wanted to convey its delicate, poignant beauties. It really was a case of the tutor generously helping the student take the lead.

That was in 2004. A couple of years later I gave my final solo public recital, at the Holst Room of Morley College. Recalling the discomfort of having to play five different composers at my diploma performance, I narrowed the programme to just two, Beethoven and Chopin. The programme was very much a labour of love, Beethoven's C Minor Variations, Chopin's D flat Nocturne (again!), his four Mazurkas opus 24, and his thrilling Polonaise in A to finish. Some years later, my very final recital, to a smaller, invited audience, would be confined to a single composer. But more of that anon.

A couple of years after that Morley College recital I decided I had had enough of Gwenneth's class. That had nothing to do with Gwenneth's excellent teaching. I was becoming increasingly frustrated with the attitude of several class members, especially a group of elderly ladies who had been in the class for decades and were going nowhere anytime soon. They were not particularly good pianists and did not take part in performances. They obtained their satisfaction from sitting in the front row, scores open, pens ready to pounce on any errors committed by the person playing, nearly always in pieces they could not have played themselves. Some of us nicknamed them the *tricoteuses*, after the lady knitters who during the French Revolution sat in front of the guillotine watching the heads of aristocrats tumbling into the baskets. But for me it had long since ceased to be a joke. I was also engaged by then in a personal long-term project, with which I found little sympathy or support among the class members.

That project, to which I will return shortly, was however enthusiastically supported at the Hereford Summer School, which I continued to attend every year up to 2011, playing in the students' concert every year except one. On five occasions I played Bach, including what I could confidently declare was a world premiere. It was a transcription I had made myself of the slow movement of one of his trio sonatas for organ. These sonatas have very demanding and independent parts for hands and pedal. In looking through this movement at the piano one day, I discovered that with one or two minor tweaks the three voices could be made to lie under two hands. I could not find an available transcription made by any of those composers with a penchant for such things, such as Liszt or Busoni or Kempff. So I resolved to have a go myself. After all, how hard could it be? The answer, as I soon found out, was very hard indeed. It took me several months of trial and error, for a piece lasting only a few minutes.

There was actually a sixth occasion on which I played Bach at a Hereford students' concert, but not this time as a soloist. A member of Andrew Ball's class over many years was Sister Madeleine, a lively nun in her eighties, with a serene disposition, a ready smile for all, a mischievous sense of humour and always a twinkle in her eye. Her powers of silent persuasion were astonishing and, I was prepared to believe, divinely inspired. She would get off a train, place her suitcase on the platform and smile. In seconds, so it seemed, porters would arrive from every direction to help her. *Porters!* These days! It was uncanny. She played as beautifully as anybody I have heard and with a sensuality some deemed rather inappropriate for a nun, though I never saw a problem myself. Is there any more sensual music than that of Hildegard of Bingen?

As with me, Bach was her favourite. She was often teased about the state of her musical texts, on which she made liberal and messy use of Tippex to erase fingerings about which she had changed her mind. I too am always changing my mind about fingerings, even when I think I have firmly decided on them and written them in in ink, but I use the much tidier gummed paper. One year, Sister Madeleine had decided to play at the students' concert the lovely slow movement of Bach's F Minor concerto. Expecting to play it as a solo she had freely basted her score with Tippex fluid so as to write in the changes necessary to incorporate at least some of the accompaniment into her part. But it would still not be satisfactory. The heart-stopping accompanying pizzicato strings could not be played along with the melody by a single player at one piano. The recital room used for the concerts had two pianos so I offered to accompany her. I did the pizzicato bits in the form of lightly spread chords. It was a wonderful experience to play with her and the performance was warmly received. Sister Madeleine passed away a few years ago, in her late eighties. Sadly for us, yes, because she was missed and still is, but not sadly for her. Her faith was strong and she knew she had led a full and rich life. Her memory always brings a smile to one's lips.

Another piece I played at a students' concert was that exquisitely atmospheric Debussy tone-poem *Pas sur La Neige* (Footsteps on the Snow). It was a real test of nerve to play a piece which says so much so quietly with so few notes. 'Don't project: draw them in,' Stephen Kovacevich had said at that master class in the Queen Elizabeth Hall. I had absorbed the lesson and it worked.

2011 saw the retirement from the School of John Barstow, the musical director, a blunt Yorkshireman with a caustic wit and a wealth of hilarious stories. I had never been in John's class, but he had always been ready in a corridor or over lunch with a helpful word of praise and encouragement. That year I had resurrected that old Schumann-Liszt favourite, *Widmung*, which I had thoroughly reworked, taking it to pieces and putting it together again and giving it a fresh coat of paint. Andrew was very pleased with the result and encouraged me to play it at the students' concert on the last evening. I did so, prefacing my performance with a few words of thanks to John, who was sitting near the front, and telling him that the 'Widmung', the dedication, was on this occasion specially for him. After I had finished and risen to acknowledge the applause, I was somewhat startled when he jumped out of his seat, rushed up and threw his arms around me. Whether or not it was the performance or the dedication which drove him to do it, I will never know. I like to think it was a bit of both.

For various reasons unconnected with music I was unable to attend the School over the next few years. I did attend in 2017, by which time it had relocated to Walsall. I joined the class of James Lisney, one of the most thoughtful and poetic musicians I have ever met. I had expected to resume regular attendance and was ready to do so for each of the following three years. In 2018 I boycotted the event at the last moment because of a decision by the organisers made on the basis of a ludicrously over-sensitive interpretation of new data protection regulations not to send out class lists in advance. The following year I was prevented by illness from attending, while in 2020 the event in its physical form fell prey to the coronavirus. The course still went ahead in that year, though only through distance technology such as Zoom, for which I had neither the facilities nor the inclination. At the time of writing I still hope to attend the 2021 course.

Securing the Reading Diploma did not serve to increase the size of my practice. My intention was only to ensure that I had a reputable qualification specifically for teaching, one which would build on the experience I had already gained and provide a solid foundation of reflection and self-awareness for the future. That future in terms of private teaching for fees was to last only a few years. Economic conditions were worsening. Enquiries were now few and far between and soon almost dried up altogether. It was also the case that I had stopped actively seeking new pupils. A new interest, that of fiction writing, was taking up an increasing portion of my time and energy. I did however make a silent pledge that I would never suddenly retire from teaching and leave my remaining pupils in the lurch. I would continue to teach them for as long as they wanted to be taught by me. My diary records my last lesson as 30 July 2012. That one remaining pupil was the one whose mother I had found distributing leaflets to pay for her lessons.

So my teaching career stopped there? Well, not quite, as we shall see.

It will shortly be time to explain those rather cryptic references above to a certain project which was to occupy me for many years. I will need to go back to Morley College in 1998. But first, the final interlude.

INTERLUDE IX

CODA

What sort of a person is a pianist? Is he a pianist because he has a good technique? No, of course not; he has a good technique because he is a pianist, because he finds meaning in sounds, the poetic content of music, its regular structure and harmony. That is what technique is needed for; a technique that is adequate to the force, height and clarity of the spiritual image.
Heinrich Neuhaus[5]

There are countless books on piano technique, and some may promise to take you to the pinnacle of pianistic accomplishment (literally, as in the case of Clementi's *Gradus ad Parnassum*!). These interludes make no such claim. They deal only with basics, in the belief that all progress at the piano should be made on solid foundations. If you have worked your way through them and done all the exercises conscientiously you may well be wondering what comes next. That is up to you. This 'coda' contains some signposts you may find helpful.

Music and 'Music'

Most musical traditions in the world are aural, in the sense that they are acquired and passed on by listening and imitation. The Western classical tradition is something of an exception in that it has developed a strong, some would say excessive, dependence on being written down, using a system of symbols on parallel lines called musical notation. Those who can interpret those symbols are said, confusingly, to be able to 'read music', whether or not they can also play or sing. You may even have been told that before you can play you will need to learn to 'read music'. You now know that is not true.

All references to 'music' in the sense of notation I will from now on put in inverted commas. It is a curious and misleading use of the word. It is often said that some musicians can play or sing 'without the music' when what is meant is that they do so without the aid of a book or score containing the notation. But of course the essence of music without the inverted commas is that it consists of sounds intended to be heard.

If you have worked through the above interludes you will have found, perhaps to your surprise, that you can go a very long way indeed without being able to read 'music'. You can name the notes. You understand about bars, accents and stresses. You know the difference between pulse and rhythm. You can play a tune with both hands using all the fingers, and in one hand with an independent accompaniment in the other. You can choose how loud or soft you want to play and at what speed. You may even have initiated yourself into the mysteries of the pedals. If you are one of the fortunate few who have a natural ability to play directly from the aural images you have developed through listening – 'playing by ear' – you will be able to go a lot further without the aid of 'music'. But for most of us, the ability to read notation can be the key to unlocking a whole treasure-trove of music which might otherwise be denied to us. There are plenty of manuals to help you do this.

One word of warning. The score (or notation, or 'music') is only ever a guide. Composers of the baroque era such as Bach did not include markings for loudness or softness – the technical term for this is 'dynamics' – because they were not writing with the piano in mind. Rarely did they give indications for speed. They did not always include all the notes they would expect to be played. Where markings for speed and dynamics are found in scores of music of the period the likelihood is that they have been added by editors. They do not carry the authority of the composer's intentions. The respect they merit depends on the competence of the editor, a very variable factor indeed. Even scores of later periods when composers indicated far more of their intentions still leave much room for the performer's own interpretation.

What about those black notes?

As pointed out in the first interlude, black notes are not qualitatively differently from the white ones you have played so far. Play a scale from middle C to the C above, but this time take in all the black notes as they occur and listen carefully. What you have just played is called a chromatic scale, built up with intervals called a semitone, which is half a tone.

Now go back to the scale of C using just the white notes and listen to the intervals, that is, the size of the jump in pitch from one note to the next. They go up as follows, starting with the jump from C to D: tone – tone – semitone – tone – tone – tone – semitone. You can reproduce this pattern by beginning on any note. Try playing the same scale but start five notes higher, on G, again using only white notes. It will sound a bit 'off' at the top. This is because the pattern is not the same as before. The final interval is now a tone instead of a semitone. To correct this you need to play the black note just above the F instead of the F. This is called a sharp, because you are sharpening the F, that is, taking it up a semitone. If you then play the scale starting a further five notes up, on D, you will need to use two black notes, or sharpen two white notes, to get the same pattern. And so on.

Why does this matter? Try playing our tune starting on G, and using only white notes. It works fine. Now try in on D. It will not work. The third note up (F) sounds flat and needs to be sharpened. Combinations of black and white notes enable us to play the same tune starting on different notes. This is called playing in different keys, the starting note being the key note. All this is within the system known as diatonic. (There are different systems but this is the most common one.) As well as keys the diatonic system has what are called modes, usually just two, major and minor. What you have played so far is in the major mode. To get a feel for the minor mode, commonly associated with moods of sadness, play the five finger exercise from C up to

G and down again, but instead of white note E play the black note immediately below. What you have done here is flatten the E. So depending on the context, the black notes are called sharps or flats.

It is possible, and very useful, especially for singers, to get a feel for the diatonic major scale without the need to identify a specific key note. This is done by using a code known as 'tonic sol-fa' in which the key note is called 'doh', whatever it happens to be. The notes above 'doh' have their own code names. No better means has been devised for learning this code than the song *Doh-Ray-Me* from the Rodgers and Hammerstein Musical *The Sound of Music*. (It is interesting that Maria never teaches the Von Trapp children to 'read music' yet they become a very accomplished choir!) There is a huge body of theoretical literature about keys and modes and you will only want to study it if the subject presents a special interest to you. For the developing pianist it is sufficient to have a sense of the different keys and the different moods they convey, both between and within pieces, and how the language of key enriches the whole vocabulary of the music you play.

So what exactly is Technique?

It is common to read or hear reviews of pianists' performance to the effect that they display plenty of technique, whatever reservations the reviewers may have on other aspects of the performance. By 'technique' the reviewers mean simply that the pianists can play fast. You may have come to these pages with the understanding that technique means speed and have been wondering where we get on to the bit where you learn to play fast. But if that is your sole pianistic ambition you will need to look elsewhere for advice.

This equation of speed with technique is, as far as I can tell, unique to pianists. Nobody praises a singer for fast singing. Nor, for that matter, a violinist for fast playing. Certainly not a tuba player. Violinists and singers are praised for their tone, which is rightly considered the essence of their technique. So why are pianists expected to show technique solely according to their speed, however rough the result?

I believe it has a lot to do with something I mentioned in the first interlude, that almost anyone with access to a decent piano can produce note for note a perfectly satisfactory tone, in isolation as good as any which could be produced by the world's leading pianists. The quality of the tone of a single note played with controlled key descent (that is, not banged or thumped) depends on the instrument alone. Technique comes into the picture when we move beyond the single note to the control of tone within and between phrases, to the shaping of dynamics, to balance between the hands and between parts of the hand, to the creation of a singing cantabile *legato*, to the sensitive use of the pedals, to the convincing interpretation of large-scale movements. I could go on. Technique is about a million things, none of which is about speed and only speed. Playing effective *legato* very slowly is an advanced technique, calling for control of line to be maintained against the fading effect of notes widely spaced in time. Balancing three levels of dynamics, all of them quiet, at a slow speed, as required in the slow movements of

Beethoven's *Pathétique* and *Moonlight* piano sonatas, requires a very high level of technical control indeed. But all these qualities are subtle and are simply not on the radar of many critics and commentators. Far easier just to get out the speedometer.

So do not be deceived and adopt speed as an aim in itself. No other instrumentalist or vocalist would do this. Of course, some passages or pieces are meant to be fast. *The Flight of the Bumble Bee* will not work at slow speeds. But it requires much more than simple haste of execution. It calls for clarity, precision, a sense of shape and purpose, and, yes, a sense of humour. Performances which are not necessarily the fastest but have these qualities will win every time over ones that put speed above everything else. If you lack the dexterity to play faster passages or pieces, there are plenty of exercises to help you. But always remember to play exercises with the same aim in view as you would have in playing a piece of music you love. Namely, musicality. Ugly-sounding exercises will produce ugly-sounding music.

So what is technique? Technique is the production of sound in a way which conveys musical meaning according to the intentions of the composer and your interpretative insights. No more, no less.

Practice

Practice makes perfect. Actually, it doesn't. When it comes to the piano, perfection does not exist. But it does make progress for you so long as it is the right sort of practice, that is, regular, focussed and concentrated.

Repeating the same mistakes over and over again only reinforces those mistakes. So make practice part of your regular routine, daily if possible. A few minutes a day is better than one hour at weekends. Focus on what you want to achieve, and make sure your objectives are manageable. If you cannot say in all honesty that you are at an advanced level then don't tackle advanced pieces. You will only get frustrated and demotivated. This is perhaps the most frequent single cause why people give up the piano. There are no short cuts to the top of Parnassus. And above all, concentrate. Listen carefully and measure what you are playing against the objectives you have set yourself for just that session. Be realistic. Your objective might be a smoother legato in one hand in a particular bar, not mastering the finale of the *Emperor* concerto in one go. Don't repeat what is already going well. Focus on problems and get them sorted, if necessary with the help of a qualified teacher.

Final Thoughts

Always remember the three-word slogan. Put them on your wall or mount them on your music stand. Repeat them to yourself before you start your practice.

Hearing. Playing. Listening.

Nothing now remains but to wish you joy and success with all your musical adventures.

SEVENTEEN

ASCENT OF GOLD MOUNTAIN

We shall not cease from exploration
And the end of all our exploring
Will be to arrive where we started
And know the place for the first time.
T S Eliot, *Four Quartets*

Katherina's Morley College class of 1998 included an adventurous pianist who, having tackled the complete cycle of twenty-four Chopin preludes, decided to climb an even more forbidding peak, Bach's monumental masterpiece, the so-called *Goldberg Variations*. This is a series of thirty variations on the harmonic sequence set out in the beautiful opening Aria. I will describe the structure and content of the work in more detail later on. The work's size and complexity make it a forbidding challenge. Our adventurous pianist did very well with the Aria and the first few variations. He left the class shortly afterwards, for reasons unconnected with this particular adventure. But he had planted a seed in Katharina's mind. Her inspired idea was to divide the thirty variations plus Aria among class members willing to take part in a public performance in the college's Holst Room.

Put far too simply, the variations can be divided into three broad categories, character pieces such as a gigue or fugue or overture, brilliant toccata-like virtuoso movements and closely worked canons at different intervals. I was allocated three variations comprising one canon, one character piece and one toccata, the last just happening to be the most challenging of them all. We prepared our movements over some months. During this process it became clear that the real difficulty of the piece resides not so much in the individual movements as in the challenge of mastering the whole work. As Katharina herself put it, 'just playing one or two movements is not hard – what's hard is playing them all.' To my ears it sounded like a challenge. The advantage of working as a class was that we could each concentrate on our individual assignments while learning through the efforts of others how the whole work was structured.

The performance itself, in February 1999, was a great success, if success can be measured by a full house and an extremely enthusiastic reception. And that is surely a perfectly valid measure of success. Within the whole there were many individual successes, especially for those with no experience of public performance and little familiarity with the styles called for by the music. Seen in that context, those who struggled the most can be seen to have triumphed the most. What they achieved was a tribute to Katharina's inspirational guidance and their own determined efforts.

The thought of learning the whole piece had taken root in my mind, though it would be some years before I could start the enterprise in earnest. For each of three consecutive sessions at the Hereford Summer School I brought one third of the work, to subject it to Andrew's and the class's patient scrutiny. I played three of the movements at three successive students' concerts. (John Barstow was worried for a while that I intended to play the whole work at those concerts over a span of thirty years.) I also brought it to Gwenneth's class at Morley College, where it was met with something like suspicion and bewilderment on the part of some of the class members. My wish to devote more of my time and effort to the piece was another of the reasons why I left that class.

After several more years of study I still found the idea of a full public performance daunting. But what about a smaller, private invitation event? I contacted Samir Saleh, the international jurist I have already mentioned, like me a former pupil of Ricci and a member of the London Piano Circle. He graciously agreed to host. His Bosendorfer and the intimate acoustics of his living room would be ideal. The plan was that I would give a short introduction followed by a complete performance, while Samir would provide the refreshments. We agreed that we would make twelve places available for our audience, eight of them reserved for members of the London Piano Circle. In the event, very few London Piano Circle members showed any interest. Their priority was usually to attend events where they could play, and this was not one of them. Of those who were interested, some chose quite understandably to give priority to another, sadder event. The inspiration for the whole idea, Katharina herself, had died, and her funeral was on the same day as my performance. I dedicated it to her.

The *Goldberg Variations* is a challenge for its audience as well as its performer, as, if the following anecdote is true, the young Rudolf Serkin found to his cost. He decided to play the whole work as encore to a chamber concert in which he had taken part. By the time he had finished, the audience was down to three. It was however a distinguished threesome, consisting of Adolf Busch, Albert Einstein and Artur Schnabel. There are two possible lessons to be drawn from this. If you are going to play the whole work as an encore, lock the doors first. If that is not possible, make sure that what is left of your audience consists of distinguished individuals. The possibility of locking my audience in was not open to me but I had the next best thing in my favour. An invited audience in a private home is not likely to walk out for fear of offending both performer and host. And as far as I was concerned my select audience was distinguished indeed by virtue of having the taken the time and trouble to be present and to be prepared to devote their attention and concentration to what would take place.

Before starting to play I gave a short talk. The following comments are based on the notes I used for my talk.

What is special about the *Goldberg Variations*? Without doubt it is one of the greatest products of one of the greatest minds in human history. It has everything: comedy, tragedy, romance, humanity. In its combination of humanity and the highest artistic achievement the only comparison which I think comes close is to be found in the great plays of Shakespeare. This is Bach at his most accomplished, but also Bach reaching out to all mankind.

The work really is unique, a hugely ambitious experiment, a thirty-two-movement work built on the foundation of a single harmonic sequence, embracing a vast array of forms and styles, some looking back to Renaissance polyphony, others looking forward to musical developments many decades further on.

Bach composed the work over the period 1739-40. He was fifty-five when he finished it, entering the last decade of his working life, when he was focussing on creating a series of huge musical monuments, such as the B Minor Mass, the *Musical Offering*, and the *Art of Fugue*. He never called it by the title by which we have come to know it. On the title-page of the version he prepared for publication, which bears no personal dedication, he describes it as an *Aria mit verschiedenen Variationen*, which translates rather awkwardly as different or varied variations. Goldberg was a young harpsichordist at the court of Count Kayserlinck in Dresden. He was only twelve when Bach began to write the work. Bach's son Wilhelm Friedemann worked at that court and it is known that his father visited him there. He may well have taken with him a copy of the Variations and left it there with a personal dedication to the Count. Wilhelm Friedemann was a noted virtuoso performer on the organ and harpsichord, and it is most likely that the more technically demanding movements were written with him in mind. It is certainly plausible that the young Goldberg would have come across it and learned it in whole or part, perhaps with the guidance of Wilhelm Friedemann. But the idea that the work was written specially for Goldberg at the instance of the Count so that he could play it to ease the Count's insomnia is the stuff of a legend put about many years after Bach's death by his first biographer, Forkel.

'Aria with Variations' is actually a misleading description. The work is not a theme and variations at all. The Aria which starts the work is itself a variation, on a chord or harmony sequence which is never heard separately but is the basis for every single movement.

Bach liked to plan his large works like an architect. The structure is framed by two statements of the Aria. The thirty so-called variations are grouped into threes. A character piece such as a dance is followed by a lively, often virtuosic movement, then a canon. The large number of canons is very unusual, suggesting a special interest in canon on Bach's part at this stage of his career. It is the most rigorous and demanding form of composition. The form itself is very easy to understand. Examples all schoolchildren used to learn are *London's Burning* and *Frère Jacques*, where one voice follows another with exactly the same music, so the lines combine to make harmonies. Bach's canons here are of course more complicated. For one thing no two are at the same interval. In the first, the following voice has exactly the same notes. In the second, the following voice comes in one note higher, that is, at an interval of a second. And so on throughout the work, through to the interval of a ninth. In two of the canons, the following line is upside down (inversion). But what is most interesting is what Bach here does with the canon form. It was popular enough then as an intellectual and technical exercise. But Bach made his canons deeply expressive, something nobody had done before, not even him.

Where we would expect the canon at the tenth (Variation Thirty) Bach is coming to the end of the work so he wanted something more uplifting. He gives us a so-called quodlibet, or medley of popular tunes. When the Bach family and circle of friends met for a musical evening, they would often indulge in a quodlibet, having fun singing popular tunes of the day, not just one after the other but at the same time. When Bach first played this movement to his friends they would have recognised the tunes right away and probably sang along. The tunes do not have great lyrics. One is a critique of vegetarianism at its least appealing. 'Cabbage and beet have driven me away; if my mother had cooked some meat I would have stayed longer.' It is perhaps a strange way to bring to a conclusion a work which has contained some of the most sustained flights of musical imagination you will find anywhere. But Shakespeare does something similar in the epilogues to some of his comedies, coming down to earth, reaching out to his audience. This is not a work which looks upward to heaven, like the B Minor Mass. It looks out to mankind, primarily through his family and friends.

And of course it is not quite the end. The work concludes with a repeat of the sublime Aria. There is plenty of convincing evidence that Bach wrote the Aria especially for his beloved wife, Anna Magdalena, while always intending it to serve as the basis for the variations. She copied it into a notebook he had bought for her some years before, a sort of musical diary and collection of her favourite songs and pieces. When the Aria comes back at the end, it is as if the whole piece has come full circle, and the place to which it returns is his own domestic hearth.

That would be touching enough, if it were just a matter of a favourite tune coming back. But there is a much deeper effect, something we can all feel without knowing anything about the background to the work. The Aria has exactly the same notes when it comes back, but we hear it differently. It is as if it has never been away. Of course, it hasn't. The tune has been away but the harmonic sequence which underlies it has been there throughout. When the Aria returns we hear not so much the tune this time, but what lies beneath. T S Eliot in his *Four Quartets* summarises the effect perfectly in the famous lines quoted at the head of this chapter.

This sense of an unchanging silent centre beneath the at times bewildering surface noise and activity is perhaps the most profound message of Bach's masterpiece. It is a message which lies at the heart of many of the world's great religions. And it is at this point, despite the work being so clearly rooted in the everyday joys and sorrows of human life, that we can understand the *Goldberg Variations* as a religious work. Not one pointed towards heaven, maybe, but to the divine within the heart and soul of mankind.

My main concern with the performance was whether I would have enough stamina to get to the end. I had never before played such a long and demanding piece to an audience, and at sixty-four I was not getting any younger. I had run a couple of marathons many years before, and I trained in much the same way, building up my endurance, mental and physical. I did not take the risk of playing the repeats, except for some towards the end. Certainly my fingers had nothing left in the tank when I came to hold that final chord, listening to the sound ebbing away. It was an extraordinary moment, a truly quasi-religious experience. I had wanted a period of silence afterwards, but had forgotten to ask for it in advance. One of my audience could not resist breaking in with applause. Well, the spell had to be broken some time. I stood up, signalled for silence and thanked them for coming, and especially Samir for his hospitality. Samir had to our delight prepared some cakes on the theme of theme and variations!

Samir later suggested that I should make a recording of the work. I did this at home over the following months, using basic equipment which captured the sound well enough but had no facility for spot-editing. So I had to do each variation in a single take and in the order in which it had been written. After each take I would have to decide whether to leave it on the disc or have another go. There was a trade-off to be made. The most accurate takes were musically the dullest. So I did them again, taking more risks. My final version certainly has its fair share of wrong notes. I tried to remember Ricci's advice to play wrong notes with conviction.

Though Samir and I discussed the possibility of a repeat performance our plans did not materialise. I have never again played the whole work through at a sitting, though it remains part of me and I revisit it from time to time. When I returned to the Hereford Summer School in 2017 I played to the class the sublime Variation Twenty-five in G minor, a movement called 'the black pearl' by legendary harpsichordist, Wanda Landowska, who was the first to record the entire work. Pianist Andras Schiff has called this variation a 'miracle of creation.' And so it surely is.

EIGHTEEN

DA CAPO

So I had come full circle. I had played Bach at my first performance at the age of nine, and Bach again over fifty years later at my last. Now in my seventies I continue to practise a couple of hours a day when I can. For the last few years I have only played Bach.

I have also returned to teaching, though not as before. During my time at Morley and Hereford I had often thought that taking master-classes would be the form of teaching I would enjoy most. There is welcome variety in student and repertoire, and the opportunity to share the burden by inviting members to contribute their own ideas and suggestions. The pressure of coaching for examinations is absent. There is, or should be, only a culture of love of the piano and its music and a willingness to explore and discover together.

An opportunity to arrange such an environment in my own home came in 2016 when I joined my local branch of the University of the Third Age (U3A). It is not actually a university. It does not award degrees. It provides a framework for people who have retired from full-time work to share and pursue interests with others in the same situation. There were several practical music groups, including a choir, a ukulele orchestra and a guitar group, but nothing specifically for pianists. I offered to form a piano group and waited, more in hope than expectation, for expressions of interest.

The proposal did in fact stimulate a large number of such expressions. Quite a few of these were from people who had never played and wanted to start, though I had always made it clear that the group could not cater for complete beginners. Of those interested who did play or had played in the past only a few got as far as coming along to the inaugural meeting and not all of those stayed on. Clearly there are plenty of retired people out there with an active interest in the piano and who would be in a very good position to benefit from taking part. They would have the services of a qualified and experienced leader and a supportive group atmosphere at no cost to themselves, other than that of transport and the nominal fee they had already paid to be members of the U3A. So what was holding them back?

I can of course only speculate. I believe it has a lot to do with that curse of self-consciousness and self-criticism which afflicts so many adult pianists. If they have not played for years, or done so only in isolation, then it does take courage to expose to others what they see as their faults and limitations. Even those who achieved a high standard of playing in their younger years may find that physical and/or mental problems later on have erected barriers they perceive as insuperable. If habits of poor posture creating physical tensions have crept in over the years, or if powers of concentration have been affected by various conditions or just by the pressures and distractions of adult life, then it may simply seem too much of a challenge to start to tackle these difficulties. Even when the barriers are purely psychological they are just as real to the individual as physical ones.

The group did eventually get going with a settled membership of just five including myself, the most I could accommodate in my front room. We had to suspend operations earlier in 2020 because of the coronavirus, later resuming with membership reduced to four to enable social distancing and other requirements to be observed within the house. During the regional tier system we were able to meet just the once in a local hall with a piano, before the full lockdown resumed. At the time of writing we are again meeting at home with five members, while observing social distancing as far as possible. The way ahead is still deeply uncertain. Summer schools and other classes with much larger memberships than our group were until recently limited to online activity. This is certainly better than nothing. For many U3A groups and other forms of learning activity, online works as well as anything else. My own view is that it does not work with the piano, where as a teacher and leader I would always want to be in the same physical space as the player. There are so many aspects of piano playing which require attention if they are to be noticed and developed. Only in the same space can the sound quality be properly enjoyed and assessed. The actions of a pianist while playing need to be observed in the round, not just in front of a camera, if problems are to be identified and addressed.

Within the membership there is a wide range of

experience and abilities, which, given my problems in the past with so-called 'advanced' classes at Morley and Hereford, is how I always wanted it. One had reached grade 8 (advanced) by the age of eighteen and continued his studies until his early forties. There was then a fifteen year absence before he took up the piano again, without tuition but with encouragement from friends. The other two are largely self-taught. One started quite late in life. Both managed to keep in touch with their playing up to the time they joined the group.

At each meeting members take it in turns to play a piece of their own choice, then the others chip in with constructive comments and suggestions. A particular pleasure for me is to hear my piano played by people other than myself in an informal group atmosphere. As anyone (not everybody, of course) can get tired of the sound of their own voice, so you can get tired of the sound of your own playing. The range of music which members have brought to meetings is extraordinarily wide. One delights in bringing along obscure arrangements of well-known tunes he has picked up in second-hand bookshops. Another has tackled some of the most forbidding pieces in the classical repertoire, with Liszt, Chopin, Rachmaninov and Beethoven featuring strongly. Another has a particular liking for Scott Joplin. At least one piece has emerged which has had such an effect on me that I have been prompted to learn it for myself. It is rare now that I tackle anything which is completely new to me. The piece in question is Busoni's elegiac and sonorous arrangement of a chorale from Bach's Little Organ Book, *Ich Ruf' zu Dir* (I call out to Thee). Most important of all, members seem to enjoy the meetings.

We take learning seriously but have plenty of fun and good humour along the way.

My membership of the U3A and leadership of the piano group did throw up a rare performing opportunity, at an event in 2018 to celebrate the tenth anniversary of the local branch. The event took place in the above-mentioned hall. Various talents from the dance and musical groups were showcased, and the piano group was invited to contribute. When I first saw the piano, a medium-sized grand, I was apprehensive. It was well over a hundred years old! But it had been well maintained and was a pleasure to play. A salutary reminder for those concerned about the cost of a piano that if well maintained a good quality piano will keep its value far longer than the average human life span in the developed world! For the first time in many years I performed in a duet, calling on the services of another member of the group to take the lower part. Given the crowded schedule we confined ourselves to a single piece over in a couple of minutes, *The Lady from Brazil,* a samba by Thomas Johnson. It was good fun and well appreciated by the youthful (in spirit) audience.

In the light of our local experience, I wondered what interest in the piano there may be in the wider U3A community. I had a letter published in the national U3A journal, Third Age Matters. In the letter I described briefly how our group had come into being and invited comments or questions on setting up similar groups and on the wider issues facing those returning to the piano in retirement after a long absence. I was astonished at the number of responses I received, about three dozen, from all parts of the country. I learned that there are a few other piano groups such as ours, mostly on a rather more informal, social model. In one, consisting of about a dozen members, they meet to play once a month and then have refreshments, during which time they may discuss issues which had arisen during the session, but without any intensive or focussed response or analysis. It is a perfectly valid model, if that is what the members want, and probably the only feasible one for a group of that size. But I could not help wondering if it left some members wishing for more feedback and practical advice to enable them to progress in the way they would like. The vast majority of the responses to my letter were from pianists seeking advice on specific matters to do with repertoire and technique. In my replies I did my best to help them, drawing in particular on the material in Interlude V above on why adults give up the piano and what can be done about it. As I was working through the responses it occurred to me that I was undertaking on an informal basis a role which could and should be established formally. The U3A keeps a list of national subject advisers, each with their own webpage, available to advise any member anywhere in the country on their chosen subject. The only musical instrument subject adviser at the time was for that very popular U3A instrument, the ukulele. I have now added my name as piano playing adviser and the queries continue to arrive.

POSTLUDE

This has been a story of adventure and discovery, and also of good fortune. I have been exceptionally fortunate in my teachers over the years. I have also been fortunate in the opportunities which have come my way for playing with and for others.

You have met some of these friends, teachers and collaborators in these pages. Where are they now? Quite a few have passed away, as of course would be expected of those who taught me in childhood. If I had been writing this only a few months ago I would have been delighted to record that Jimmy Firth was still alive, at the age of ninety-one, having been musically active in his native Crosby into his eighties. But Jimmy too has passed, in January of 2020. To the best of my knowledge Wilfred Simenauer, about the same age as Jimmy, is still alive in his re-adopted native land of New Zealand. While Gwenneth Pryor still takes an advanced class at Morley College, Katharina and Ricci have both died in recent years, at the end of long and fulfilling lives. Raphael Terroni died in 2012, much too young at the age of sixty-seven. Even younger when he passed, at only fifty-seven, was the Welsh composer, William Mathias, though he nonetheless left behind him a large and impressive body of work. My friend Christine is still active in her church and sings with the outstanding Wimbledon Choral Society. Michael Longford died in 2015, after publishing two fascinating volumes of autobiography, one of which is a classic of its kind, describing his life as a colonial administrator in pre-independence Tanganyika[6]. David Crystal is as active and productive as ever. Accounts vary as to the number of books he has written, edited or contributed to. Only he knows the truth, or maybe not. But all estimates are comfortably into three figures.

Certainly there have been dark times and setbacks in my journey. It is not just that music has been a consolation in difficult times. That is true for many who do not play and find listening to be sufficient. No, the fire of music was only lit and kept alive within me in the way that it was because of those same dark shadows of family tension and grievance I have only briefly described. Paradoxically it was that very darkness which created the light. For me, music could never be just a hobby. It has been a lifelong search for a light which was missing from childhood. It was both a means to confront the darkness and to avoid being overwhelmed by it. Emotional release, a need to reach out and be understood, a means of finding and expressing meaning in a world so often without it – music and its expression through the medium of the piano has been all those things for me. I do not like to think what paths my life would have taken without it, but I cannot imagine they would have been anything but destructive, of self and others. As it is, I have never found trust easy to give or receive; a lasting legacy of my upbringing. Depression and intolerance of anything I perceive as a failure in myself have also formed part of that legacy. Addressing these issues by writing about them has helped significantly. I would never argue that music can be a cure for depressive illness. I have suffered from depressive episodes and even suicidal thoughts at various times in my life. At such times, as all who have suffered in similar ways will testify, the mind and soul are too preoccupied to respond to anything which is life-enhancing, least of all to take part in its creation or its promulgation. But when recovery starts to beckon, music can be among the first of the forces within and around us to offer a helping hand.

If I consider what could be called the landmarks in my musical journey it seems fair to say that I have been engaged in a process of almost continuous catch-up. Resuming lessons at forty-eight after a thirty-two year gap, first solo recital at fifty, diploma at fifty-five, starting to teach at fifty-six, playing the *Goldberg Variations* at sixty-four. All these are things one could reasonably expect to happen at a younger age if they are to happen at all. Perhaps those who are younger than any of those ages I have mentioned and still have the necessary physical and mental capacities can take some comfort in the thought that it may not be too late to achieve their musical ambitions, whatever they may be. My journey will also make it clear to them that opportunities are always there, if you look out for them. And of course having spotted them, you have to take them. There is nothing to lose and so much to gain.

Finally, a word about criticism, especially the criticism which is bred by envy. All musicians, amateur or professional, who aim for a degree of excellence will come in for a great deal of ill-informed and unjustified criticism.

That just seems to be the way it is. Indeed, amateurs may suffer more in this respect. Professional musicians as far as I can observe, and I have met many, generally have a mutual respect for each other's abilities and accomplishments, even when they do not share all their aims and values. But a surprising number of amateurs seem poisoned by envy and resentment. They seem not to understand that those who can play better than they do have worked and studied harder and practised more. It is only amateurs, and I stress that this is only true of some, who believe they can tackle difficult advanced pieces with minimal and unfocussed practice, far less than they know that professionals practise. At its worst this is sheer arrogance. At best it is an excuse for underachievement.

At times, any of us may feel envy about the musical achievements of others, because there are always those above us on the ladder. What about those who scale the very heights of musical achievement? We might with justice envy them if their gifts were entirely the result of chance and the outcomes as effortless as they often appear. But I do believe that is rarely or perhaps never the case. Very few if any so-called natural geniuses will have had 'normal' childhoods, even if they found them fulfilling. There always have to be sacrifices. When the great guitarist Segovia first heard the young John Williams, he declared that 'God had laid a finger on his brow.' It was an expression I did not at first understand. It sounded as if Williams' gifts were simply bestowed, without effort on his part. But Segovia understood from his own experience that the finger was not just a gift but also a burden, an inner lifelong drive to achieve perfection at whatever cost. A lady once approached the great violinist Fritz Kreisler after a concert and told him she would give her life to play as he did. 'I did give my life,' is what he replied. Our natural envy for the supreme artists we hear should always be tempered with the thought of the price they pay for the gifts they bestow on us.

On the much lower rung of the ladder where I find myself, I have certainly had my share of unfair criticism. I will not pretend that I take kindly to it. It hurts, badly. I have no interest in the motives which drive these critics. Their problems are their own. Positive, constructive, well-informed criticism on the other hand is the life-blood of progress. Every opportunity should be taken to find teachers and colleagues who can offer it. In the words of Polonius in *Hamlet,* you should grapple them to your soul with hoops of steel.

London   July 2021

APPENDIX
THE CHOSEN CHILD/EMOTIONAL INCEST SYNDROME

Some may find my accounts above of my deeply dysfunctional relationship with my family, and with my mother in particular, to be both bewildering and distressing. Others may find them painfully familiar. It may perhaps be some consolation to the latter to know, if they do not already, that my mother's abusive pattern of behaviour has a name, indeed more than one name. It is a recognised syndrome, sometimes called 'chosen child'. Another name for it is emotional incest. This is when a parent chooses a child to fill in the gaps in their own life, to succeed where they failed, to provide the image they always wanted to present to the world but were unable to do so. This is nothing like normal, healthy parental ambition. It is not about the child at all, but about the parent. The pressures on the child to succeed are immense, incompatible with any normal childhood. Inevitably, because the object of this form of abuse is only a child, there will be failures, often defined by the abuser as not immediately achieving the best possible success. The child is then subjected to the parent's anger and is forced to carry a huge weight of guilt. Low self-esteem is inevitable. I suspect that children who display an early aptitude for something artistic, something which can be displayed with pride to the world, have a more than average chance of being the victim of this form of abuse.

For anybody reading this who is or has been such a victim, I will say only this. The failures are your parent's, not yours. The guilt is theirs, not yours. *It is not your fault.* It is not within the scope of this book to explore this syndrome in detail. Others have done that with admirable thoroughness and compassion. I can in particular recommend a book by Dr Patricia Love[7]. I was into my forties when I discovered this book by chance in a New York bookstore. The relief to discover that I was not to blame for my mother's anger and unhappiness was immense. And do not believe anyone who says that this is all about mental illness. My mother did experience episodes of severe mental illness later in life, but at those times the illness blunted her cruelties. The syndrome, whatever its origins, was there in my life from the start. In its most extreme form, likely to be found when the abuser has in their turn experienced some form of abuse in their own childhood, it is deliberate, conscious abuse and its effects are wide-ranging and long-lasting.

REFERENCES

1. Simenauer, W. (2011). *Slaving over a Hot Cello.* Saarbrucken, Germany: Lambert Academic Publishing.

2. Crystal, D. (2009). *Just a Phrase I'm Going through.* Abingdon: Routledge.

3. Schumann, R., Isserlis S. (2016). *Robert Schumann's Advice to Young Musicians, Revisited by Steven Isserlis.* London: Faber and Faber Ltd.

4. Kentner, L. (1976). *Yehudi Menuhin Music Guides – Piano.* London: MacDonald.

5. Neuhaus, H., trans Leibovitch, K. (1993). *The Art of Piano Playing.* London: Kahn and Everill.

6. Longford, M. (2001). *The Flags Changed at Midnight.* Leominster: Gracewing.

7. Love, P. (1990). *The Emotional Incest Syndrome.* New York: Bantam Books.

INDEX